Copyrights, Patents and Trademarks

Protect Your Rights
Worldwide

To Diana,
my sweetheart forever

Copyrights, Patents and Trademarks
Protect Your Rights Worldwide

Hoyt L. Barber

LIBERTY HALL
PRESS™

LIBERTY HALL PRESS books are published by LIBERTY HALL PRESS, a division of TAB BOOKS. Its trademark, consisting of the words ''LIBERTY HALL PRESS'' and the portrayal of Benjamin Franklin, is registered in the United States Patent and Trademark Office.

First Edition
Second Printing

© 1990 by TAB BOOKS
Printed in the United States of America

Library of Congress Cataloging-in-Publication Data

Barber, Hoyt L.
Copyright, patents, and trademarks : protect your rights worldwide
/ by Hoyt L. Barber.
p. cm.
ISBN 0-8306-0233-x (pbk.)
1. Intellectual property—United States—Popular works.
2. Intellectual property—Popular works. I. Title.
KF2980.B37 1989
346.730498—dc20
[347.30648]   89-12641
                                                  CIP

TAB BOOKS offers software for sale.
For information and a catalog, please contact:

TAB Software Department
Blue Ridge Summit, PA 17294-0850

Questions regarding the content of this book
should be addressed to:

Reader Inquiry Branch
Division of TAB BOOKS
Blue Ridge Summit, PA 17294-0214

Vice President & Editorial Director: David J. Conti
Book Editor: Roman H. Gorski
Production: Katherine Brown
Cover Design: Lori E. Schlosser

Contents

Part 4 Intellectual Property Protection in Foreign Countries 181

Part 5 Resources 239

Index 255

Introduction

Copyrights, Patents, and Trademarks: Protect Your Rights Worldwide provides an abundance of information on the various forms of intellectual property protection. It explains in detailed, step-by-step procedures, how to obtain exclusive protection for unique ideas, inventions, names, identifying marks, or artistic, literary, musical, photographic or cinematographic works.

You can now have available valuable facts and information on intellectual property protection at your fingertips. The material and instructions in this book will save you unnecessary expense and time-consuming research. The information is organized to provide fast comprehension, so that it may be implemented immediately. Forms are included for Federal copyright, patent, and trademark registration.

The subject of intellectual property protection is extensive. The purpose of this book is to simplify the process of securing a copyright, patent, or trademark in most countries where protection would be beneficial. The information disclosed here will be useful to know even before embarking on any creative endeavor that you hope someday will find its way into the marketplace. Most ideas developed for maximum commercial value will need to be legally protected from encroachment and undesirable imitation. Writers, designers, artists, photographers, inventors, composers, musicians, performers, and many others can now get regional, national, or international protection for their creations.

This book is divided into five parts. Part 1 discusses copyrights. Part 2 covers patents. Part 3 details Federal trademarks and seven key areas of state trademarks. Part 4 is an international whirlwind tour of copyrights, patents, and trademarks, including a country-by-country profile of over 60 foreign lands from Algeria to Zambia. Part 5 provides valuable contacts, sources of additional information, and suggested books to read. All forms have been placed at the end of the appropriate part.

Intellectual Property Protection

Intellectual property includes copyrights, patents, trademarks, and unfair competition. Comprehensive laws govern all areas of intellectual property in the United States and many foreign countries. Specific rights are conferred that protect the creators of unique ideas, inventions, literary and other works, names, products, and more from unauthorized use. Intellectual property can be divided into two categories:

1. Industrial property
   a) Patents
   b) Trademarks
   c) Trade secrets
   d) Unfair competition laws
2. Literary property
   a) Copyrights

Industrial property protection protects industrial designs, inventions, and trademarks against unfair competition. *Literary property* protection includes the copyright protection of artistic, cinematographic, literary, musical, and photographic works.

Part 1
Copyrights

COPYRIGHT PROTECTION

Categories of Copyright Protection

Authors are entitled to copyright protection for their original works. Once the author's work has taken a tangible form, it can be copyrighted under one of the following seven categories:

1. Literary works
2. Musical works, including any accompanying words
3. Dramatic works, including any accompanying music
4. Pantomines and choreographic works
5. Pictorial, graphic and sculptural works
6. Motion pictures and other audiovisual works
7. Sound recordings

When Does Copyright Begin?

Upon creation, a work is automatically protected by copyright. A work is not only copyrighted once it's completed, it is also protected during the course of creation. Once it becomes tangible for the first time, even if the work is incomplete (such as a first draft of a manuscript or the first chapter of a manuscript), then it receives full protection under the copyright law.

Copyright protection extends to published and unpublished works. It gives the author the exclusive right to use the copyrighted work to his benefit, including the right to authorize others to use the work. The author may reproduce it, prepare derivative works, distribute copies or phonorecords, and perform and display the copyrighted work publicly.

Benefits of Registration

Although an author's work is automatically protected by copyright, there are advantages to registering the work with the Copyright Office:

- Registration establishes a public record of the copyright claim.
- Registration is ordinarily necessary before any infringement suits can be filed in court.
- If made before or within five years of publication, registration will establish prima facie evidence in court of the validity of the copyright and of the facts stated in the certificate.
- If registration is made within three months after publication of the work or prior to an infringement of the work, statutory damages and attorney's fees will be available to the copyright owner in court actions. Otherwise, only an award of actual damages and profits is available to the copyright owner.

The New Copyright Law

On October 19, 1976, President Gerald Ford signed a bill to revise the U.S. copyright law. The new law is now known as Public Law 94-553 (90 Stat. 2541) and became effective on January 1, 1978. This law overrides the former Copyright Act of 1909.

Major changes in the copyright law occurred as a result of the introduction of this bill, known as the Copyright Revision Bill. Only pertinent changes will be pointed out in this book as they apply to the material covered; all other information is current. Works presently being copyrighted will be governed by the January 1, 1978, changes.

Publication

Publication is an important element of copyright; however, it's no longer the key to obtaining a statutory copyright. The Copyright Act defines *publication* as follows:

> Publication is the distribution of copies or phonorecords of a work to the public for sale or other transfer of ownership, or by rental, lease or lending. The offering to distribute copies or phonorecords to a group of persons for purposes of further distribution, public performance, or public display, constitutes publication. A public performance or display of a work does not of itself constitute publication.

Copyright Notice

Publicly distributed copies should bear a copyright notice. This also applies to published works as they are intended for public distribution. When a copyright is placed on copies of a work for public distribution, it's mandatory to satisfy deposit requirements for registration compliance.

The owner of the copyright is responsible to comply with the copyright notice requirement; otherwise, certain additional rights may be lost. This also applies to works published outside the United States.

The following is a correct example of how the copyright notice should be displayed:

© 1990 Hoyt L. Barber

The notice must contain three important ingredients:

1. The symbol. The letter *c* in a circle, or the word *Copyright*, or the abbreviation *Copr.*
2. The year of the first publication of the work. "The year date may be omitted where a pictorial, graphic, or sculptural work, with accompanying textual matter, if any, is reproduced in or on greeting cards, postcards, stationery, jewelry, dolls, toys, or any useful article."
3. The name of the owner of a copyright. The "c in a circle" is only required on "visually perceptible copies." Because audio tapes and phonograph discs are

"phonorecords" and not "copies," they aren't required to bear the "c in the circle."

Notice for Phonorecords of Sound Recordings

The notice for phonorecords of sound recordings also contain three elements, but these are actually in the sound recording itself.

1. The symbol P, the letter *P* within a circle.
2. The year of first publication of the sound recording.
3. The name of the owner of the copyright. "If the producer of the sound recording is named on the phonorecord labels or containers, and if no other name appears in conjunction with the notice, the producer's name shall be considered a part of the notice."

Position of the copyright notice should be "permanently legible to an ordinary user of the work under normal conditions of use and should not be concealed from view upon reasonable examination." Its purpose is to give reasonable notice of the claim of copyright. Each category that a work falls under has its own guidelines for displaying the notice.

Unpublished works don't require a copyright notice, but a notice may still be affixed to alert others that it is protected under copyright law. The following notice is sufficient:

"Unpublished Work © 1990 Hoyt L. Barber"

WHO CAN CLAIM COPYRIGHT?

Copyright protection may be claimed by the author or those deriving their rights from the author. The author of a "work made for hire" is the employer or person who hired the author to create the work.

Collaborative Works

Collaborative works are jointly owned by the authors, unless there is an agreement which stipulates another arrangement between the parties involved. A separate contribution to a collective work is individually protected by copyright, even if the collective work is copyrighted by someone else (i.e., a book containing 20 individual copyrighted stories, authored by different individuals, but compiled and collectively copyrighted by the editor).

Unpublished Collections

A *collection* is an orderly combination of copyrightable elements that bear a single title. An example of a work of this nature, although it has been published, is a book entitled *The Creative Process*. The editor, Brewster Ghiselin, compiled 38 previously published short stories by famous individuals like Einstein, Van Gogh, Moore, etc. Although each story bears its own copyright, Mr. Ghiselin's publisher secured a copyright for his collective work, and also protected the introduction to the book. This practice does not invalid or lessen the individual author's copyright claim or protection.

A collective work is made up of distinctly individual contributions or parts. Each element of the collection can stand as a work on its own merit, and may consist of a contribution by one or more authors. An aviation magazine writer, for instance, might choose to assemble some of his previously published and unpublished articles on flying into book form, thereby creating a collective work.

National Origin of the Work

Any unpublished work is entitled to copyright protection regardless of the author's nationality or domicile.

One of the following requirements must be met for a published work to be eligible:

- "On the date of first publication, one or more of the authors is a national or domiciliary of the United States or is a national, domiciliary, or sovereign authority of a foreign country that is a party to a copyright treaty to which the United States is also a party, or is a stateless person wherever that person may be domiciled.

- "The work is first published in the United States or in a foreign nation that, on the date of first publication, is a party to the Universal Copyright Convention.

- "The work comes within the scope of a Presidential proclamation."

COPYRIGHT DURATION

As previously mentioned, a work is automatically protected by copyright immediately upon creation. This is known as being "fixed in tangible form for the first time." The copyright term is the life of the author plus an additional 50 years after the author's death. If the work was co-authored, the term is 50 years in addition to the life of the last surviving author.

If it's an *anonymous work*—one made for hire or a pseudonymous work—the copyright duration is 75 years from publication or 100 years from its creation, whichever is shorter.

Works copyrighted before January 1, 1978 (old law) and works copyrighted on the date the work was published (or when it was registered if it was in unpublished form) are both 28 years from the date of copyright. These copyrights were eligible for renewal during the 28th year of the term. Pre-1978 copyrights may still be renewed under the new law for a term of 28 to 47 years. To secure the additional 47-year period, the copyright must be renewed at the proper time. The time limits for renewal registration begin on December 31 of the 27th year of the copyright and extend through December 31 of the 28th year. This affords the copyright holder (under the old law) a total of 75 years of protection. If renewal isn't made within the allotted period, copyright protection will be permanently lost.

REGISTRATION PROCEDURES

Let's take a general look at the registration procedures here:

1. Complete the appropriate application form.
2. Enclose a $10 nonrefundable filing fee (per application).
3. Deposit of the work being registered (nonrefundable).

Here are the deposit requirements:

- "If the work is unpublished, one complete copy or phonorecord.
- "If the work was first published in the United States on or after January 1, 1978, two complete copies or phonocopies of the best edition.
- "If the work was first published in the United States before January 1, 1978, two complete copies or phonorecords of the work as first published.
- "If the work was first published outside the United States, whenever published, one copy or phonorecord of the work as first published.
- "If the work is a contribution to a collective work, and published after January 1, 1978, one complete copy of the phonorecord of the best edition of the collective work.

Renewal of a copyright is simple. Complete the RE form and return it with a nonrefundable $6.00. Each renewal must be accompanied by an application form and payment.

Deposit Requirements

All works bearing a copyright notice are required to meet the deposit requirements within three months of publication. Two copies of the work at the time of registration must be furnished with the Copyright Office. One copy is for use by the Library of Congress and the other is to meet the registration requirement. Failure to provide the required deposit within the allotted period might result in fines and other penalties.

The Copyright Applicant

A copyright application may be legally filed by any one of the following persons or organizations:

- The author of the work. In the case of a "work for hire" arrangement, it's the employer, person or organization who contracts the author's services.
- The copyright claimant. Ownership of the rights in a copyrighted work may be obtained from the author. The person or organization possessing legal title to the copyrighted work is known as the "claimant." An example is a publishing

agreement which stipulates that the publisher of a particular work will secure the copyright in the publisher's name. The publisher legally owns the copyright, however the extent of the publisher's rights and the term are governed (or at least should be) by a written agreement. When the contract is terminated, the rights should revert back to the creator of the work.

- The owner of exclusive right(s). Exclusive rights which make up a copyright can be subdivided and can be transferred or owned separately, even if limited by time or place of effect. An owner of a particular exclusive right in a copyright is considered a "copyright owner" and is entitled to register a claim in the work.

- The authorized agent of the author, copyright claimant, or owner of exclusive right(s).

Copyright Application Forms

The following forms are used for different types of works. The work may be published or unpublished. Each form is accompanied by easy-to-follow instructions.

- *Form TX:* Nondramatic literary works, excluding periodicals or serial issues. This includes fiction, nonfiction, poetry, textbooks, reference works, directories, catalogs, advertising copy, compilations of information, and computer programs.

- *Form PA:* Works prepared for the purpose of being "performed" directly before an audience or indirectly "by means of any device or process." This includes 1) musical works, including any accompanying words; 2) dramatic works, including any accompanying music; 3) pantomimes and choreographic works; and 4) motion pictures and other audio visual works.

- *Form VA:* Visual arts. This consists of "pictorial, graphic, or sculptural works," including two-dimensional and three-dimensional works of fine, graphic and applied art, photographs, prints and art reproductions, maps, globes, charts, technical drawings, diagrams and models.

- *Form SR:* Sound recordings. This should be used where the copyright claim is limited to the sound recording itself, and can also be used where the same copyright claimant is seeking simultaneous registration of the underlying musical, dramatic, or literary work embodied in the phonorecord.

- *Form SE:* Each individual serial work must be registered on form SE. A serial is a work issued or intended to be issued in successive parts bearing numerical or chronological designations and intended to be continued indefinitely.

Filing the Application

Make a practice of providing the Copyright Office with everything required at one time. This will prevent unnecessary delays! Your registration package should contain:

1. Completed application
2. Appropriate fee (nonrefundable)
3. Required deposit (nonreturnable)

Once you've double-checked the contents of the mailing envelope and are certain everything is in proper order, address it to:

REGISTER OF COPYRIGHTS
Copyright Office
Library of Congress
Washington, D.C. 20559

Do not mail cash! A money order, check or bank draft is acceptable and should be made payable in U.S. dollars to the "Register of Copyrights." Foreign checks are not accepted. Attach the payment securely to the application.

Regardless of the time required to process your application, the copyright registration is effective on the date it's received by the Copyright Office, if all requirements are met. Within 120 days you will either receive a Certificate of Registration of copyright or a letter explaining why the application is rejected. If further information is required, a copyright examiner will write or call the applicant.

WHAT CAN'T BE COPYRIGHTED?

- Blank forms
- Catchwords, catch phrases, mottoes, slogans, or short advertising expressions (refer to Part 3, Trademarks)
- Common or standard works
- Devices or inventions (refer to Part 2, Patents)
- Ideas, methods, systems, principles, concepts
- Mere listings of ingredients, such as a recipe or formula, unless there is substantial literary expression in the directions or if there is a compilation of recipes.
- Names of businesses, organizations or groups (refer to Part 3, Trademarks)
- Names of products or services (refer to Part 3, Trademarks)
- Names or pseudonyms of individuals, such as a pen or stage name
- Patents and trademarks

- Titles of works
- Works in the public domain
- Works of the U.S. Government

FAILURE TO PUBLISH THE COPYRIGHT NOTICE

The copyright notice should be correctly included in published works or phonorecords to ensure full copyright protection. Failure to properly display the copyright notice is known as "omission of notice" but does not automatically invalidate the copyright. Permanent loss or a shortened term of copyright protection may result if the omission is not corrected. In addition, here are the types of errors which the Copyright Office considers the same as an omission:

- "A notice that does not contain the symbol © (the letter c in a circle), or the word "Copyright" or the abbreviation "Copr." or, if the work is a sound recording, the symbol ℗ (the letter P in a circle).
- "A notice dated more than one year later than the date of first publication.
- "A notice without a name or date that could reasonably be considered part of the notice.
- "A notice that lacks the statement required for words consisting preponderantly of U.S. government material.
- "A notice located so that it does not give reasonable notice of the claim of copyright.

"The omission of notice does not affect the copyright protection and no corrective steps are required if:

1. "The notice is omitted from no more than a relatively small number of copies or phonorecords distributed to the public, or
2. "The omission violated an express written requirement that the published copies or phonorecords bear the prescribed notice.

"In all other cases of omission, to preserve copyright:

1. "The work must have been registered before it was published in any form or before the omission occurred or it must be registered within five years after the date of publication without notice and
2. "The copyright owner must make a reasonable effort to add the notice to all copies or phonorecords that are distributed to the public in the United States after the omission is discovered."

If corrective measures aren't implemented according to the Copyright Office guidelines, all copyright protection will be lost forever and the work will become public domain.

UNFAIR FOREIGN COMPETITION

Refer to Part 3, Trademarks, for further information on how to protect copyrighted goods from unfair foreign competition in the United States.

INSTRUCTIONS FOR COMPLETION OF COPYRIGHT FORMS

The forms on the following pages are accompanied by easy-to-follow instructions. Read each step before completing the next space on the form. If additional copies are required, the forms in this book can be photocopied or you can write to the Copyright Office for extra sets. Forms should always be typed or legibly handwritten in black ink.

COPYRIGHT FORMS

Filling Out Application Form TX

Detach and read these instructions before completing this form. Make sure all applicable spaces have been filled in before you return this form.

BASIC INFORMATION

When to Use This Form: Use Form TX for registration of published or unpublished non-dramatic literary works, excluding periodicals or serial issues. This class includes a wide variety of works: fiction, non-fiction, poetry, textbooks, reference works, directories, catalogs, advertising copy, compilations of information, and computer programs. For periodicals and serials, use Form SE.

Deposit to Accompany Application: An application for copyright registration must be accompanied by a deposit consisting of copies or phonorecords representing the entire work for which registration is to be made. The following are the general deposit requirements as set forth in the statute:

Unpublished Work: Deposit one complete copy (or phonorecord).

Published Work: Deposit two complete copies (or phonorecords) of the best edition.

Work First Published Outside the United States: Deposit one complete copy (or phonorecord) of the first foreign edition.

Contribution to a Collective Work: Deposit one complete copy (or phonorecord) of the best edition of the collective work.

The Copyright Notice: For published works, the law provides that a copyright notice in a specified form "shall be placed on all publicly distributed copies from which the work can be visually perceived." Use of the copyright notice is the responsibility of the copyright owner and does not require advance permission from the Copyright Office. The required form of the notice for copies generally consists of three elements: (1) the symbol "©", or the word "Copyright," or the abbreviation "Copr."; (2) the year of first publication; and (3) the name of the owner of copyright. For example: "© 1981 Constance Porter." The notice is to be affixed to the copies "in such manner and location as to give reasonable notice of the claim of copyright."

For further information about copyright registration, notice, or special questions relating to copyright problems, write:

> Information and Publications Section, LM-455
> Copyright Office
> Library of Congress
> Washington, D.C. 20559

LINE-BY-LINE INSTRUCTIONS

1 SPACE 1: Title

Title of This Work: Every work submitted for copyright registration must be given a title to identify that particular work. If the copies or phonorecords of the work bear a title (or an identifying phrase that could serve as a title), transcribe that wording *completely* and *exactly* on the application. Indexing of the registration and future identification of the work will depend on the information you give here.

Previous or Alternative Titles: Complete this space if there are any additional titles for the work under which someone searching for the registration might be likely to look, or under which a document pertaining to the work might be recorded.

Publication as a Contribution: If the work being registered is a contribution to a periodical, serial, or collection, give the title of the contribution in the "Title of this Work" space. Then, in the line headed "Publication as a Contribution," give information about the collective work in which the contribution appeared.

2 SPACE 2: Author(s)

General Instructions: After reading these instructions, decide who are the "authors" of this work for copyright purposes. Then, unless the work is a "collective work," give the requested information about every "author" who contributed any appreciable amount of copyrightable matter to this version of the work. If you need further space, request additional Continuation sheets. In the case of a collective work, such as an anthology, collection of essays, or encyclopedia, give information about the author of the collective work as a whole.

Name of Author: The fullest form of the author's name should be given. Unless the work was "made for hire," the individual who actually created the work is its "author." In the case of a work made for hire, the statute provides that "the employer or other person for whom the work was prepared is considered the author."

What is a "Work Made for Hire"? A "work made for hire" is defined as: (1) "a work prepared by an employee within the scope of his or her employment"; or (2) "a work specially ordered or commissioned for use as a contribution to a collective work, as a part of a motion picture or other audiovisual work, as a translation, as a supplementary work, as a compilation, as an instructional text, as a test, as answer material for a test, or as an atlas, if the parties expressly agree in a written instrument signed by them that the work shall be considered a work made for hire." If you have checked "Yes" to indicate that the work was "made for hire," you must give the full legal name of the employer (or other person for whom the work was prepared). You may also include the name of the employee along with the name of the employer (for example: "Elster Publishing Co., employer for hire of John Ferguson").

"Anonymous" or "Pseudonymous" Work: An author's contribution to a work is "anonymous" if that author is not identified on the copies or phonorecords of the work. An author's contribution to a work is "pseudonymous" if that author is identified on the copies or phonorecords under a fictitious name. If the work is "anonymous" you may: (1) leave the line blank; or (2) state " anonymous" on the line; or (3) reveal the author's identity. If the work is "pseudonymous" you may : (1) leave the line blank; or (2) give the pseudonym and identify it as such (for example: "Huntley Haverstock, pseudonym"); or (3) reveal the author's name, making clear which is the real name and which is the pseudonym (for example: "Judith Barton, whose pseudonym is Madeline Elster"). However, the citizenship or domicile of the author **must** be given in all cases.

Dates of Birth and Death: If the author is dead, the statute requires that the year of death be included in the application unless the work is anonymous or pseudonymous. The author's birth date is optional, but is useful as a form of identification. Leave this space blank if the author's contribution was a "work made for hire."

Author's Nationality or Domicile: Give the country of which the author is a citizen, or the country in which the author is domiciled. Nationality or domicile **must** be given in all cases.

Nature of Authorship: After the words "Nature of Authorship" give a brief general statement of the nature of this particular author's contribution to the work. Examples: "Entire text"; "Coauthor of entire text"; "Chapters 11-14"; "Editorial revisions"; "Compilation and English translation"; "New text."

3 SPACE 3: Creation and Publication

General Instructions: Do not confuse "creation" with "publication." Every application for copyright registration must state "the year in which creation of the work was completed." Give the date and nation of first publication only if the work has been published.

Creation: Under the statute, a work is "created" when it is fixed in a copy or phonorecord for the first time. Where a work has been prepared over a period of time, the part of the work existing in fixed form on a particular date constitutes the created work on that date. The date you give here should be the year in which the author completed the particular version for which registration is now being sought, even if other versions exist or if further changes or additions are planned.

Publication: The statute defines "publication" as "the distribution of copies or phonorecords of a work to the public by sale or other transfer of ownership, or by rental, lease, or lending"; a work is also "published" if there has been an "offering to distribute copies or phonorecords to a group of persons for purposes of further distribution, public performance, or public display." Give the full date (month, day, year) when, and the country where, publication first occurred. If first publication took place simultaneously in the United States and other countries, it is sufficient to state "U.S.A."

4 SPACE 4: Claimant(s)

Name(s) and Address(es) of Copyright Claimant(s): Give the name(s) and address(es) of the copyright claimant(s) in this work even if the claimant is the same as the author. Copyright in a work belongs initially to the author of the work (including, in the case of a work made for hire, the employer or other person for whom the work was prepared). The copyright claimant is either the author of the work or a person or organization to whom the copyright initially belonging to the author has been transferred.

Transfer: The statute provides that, if the copyright claimant is not the author, the application for registration must contain "a brief statement of how the claimant obtained ownership of the copyright." If any copyright claimant named in space 4 is not an author named in space 2, give a brief, general statement summarizing the means by which that claimant obtained ownership of the copyright. Examples: "By written contract"; "Transfer of all rights by author"; "Assignment"; "By will." Do not attach transfer documents or other attachments or riders.

5 SPACE 5: Previous Registration

General Instructions: The questions in space 5 are intended to find out whether an earlier registration has been made for this work and, if so, whether there is any basis for a new registration. As a general rule, only one basic copyright registration can be made for the same version of a particular work.

Same Version: If this version is substantially the same as the work covered by a previous registration, a second registration is not generally possible unless: (1) the work has been registered in unpublished form and a second registration is now being sought to cover this first published edition; or (2) someone other than the author is identified as copyright claimant in the earlier registration, and the author is now seeking registration in his or her own name. If either of these two exceptions apply, check the appropriate box and give the earlier registration number and date. Otherwise, do not submit Form TX; instead, write the Copyright Office for information about supplementary registration or recordation of transfers of copyright ownership.

Changed Version: If the work has been changed, and you are now seeking registration to cover the additions or revisions, check the last box in space 5, give the earlier registration number and date, and complete both parts of space 6 in accordance with the instructions below.

Previous Registration Number and Date: If more than one previous registration has been made for the work, give the number and date of the latest registration.

6 SPACE 6: Derivative Work or Compilation

General Instructions: Complete space 6 if this work is a "changed version," "compilation," or "derivative work," and if it incorporates one or more earlier works that have already been published or registered for copyright, or that have fallen into the public domain. A "compilation" is defined as "a work formed by the collection and assembling of preexisting materials or of data that are selected, coordinated, or arranged in such a way that the resulting work as a whole constitutes an original work of authorship." A "derivative work" is "a work based on one or more preexisting works." Examples of derivative works include translations, fictionalizations, abridgments, condensations, or "any other form in which a work may be recast, transformed, or adapted." Derivative works also include works "consisting of editorial revisions, annotations, or other modifications" if these changes, as a whole, represent an original work of authorship.

Preexisting Material (space 6a): For derivative works, complete this space and space 6b. In space 6a identify the preexisting work that has been recast, transformed, or adapted. An example of preexisting material might be: "Russian version of Goncharov's 'Oblomov'." Do not complete space 6a for compilations.

Material Added to This Work (space 6b): Give a brief, general statement of the new material covered by the copyright claim for which registration is sought. **Derivative work** examples include: "Foreword, editing, critical annotations"; "Translation"; "Chapters 11-17." If the work is a **compilation**, describe both the compilation itself and the material that has been compiled. Example: "Compilation of certain 1917 Speeches by Woodrow Wilson." A work may be both a derivative work and compilation, in which case a sample statement might be: "Compilation and additional new material."

7 SPACE 7: Manufacturing Provisions

General Instructions: The copyright statute currently provides, as a general rule, that the copies of a published work "consisting preponderantly of nondramatic literary material in the English language" be manufactured in the United States or Canada in order to be lawfully produced and publicly distributed in the United States. If the work being registered is unpublished or not in English, leave this space blank. Complete this space if registration is sought for a published work "consisting preponderantly of nondramatic literary material that is in the English language." Identify those who manufactured the copies and where those manufacturing processes were performed. As an exception to the manufacturing provisions, the statute prescribes that, where manufacture has taken place outside the United States or Canada, a maximum of 2000 copies of the foreign edition may be imported into the United States without affecting the copyright owners' rights. For this purpose, the Copyright Office will issue an Import Statement upon request and payment of a fee of $3 at the time of registration or at any later time. For further information about import statements, write for Form IS.

8 SPACE 8: Reproduction for Use of Blind or Physically Handicapped Individuals

General Instructions: One of the major programs of the Library of Congress is to provide Braille editions and special recordings of works for the exclusive use of the blind and physically handicapped. In an effort to simplify and speed up the copyright licensing procedures that are a necessary part of this program, section 710 of the copyright statute provides for the establishment of a voluntary licensing system to be tied in with copyright registration. Copyright Office regulations provide that you may grant a license for such reproduction and distribution solely for the use of persons who are certified by competent authority as unable to read normal printed material as a result of physical limitations. The license is entirely voluntary, nonexclusive, and may be terminated upon 90 days notice.

How to Grant the License: If you wish to grant it, check one of the three boxes in space 8. Your check in one of these boxes, together with your signature in space 10, will mean that the Library of Congress can proceed to reproduce and distribute under the license without further paperwork. For further information, write for Circular R63.

9,10,11 SPACE 9, 10, 11: Fee, Correspondence, Certification, Return Address

Deposit Account: If you maintain a Deposit Account in the Copyright Office, identify it in space 9. Otherwise leave the space blank and send the fee of $10 with your application and deposit.

Correspondence (space 9): This space should contain the name, address, area code, and telephone number of the person to be consulted if correspondence about this application becomes necessary.

Certification (space 10): The application can not be accepted unless it bears the date and the **handwritten signature** of the author or other copyright claimant, or of the owner of exclusive right(s), or of the duly authorized agent of author, claimant, or owner of exclusive right(s).

Address for Return of Certificate (space 11): The address box must be completed legibly since the certificate will be returned in a window envelope.

FORM TX

UNITED STATES COPYRIGHT OFFICE

REGISTRATION NUMBER

TX	TXU

EFFECTIVE DATE OF REGISTRATION

Month	Day	Year

DO NOT WRITE ABOVE THIS LINE. IF YOU NEED MORE SPACE, USE A SEPARATE CONTINUATION SHEET.

1 **TITLE OF THIS WORK ▼**

PREVIOUS OR ALTERNATIVE TITLES ▼

PUBLICATION AS A CONTRIBUTION   If this work was published as a contribution to a periodical, serial, or collection, give information about the collective work in which the contribution appeared.   **Title of Collective Work ▼**

If published in a periodical or serial give: **Volume ▼**   **Number ▼**   **Issue Date ▼**   **On Pages ▼**

2 **a** **NAME OF AUTHOR ▼**

DATES OF BIRTH AND DEATH
Year Born ▼   Year Died ▼

Was this contribution to the work a "work made for hire"?
☐ Yes
☐ No

AUTHOR'S NATIONALITY OR DOMICILE
Name of Country
OR { Citizen of ▶ _____
Domiciled in ▶ _____

WAS THIS AUTHOR'S CONTRIBUTION TO THE WORK
Anonymous?   ☐ Yes ☐ No
Pseudonymous?   ☐ Yes ☐ No
If the answer to either of these questions is "Yes," see detailed instructions.

NATURE OF AUTHORSHIP   Briefly describe nature of the material created by this author in which copyright is claimed. ▼

NOTE

Under the law, the "author" of a "work made for hire" is generally the employer, not the employee (see instructions). For any part of this work that was "made for hire" check "Yes" in the space provided, give the employer (or other person for whom the work was prepared) as "Author" of that part, and leave the space for dates of birth and death blank.

b **NAME OF AUTHOR ▼**

DATES OF BIRTH AND DEATH
Year Born ▼   Year Died ▼

Was this contribution to the work a "work made for hire"?
☐ Yes
☐ No

AUTHOR'S NATIONALITY OR DOMICILE
Name of country
OR { Citizen of ▶ _____
Domiciled in ▶ _____

WAS THIS AUTHOR'S CONTRIBUTION TO THE WORK
Anonymous?   ☐ Yes ☐ No
Pseudonymous?   ☐ Yes ☐ No
If the answer to either of these questions is "Yes," see detailed instructions.

NATURE OF AUTHORSHIP   Briefly describe nature of the material created by this author in which copyright is claimed. ▼

c **NAME OF AUTHOR ▼**

DATES OF BIRTH AND DEATH
Year Born ▼   Year Died ▼

Was this contribution to the work a "work made for hire"?
☐ Yes
☐ No

AUTHOR'S NATIONALITY OR DOMICILE
Name of Country
OR { Citizen of ▶ _____
Domiciled in ▶ _____

WAS THIS AUTHOR'S CONTRIBUTION TO THE WORK
Anonymous?   ☐ Yes ☐ No
Pseudonymous?   ☐ Yes ☐ No
If the answer to either of these questions is "Yes," see detailed instructions.

NATURE OF AUTHORSHIP   Briefly describe nature of the material created by this author in which copyright is claimed. ▼

3 **YEAR IN WHICH CREATION OF THIS WORK WAS COMPLETED**   This information must be given in all cases.   ◀ Year

DATE AND NATION OF FIRST PUBLICATION OF THIS PARTICULAR WORK
Complete this information ONLY if this work has been published.
Month ▶ _____ Day ▶ _____ Year ▶ _____   ◀ Nation

4 **COPYRIGHT CLAIMANT(S)** Name and address must be given even if the claimant is the same as the author given in space 2.▼

See instructions before completing this space.

TRANSFER If the claimant(s) named here in space 4 are different from the author(s) named in space 2, give a brief statement of how the claimant(s) obtained ownership of the copyright.▼

DO NOT WRITE HERE OFFICE USE ONLY

APPLICATION RECEIVED

ONE DEPOSIT RECEIVED

TWO DEPOSITS RECEIVED

REMITTANCE NUMBER AND DATE

MORE ON BACK ▶   • Complete all applicable spaces (numbers 5-11) on the reverse side of this page.
• See detailed instructions.   • Sign the form at line 10.

DO NOT WRITE HERE
Page 1 of _____ pages

EXAMINED BY	FORM TX
CHECKED BY	
☐ CORRESPONDENCE Yes	FOR COPYRIGHT OFFICE USE ONLY
☐ DEPOSIT ACCOUNT FUNDS USED	

DO NOT WRITE ABOVE THIS LINE. IF YOU NEED MORE SPACE, USE A SEPARATE CONTINUATION SHEET.

PREVIOUS REGISTRATION Has registration for this work, or for an earlier version of this work, already been made in the Copyright Office?

☐ **Yes** ☐ **No** If your answer is "Yes," why is another registration being sought? (Check appropriate box) ▼

☐ This is the first published edition of a work previously registered in unpublished form.

☐ This is the first application submitted by this author as copyright claimant.

☐ This is a changed version of the work, as shown by space 6 on this application.

If your answer is "Yes," give: **Previous Registration Number** ▼   **Year of Registration** ▼

5

DERIVATIVE WORK OR COMPILATION Complete both space 6a & 6b for a derivative work; complete only 6b for a compilation.

a. Preexisting Material Identify any preexisting work or works that this work is based on or incorporates. ▼

b. Material Added to This Work Give a brief, general statement of the material that has been added to this work and in which copyright is claimed. ▼

See instructions before completing this space.

6

MANUFACTURERS AND LOCATIONS If this is a published work consisting preponderantly of nondramatic literary material in English, the law may require that the copies be manufactured in the United States or Canada for full protection. If so, the names of the manufacturers who performed certain processes, and the places where these processes were performed **must** be given. See instructions for details.

Names of Manufacturers ▼   **Places of Manufacture** ▼

7

REPRODUCTION FOR USE OF BLIND OR PHYSICALLY HANDICAPPED INDIVIDUALS   A signature on this form at space 10, and a check in one of the boxes here in space 8, constitutes a non-exclusive grant of permission to the Library of Congress to reproduce and distribute solely for the blind and physically handicapped and under the conditions and limitations prescribed by the regulations of the Copyright Office: (1) copies of the work identified in space 1 of this application in Braille (or similar tactile symbols); or (2) phonorecords embodying a fixation of a reading of that work; or (3) both.

a ☐ Copies and Phonorecords   b ☐ Copies Only   c ☐ Phonorecords Only

See instructions.

8

DEPOSIT ACCOUNT If the registration fee is to be charged to a Deposit Account established in the Copyright Office, give name and number of Account.

Name ▼   **Account Number** ▼

CORRESPONDENCE Give name and address to which correspondence about this application should be sent. Name/Address/Apt/City/State/Zip ▼

Area Code & Telephone Number ▶

Be sure to give your daytime phone number.

9

CERTIFICATION* I, the undersigned, hereby certify that I am the

Check one ▶

☐ author
☐ other copyright claimant
☐ owner of exclusive right(s)
☐ authorized agent of

of the work identified in this application and that the statements made by me in this application are correct to the best of my knowledge.

Name of author or other copyright claimant, or owner of exclusive right(s) ▲

Typed or printed name and date ▼ If this is a published work, this date must be the same as or later than the date of publication given in space 3.

date ▶

Handwritten signature (X) ▼

10

MAIL CERTIFI-CATE TO

Certificate will be mailed in window envelope

Name ▼

Number/Street/Apartment Number ▼

City/State/ZIP ▼

Have you:
• Completed all necessary spaces?
• Signed your application in space 10?
• Enclosed check or money order for $10 payable to *Register of Copyrights*?
• Enclosed your deposit material with the application and fee?

MAIL TO: Register of Copyrights, Library of Congress, Washington, D.C. 20559.

11

* 17 U.S.C. § 506(e): Any person who knowingly makes a false representation of a material fact in the application for copyright registration provided for by section 409, or in any written statement filed in connection with the application, shall be fined not more than $2,500.

☆U.S. GOVERNMENT PRINTING OFFICE: 1985: 491-560/20,011   December 1985—200,000

Filling Out Application Form PA

Detach and read these instructions before completing this form. Make sure all applicable spaces have been filled in before you return this form.

BASIC INFORMATION

When to Use This Form: Use Form PA for registration of published or unpublished works of the performing arts. This class includes works prepared for the purpose of being "performed" directly before an audience or indirectly "by means of any device or process." Works of the performing arts include: (1) musical works, including any accompanying words; (2) dramatic works, including any accompanying music; (3) pantomimes and choreographic works; and (4) motion pictures and other audiovisual works.

Deposit to Accompany Application: An application for copyright registration must be accompanied by a deposit consisting of copies or phonorecords representing the entire work for which registration is to be made. The following are the general deposit requirements as set forth in the statute:

Unpublished Work: Deposit one complete copy (or phonorecord).

Published Work: Deposit two complete copies (or phonorecords) of the best edition.

Work First Published Outside the United States: Deposit one complete copy (or phonorecord) of the first foreign edition.

Contribution to a Collective Work: Deposit one complete copy (or phonorecord) of the best edition of the collective work.

Motion Pictures: Deposit *both* of the following: (1) a separate written description of the contents of the motion picture; and (2) for a published work, one complete copy of the best edition of the motion picture; or, for an unpublished work, one complete copy of the motion picture or identifying material. Identifying material may be either an audiorecording of the entire soundtrack or one frame enlargement or similar visual print from each 10-minute segment.

The Copyright Notice: For published works, the law provides that a copyright notice in a specified form "shall be placed on all publicly distributed copies from which the work can be visually perceived." Use of the copyright notice is the responsibility of the copyright owner and does not require advance permission from the Copyright Office. The required form of the notice for copies generally consists of three elements: (1) the symbol "©", or the word "Copyright," or the abbreviation "Copr."; (2) the year of first publication; and (3) the name of the owner of copyright. For example: "© 1981 Constance Porter." The notice is to be affixed to the copies "in such manner and location as to give reasonable notice of the claim of copyright."

For further information about copyright registration, notice, or special questions relating to copyright problems, write:

Information and Publications Section, LM-455
Copyright Office
Library of Congress
Washington, D.C. 20559

LINE-BY-LINE INSTRUCTIONS

1 SPACE 1: Title

Title of This Work: Every work submitted for copyright registration must be given a title to identify that particular work. If the copies or phonorecords of the work bear a title (or an identifying phrase that could serve as a title), transcribe that wording *completely* and *exactly* on the application. Indexing of the registration and future identification of the work will depend on the information you give here. If the work you are registering is an entire "collective work" (such as a collection of plays or songs), give the overall title of the collection. If you are registering one or more individual contributions to a collective work, give the title of each contribution, followed by the title of the collection. Example: "'A Song for Elinda' in *Old and New Ballads for Old and New People.*"

Previous or Alternative Titles: Complete this space if there are any additional titles for the work under which someone searching for the registration might be likely to look, or under which a document pertaining to the work might be recorded.

Nature of This Work: Briefly describe the general nature or character of the work being registered for copyright. Examples: "Music"; "Song Lyrics"; "Words and Music"; "Drama"; "Musical Play"; "Choreography"; "Pantomime"; "Motion Picture"; "Audiovisual Work."

2 SPACE 2: Author(s)

General Instructions: After reading these instructions, decide who are the "authors" of this work for copyright purposes. Then, unless the work is a "collective work," give the requested information about every "author" who contributed any appreciable amount of copyrightable matter to this version of the work. If you need further space, request additional Continuation Sheets. In the case of a collective work, such as a songbook or a collection of plays, give information about the author of the collective work as a whole.

Name of Author: The fullest form of the author's name should be given. Unless the work was "made for hire," the individual who actually created the work is its "author." In the case of a work made for hire, the statute provides

that "the employer or other person for whom the work was prepared is considered the author."

What is a "Work Made for Hire"? A "work made for hire" is defined as: (1) "a work prepared by an employee within the scope of his or her employment"; or (2) "a work specially ordered or commissioned for use as a contribution to a collective work, as a part of a motion picture or other audiovisual work, as a translation, as a supplementary work, as a compilation, as an instructional text, as a test, as answer material for a test, or as an atlas, if the parties expressly agree in a written instrument signed by them that the work shall be considered a work made for hire." If you have checked "Yes" to indicate that the work was "made for hire," you must give the full legal name of the employer (or other person for whom the work was prepared). You may also include the name of the employee along with the name of the employer (for example: "Elster Music Co., employer for hire of John Ferguson").

"Anonymous" or "Pseudonymous" Work: An author's contribution to a work is "anonymous" if that author is not identified on the copies or phonorecords of the work. An author's contribution to a work is "pseudonymous" if that author is identified on the copies or phonorecords under a fictitious name. If the work is "anonymous" you may: (1) leave the line blank; or (2) state "anonymous" on the line; or (3) reveal the author's identity. If the work is "pseudonymous" you may: (1) leave the line blank; or (2) give the pseudonym and identify it as such (for example: "Huntley Haverstock, pseudonym"); or (3) reveal the author's name, making clear which is the real name and which is the pseudonym (for example: "Judith Barton, whose pseudonym is Madeline Elster"). However, the citizenship or domicile of the author **must** be given in all cases.

Dates of Birth and Death: If the author is dead, the statute requires that the year of death be included in the application unless the work is anonymous or pseudonymous. The author's birth date is optional, but is useful as a form of identification. Leave this space blank if the author's contribution was a "work made for hire."

Author's Nationality or Domicile: Give the country of which the author is a citizen, or the country in which the author is domiciled. Nationality or domicile **must** be given in all cases.

Nature of Authorship: Give a brief general statement of the nature of this particular author's contribution to the work. Examples: "Words"; "Co-Author of Music"; "Words and Music"; "Arrangement"; "Co-Author of Book and Lyrics"; "Dramatization"; "Screen Play"; "Compilation and English Translation"; "Editorial Revisions."

3 SPACE 3: Creation and Publication

General Instructions: Do not confuse "creation" with "publication." Every application for copyright registration must state "the year in which creation of the work was completed." Give the date and nation of first publication only if the work has been published.

Creation: Under the statute, a work is "created" when it is fixed in a copy or phonorecord for the first time. Where a work has been prepared over a period of time, the part of the work existing in fixed form on a particular date constitutes the created work on that date. The date you give here should be the year in which the author completed the particular version for which registration is now being sought, even if other versions exist or if further changes or additions are planned.

Publication: The statute defines "publication" as "the distribution of copies or phonorecords of a work to the public by sale or other transfer of ownership, or by rental, lease, or lending"; a work is also "published" if there has been an "offering to distribute copies or phonorecords to a group of persons for purposes of further distribution, public performance, or public display." Give the full date (month, day, year) when, and the country where, publication first occurred. If first publication took place simultaneously in the United States and other countries, it is sufficient to state "U.S.A."

4 SPACE 4: Claimant(s)

Name(s) and Address(es) of Copyright Claimant(s): Give the name(s) and address(es) of the copyright claimant(s) in this work even if the claimant is the same as the author. Copyright in a work belongs initially to the author of the work (including, in the case of a work made for hire, the employer or other person for whom the work was prepared). The copyright claimant is either the author of the work or a person or organization to whom the copyright initially belonging to the author has been transferred.

Transfer: The statute provides that, if the copyright claimant is not the author, the application for registration must contain "a brief statement of how the claimant obtained ownership of the copyright." If any copyright claimant named in space 4 is not an author named in space 2, give a brief, general statement summarizing the means by which that claimant obtained ownership of the copyright. Examples: "By written contract"; "Transfer of all rights by author"; "Assignment"; "By will." Do not attach transfer documents or other attachments or riders.

5 SPACE 5: Previous Registration

General Instructions: The questions in space 5 are intended to find out whether an earlier registration has been made for this work and, if so, whether there is any basis for a new registration. As a general rule, only one basic copyright registration can be made for the same version of a particular work.

Same Version: If this version is substantially the same as the work covered by a previous registration, a second registration is not generally possible unless: (1) the work has been registered in unpublished form and a second registration is now being sought to cover this first published edition; or (2) someone other than the author is identified as copyright claimant in the earlier registration, and the author is now seeking registration in his or her own name. If either of these two exceptions apply, check the appropriate box and give the

earlier registration number and date. Otherwise, do not submit Form PA; instead, write the Copyright Office for information about supplementary registration or recordation of transfers of copyright ownership.

Changed Version: If the work has been changed, and you are now seeking registration to cover the additions or revisions, check the last box in space 5, give the earlier registration number and date, and complete both parts of space 6 in accordance with the instructions below.

Previous Registration Number and Date: If more than one previous registration has been made for the work, give the number and date of the latest registration.

6 SPACE 6: Derivative Work or Compilation

General Instructions: Complete space 6 if this work is a "changed version," "compilation," or "derivative work," and if it incorporates one or more earlier works that have already been published or registered for copyright, or that have fallen into the public domain. A "compilation" is defined as "a work formed by the collection and assembling of preexisting materials or of data that are selected, coordinated, or arranged in such a way that the resulting work as a whole constitutes an original work of authorship." A "derivative work" is "a work based on one or more preexisting works." Examples of derivative works include musical arrangements, dramatizations, translations, abridgments, condensations, motion picture versions, or "any other form in which a work may be recast, transformed, or adapted." Derivative works also include works "consisting of editorial revisions, annotations, or other modifications" if these changes, as a whole, represent an original work of authorship.

Preexisting Material (space 6a): Complete this space and space 6b for derivative works. In this space identify the preexisting work that has been recast, transformed, or adapted. For example, the preexisting material might be: "French version of Hugo's 'Le Roi s'amuse'." Do not complete this space for compilations.

Material Added to This Work (space 6b): Give a brief, general statement of the additional new material covered by the copyright claim for which registration is sought. In the case of a derivative work, identify this new material. Examples: "Arrangement for piano and orchestra"; "Dramatization for television"; "New film version"; "Revisions throughout; Act III completely new." If the work is a compilation, give a brief, general statement describing both the material that has been compiled and the compilation itself. Example: "Compilation of 19th Century Military Songs."

7,8,9 SPACE 7, 8, 9: Fee, Correspondence, Certification, Return Address

Deposit Account: If you maintain a Deposit Account in the Copyright Office, identify it in space 7. Otherwise leave the space blank and send the fee of $10 with your application and deposit.

Correspondence (space 7): This space should contain the name, address, area code, and telephone number of the person to be consulted if correspondence about this application becomes necessary.

Certification (space 8): The application cannot be accepted unless it bears the date and the **handwritten signature** of the author or other copyright claimant, or of the owner of exclusive right(s), or of the duly authorized agent of the author, claimant, or owner of exclusive right(s).

Address for Return of Certificate (space 9): The address box must be completed legibly since the certificate will be returned in a window envelope.

MORE INFORMATION

How To Register a Recorded Work: If the musical or dramatic work that you are registering has been recorded (as a tape, disk, or cassette), you may choose either copyright application Form PA or Form SR, Performing Arts or Sound Recordings, depending on the purpose of the registration.

Form PA should be used to register the underlying musical composition or dramatic work. Form SR has been developed specifically to register a "sound recording" as defined by the Copyright Act—a work resulting from the "fixation of a series of sounds," separate and distinct from the underlying musical or dramatic work. Form SR should be used when the copyright claim is limited to the sound recording itself. (In one instance, Form SR may also be used to file for a copyright registration for both kinds of works—see (4) below.) Therefore:

(1) File Form PA if you are seeking to register the musical or dramatic work, not the "sound recording," even though what you deposit for copyright purposes may be in the form of a phonorecord.

(2) File Form PA if you are seeking to register the audio portion of an audiovisual work, such as a motion picture soundtrack; these are considered integral parts of the audiovisual work.

(3) File Form SR if you are seeking to register the "sound recording" itself, that is, the work that results from the fixation of a series of musical, spoken, or other sounds, but not the underlying musical or dramatic work.

(4) File Form SR if you are the copyright claimant for both the underlying musical or dramatic work and the sound recording, *and* you prefer to register both on the same form.

(5) File both forms PA and SR if the copyright claimant for the underlying work and sound recording differ, or you prefer to have separate registration for them.

"Copies" and "Phonorecords":
To register for copyright, you are required to deposit "copies" or "phonorecords." These are defined as follows:

Musical compositions may be embodied (fixed) in "copies," objects from which a work can be read or visually perceived, directly or with the aid of a machine or device, such as manuscripts, books, sheet music, film, and videotape. They may also be fixed in "phonorecords," objects embodying fixations of sounds, such as tapes and phonograph disks, commonly known as phonograph records. For example, a song (the work to be registered) can be reproduced in sheet music ("copies") or phonograph records ("phonorecords"), or both.

FORM PA
UNITED STATES COPYRIGHT OFFICE

REGISTRATION NUMBER

_____

PA   PAU

EFFECTIVE DATE OF REGISTRATION

_____
Month   Day   Year

DO NOT WRITE ABOVE THIS LINE. IF YOU NEED MORE SPACE, USE A SEPARATE CONTINUATION SHEET.

1

TITLE OF THIS WORK ▼

PREVIOUS OR ALTERNATIVE TITLES ▼

NATURE OF THIS WORK ▼ See instructions

2

a

NAME OF AUTHOR ▼

DATES OF BIRTH AND DEATH
Year Born ▼   Year Died ▼

Was this contribution to the work a "work made for hire"?
☐ Yes
☐ No

AUTHOR'S NATIONALITY OR DOMICILE
Name of Country
OR { Citizen of ▶ _____
Domiciled in ▶ _____

WAS THIS AUTHOR'S CONTRIBUTION TO THE WORK
Anonymous?   ☐ Yes ☐ No
Pseudonymous? ☐ Yes ☐ No
If the answer to either of these questions is "Yes," see detailed instructions.

NATURE OF AUTHORSHIP Briefly describe nature of the material created by this author in which copyright is claimed. ▼

NOTE

Under the law, the "author" of a "work made for hire" is generally the employer, not the employee (see instructions). For any part of this work that was "made for hire" check "Yes" in the space provided, give the employer (or other person for whom the work was prepared) as "Author" of that part, and leave the space for dates of birth and death blank.

b

NAME OF AUTHOR ▼

DATES OF BIRTH AND DEATH
Year Born ▼   Year Died ▼

Was this contribution to the work a "work made for hire"?
☐ Yes
☐ No

AUTHOR'S NATIONALITY OR DOMICILE
Name of country
OR { Citizen of ▶ _____
Domiciled in ▶ _____

WAS THIS AUTHOR'S CONTRIBUTION TO THE WORK
Anonymous?   ☐ Yes ☐ No
Pseudonymous? ☐ Yes ☐ No
If the answer to either of these questions is "Yes," see detailed instructions.

NATURE OF AUTHORSHIP Briefly describe nature of the material created by this author in which copyright is claimed. ▼

c

NAME OF AUTHOR ▼

DATES OF BIRTH AND DEATH
Year Born ▼   Year Died ▼

Was this contribution to the work a "work made for hire"?
☐ Yes
☐ No

AUTHOR'S NATIONALITY OR DOMICILE
Name of Country
OR { Citizen of ▶ _____
Domiciled in ▶ _____

WAS THIS AUTHOR'S CONTRIBUTION TO THE WORK
Anonymous?   ☐ Yes ☐ No
Pseudonymous? ☐ Yes ☐ No
If the answer to either of these questions is "Yes," see detailed instructions.

NATURE OF AUTHORSHIP Briefly describe nature of the material created by this author in which copyright is claimed. ▼

3

YEAR IN WHICH CREATION OF THIS WORK WAS COMPLETED This information must be given in all cases.
◀ Year

DATE AND NATION OF FIRST PUBLICATION OF THIS PARTICULAR WORK Complete this information ONLY if this work has been published.
Month ▶ _____ Day ▶ _____ Year ▶ _____
◀ Nation

4

COPYRIGHT CLAIMANT(S) Name and address must be given even if the claimant is the same as the author given in space 2.▼

See instructions before completing this space.

TRANSFER If the claimant(s) named here in space 4 are different from the author(s) named in space 2, give a brief statement of how the claimant(s) obtained ownership of the copyright.▼

DO NOT WRITE HERE OFFICE USE ONLY

APPLICATION RECEIVED

ONE DEPOSIT RECEIVED

TWO DEPOSITS RECEIVED

REMITTANCE NUMBER AND DATE

MORE ON BACK ▶
• Complete all applicable spaces (numbers 5-9) on the reverse side of this page.
• See detailed instructions.
• Sign the form at line 8.

DO NOT WRITE HERE
Page 1 of _____ pages

EXAMINED BY _____

FORM PA

CHECKED BY _____

☐ CORRESPONDENCE
☐ Yes

☐ DEPOSIT ACCOUNT
☐ FUNDS USED

FOR
COPYRIGHT
OFFICE
USE
ONLY

DO NOT WRITE ABOVE THIS LINE. IF YOU NEED MORE SPACE, USE A SEPARATE CONTINUATION SHEET.

PREVIOUS REGISTRATION   Has registration for this work, or for an earlier version of this work, already been made in the Copyright Office?
☐ Yes ☐ No If your answer is "Yes," why is another registration being sought? (Check appropriate box) ▼
☐ This is the first published edition of a work previously registered in unpublished form.
☐ This is the first application submitted by this author as copyright claimant.
☐ This is a changed version of the work, as shown by space 6 on this application.
If your answer is "Yes," give: **Previous Registration Number ▼**   **Year of Registration ▼**

5

DERIVATIVE WORK OR COMPILATION   Complete both space 6a & 6b for a derivative work; complete only 6b for a compilation.
a. Preexisting Material   Identify any preexisting work or works that this work is based on or incorporates. ▼

b. Material Added to This Work   Give a brief, general statement of the material that has been added to this work and in which copyright is claimed.▼

6

See instructions
before completing
this space.

DEPOSIT ACCOUNT   If the registration fee is to be charged to a Deposit Account established in the Copyright Office, give name and number of Account.
Name ▼   **Account Number ▼**

7

CORRESPONDENCE   Give name and address to which correspondence about this application should be sent.   Name/Address/Apt/City/State/Zip ▼

Area Code & Telephone Number ▶

Be sure to
give your
daytime phone
◀ number.

CERTIFICATION*   I, the undersigned, hereby certify that I am the
Check only one ▼
☐ author
☐ other copyright claimant
☐ owner of exclusive right(s)
☐ authorized agent of_____
                            Name of author or other copyright claimant, or owner of exclusive right(s) ▲

8

of the work identified in this application and that the statements made
by me in this application are correct to the best of my knowledge.

Typed or printed name and date ▼ If this is a published work, this date must be the same as or later than the date of publication given in space 3.

_____ date ▶ _____

Handwritten signature (X) ▼

**MAIL
CERTIFI-
CATE TO**

**Certificate
will be
mailed in
window
envelope**

Name ▼

Number/Street/Apartment Number ▼

City/State/ZIP ▼

Have you:
• Completed all necessary
  spaces?
• Signed your application in space
  8?
• Enclosed check or money order
  for $10 payable to *Register of
  Copyrights?*
• Enclosed your deposit material
  with the application and fee?
MAIL TO: Register of Copyrights,
Library of Congress, Washington,
D.C. 20559.

9

* 17 U.S.C. § 506(e): Any person who knowingly makes a false representation of a material fact in the application for copyright registration provided for by section 409, or in any written statement filed in connection with the application, shall be fined not more than $2,500.

☉ U.S. GOVERNMENT PRINTING OFFICE: 1987:181-531/60,000

July 1987-100,000

Filling Out Application Form VA

Detach and read these instructions before completing this form. Make sure all applicable spaces have been filled in before you return this form.

BASIC INFORMATION

When to Use This Form: Use Form VA for copyright registration of published or unpublished works of the visual arts. This category consists of "pictorial, graphic, or sculptural works," including two-dimensional and three-dimensional works of fine, graphic, and applied art, photographs, prints and art reproductions, maps, globes, charts, technical drawings, diagrams, and models.

What Does Copyright Protect? Copyright in a work of the visual arts protects those pictorial, graphic, or sculptural elements that, either alone or in combination, represent an "original work of authorship." The statute declares: "In no case does copyright protection for an original work of authorship extend to any idea, procedure, process, system, method of operation, concept, principle, or discovery, regardless of the form in which it is described, explained, illustrated, or embodied in such work."

Works of Artistic Craftsmanship and Designs: "Works of artistic craftsmanship" are registrable on Form VA, but the statute makes clear that protection extends to "their form" and not to "their mechanical or utilitarian aspects." The "design of a useful article" is considered copyrightable "only if, and only to the extent that, such design incorporates pictorial, graphic, or sculptural features that can be identified separately from, and are capable of existing independently of, the utilitarian aspects of the article."

Labels and Advertisements: Works prepared for use in connection with the sale or advertisement of goods and services are registrable if they contain "original work of authorship." Use Form VA if the copyrightable material in the work you are registering is mainly pictorial or graphic; use Form TX if it consists mainly of text. **NOTE:** Words and short phrases such as names, titles, and slogans cannot be protected by copyright, and the same is true of standard symbols, emblems, and other commonly used graphic designs that are in the public domain. When used commercially, material of that sort can sometimes be protected under state laws of unfair competition or under the Federal trademark laws. For information about trademark registration, write to the Commissioner of Patents and Trademarks, Washington, D.C. 20231.

Deposit to Accompany Application: An application for copyright registration must be accompanied by a deposit consisting of copies representing the entire work for which registration is to be made.

Unpublished Work: Deposit one complete copy.

Published Work: Deposit two complete copies of the best edition.

Work First Published Outside the United States: Deposit one complete copy of the first foreign edition.

Contribution to a Collective Work: Deposit one complete copy of the best edition of the collective work.

The Copyright Notice: For published works, the law provides that a copyright notice in a specified form "shall be placed on all publicly distributed copies from which the work can be visually perceived." Use of the copyright notice is the responsibility of the copyright owner and does not require advance permission from the Copyright Office. The required form of the notice for copies generally consists of three elements: (1) the symbol "©", or the word "Copyright," or the abbreviation "Copr."; (2) the year of first publication; and (3) the name of the owner of copyright. For example: "© 1981 Constance Porter." The notice is to be affixed to the copies "in such manner and location as to give reasonable notice of the claim of copyright."

For further information about copyright registration, notice, or special questions relating to copyright problems, write:

Information and Publications Section, LM-455
Copyright Office, Library of Congress, Washington, D.C. 20559

LINE-BY-LINE INSTRUCTIONS

1 SPACE 1: Title

Title of This Work: Every work submitted for copyright registration must be given a title to identify that particular work. If the copies of the work bear a title (or an identifying phrase that could serve as a title), transcribe that wording *completely* and *exactly* on the application. Indexing of the registration and future identification of the work will depend on the information you give here.

Previous or Alternative Titles: Complete this space if there are any additional titles for the work under which someone searching for the registration might be likely to look, or under which a document pertaining to the work might be recorded.

Publication as a Contribution: If the work being registered is a contribution to a periodical, serial, or collection, give the title of the contribution in the "Title of This Work" space. Then, in the line headed "Publication as a Contribution," give information about the collective work in which the contribution appeared.

Nature of This Work: Briefly describe the general nature or character of the pictorial, graphic, or sculptural work being registered for copyright. Examples: "Oil Painting"; "Charcoal Drawing"; "Etching"; "Sculpture"; "Map"; "Photograph"; "Scale Model"; "Lithographic Print"; "Jewelry Design"; "Fabric Design."

2 SPACE 2: Author(s)

General Instructions: After reading these instructions, decide who are the "authors" of this work for copyright purposes. Then, unless the work is a "collective work," give the requested information about every "author" who contributed any appreciable amount of copyrightable matter to this version of the work. If you need further space, request additional Continuation Sheets. In the case of a collective work, such as a catalog of paintings or collection of cartoons by various authors, give information about the author of the collective work as a whole.

Name of Author: The fullest form of the author's name should be given. Unless the work was "made for hire," the individual who actually created the work is its "author." In the case of a work made for hire, the statute provides that "the employer or other person for whom the work was prepared is considered the author."

What is a "Work Made for Hire"? A "work made for hire" is defined as: (1) "a work prepared by an employee within the scope of his or her employment"; or (2) "a work specially ordered or commissioned for use as a contribution to a collective work, as a part of a motion picture or other audiovisual work, as a translation, as a supplementary work, as a compilation, as an instructional text, as a test, as answer material for a test, or as an atlas, if the parties expressly agree in a written instrument signed by them that the work shall be considered a work made for hire." If you have checked "Yes" to indicate that the work was "made for hire," you must give the full legal name of the employer (or other person for whom the work was prepared). You may also include the name of the employee along with the name of the employer (for example: "Elster Publishing Co., employer for hire of John Ferguson").

"Anonymous" or "Pseudonymous" Work: An author's contribution to a work is "anonymous" if that author is not identified on the copies or phonorecords of the work. An author's contribution to a work is "pseudonymous" if that author is identified on the copies or phonorecords under a fictitious name. If the work is "anonymous" you may: (1) leave the line blank; or (2) state "anonymous" on the line; or (3) reveal the author's identity. If the work is "pseudonymous" you may: (1) leave the line blank; or (2) give the pseudonym and identify it as such (for example: "Huntley Haverstock, pseudonym"); or (3) reveal the author's name, making clear which is the real name and which is the pseudonym (for example: "Henry Leek, whose pseudonym is Priam Farrel"). However, the citizenship or domicile of the author **must** be given in all cases.

Dates of Birth and Death: If the author is dead, the statute requires that the year of death be included in the application unless the work is anonymous or pseudonymous. The author's birth date is optional, but is useful as a form of identification. Leave this space blank if the author's contribution was a "work made for hire."

Author's Nationality or Domicile: Give the country of which the author is a citizen, or the country in which the author is domiciled. Nationality or domicile **must** be given in all cases.

Nature of Authorship: Give a brief general statement of the nature of this particular author's contribution to the work. Examples: "Painting"; "Photograph"; "Silk Screen Reproduction"; "Co-author of Cartographic Material"; "Technical Drawing"; "Text and Artwork."

3 SPACE 3: Creation and Publication

General Instructions: Do not confuse "creation" with "publication." Every application for copyright registration must state "the year in which creation of the work was completed." Give the date and nation of first publication only if the work has been published.

Creation: Under the statute, a work is "created" when it is fixed in a copy or phonorecord for the first time. Where a work has been prepared over a period of time, the part of the work existing in fixed form on a particular date constitutes the created work on that date. The date you give here should be the year in which the author completed the particular version for which registration is now being sought, even if other versions exist or if further changes or additions are planned.

Publication: The statute defines "publication" as "the distribution of copies or phonorecords of a work to the public by sale or other transfer of ownership, or by rental, lease, or lending"; a work is also "published" if there has been an "offering to distribute copies or phonorecords to a group of persons for purposes of further distribution, public performance, or public display." Give the full date (month, day, year) when, and the country where, publication first occurred. If first publication took place simultaneously in the United States and other countries, it is sufficient to state "U.S.A."

4 SPACE 4: Claimant(s)

Name(s) and Address(es) of Copyright Claimant(s): Give the name(s) and address(es) of the copyright claimant(s) in this work even if the claimant is the same as the author. Copyright in a work belongs initially to the author of the work (including, in the case of a work made for hire, the employer or other person for whom the work was prepared). The copyright claimant is either the author of the work or a person or organization to whom the copyright initially belonging to the author has been transferred.

Transfer: The statute provides that, if the copyright claimant is not the author, the application for registration must contain "a brief statement of how the claimant obtained ownership of the copyright." If any copyright claimant named in space 4 is not an author named in space 2, give a brief, general statement summarizing the means by which that claimant obtained ownership of the copyright. Examples: "By written contract"; "Transfer of all rights by author"; "Assignment"; "By will." Do not attach transfer documents or other attachments or riders.

5 SPACE 5: Previous Registration

General Instructions: The questions in space 5 are intended to find out whether an earlier registration has been made for this work and, if so, whether there is any basis for a new registration. As a rule, only one basic copyright registration can be made for the same version of a particular work.

Same Version: If this version is substantially the same as the work covered by a previous registration, a second registration is not generally possible unless: (1) the work has been registered in unpublished form and a second registration is now being sought to cover this first published edition; or (2) some-

one other than the author is identified as copyright claimant in the earlier registration, and the author is now seeking registration in his or her own name. If either of these two exceptions apply, check the appropriate box and give the earlier registration number and date. Otherwise, do not submit Form VA; instead, write the Copyright Office for information about supplementary registration or recordation of transfers of copyright ownership.

Changed Version: If the work has been changed, and you are now seeking registration to cover the additions or revisions, check the last box in space 5, give the earlier registration number and date, and complete both parts of space 6 in accordance with the instructions below.

Previous Registration Number and Date: If more than one previous registration has been made for the work, give the number and date of the latest registration.

6 SPACE 6: Derivative Work or Compilation

General Instructions: Complete space 6 if this work is a "changed version," "compilation," or "derivative work," and if it incorporates one or more earlier works that have already been published or registered for copyright, or that have fallen into the public domain. A "compilation" is defined as "a work formed by the collection and assembling of preexisting materials or of data that are selected, coordinated, or arranged in such a way that the resulting work as a whole constitutes an original work of authorship." A "derivative work" is "a work based on one or more preexisting works." Examples of derivative works include reproductions of works of art, sculptures based on drawings, lithographs based on paintings, maps based on previously published sources, or "any other form in which a work may be recast, transformed, or adapted." Derivative works also include works "consisting of editorial revisions, annotations, or other modifications" if these changes, as a whole, represent an original work of authorship.

Preexisting Material (space 6a): Complete this space **and** space 6b for derivative works. In this space identify the preexisting work that has been recast, transformed, or adapted. Examples of preexisting material might be "Grunewald Altarpiece"; or "19th century quilt design." Do not complete this space for compilations.

Material Added to This Work (space 6b): Give a brief, general statement of the **additional** new material covered by the copyright claim for which registration is sought. In the case of a derivative work, identify this new material. Examples: "Adaptation of design and additional artistic work"; "Reproduction of painting by photolithography"; "Additional cartographic material"; "Compilation of photographs." If the work is a compilation, give a brief, general statement describing both the material that has been compiled **and** the compilation itself. Example: "Compilation of 19th Century Political Cartoons."

7,8,9 SPACE 7, 8, 9: Fee, Correspondence, Certification, Return Address

Deposit Account: If you maintain a Deposit Account in the Copyright Office, identify it in space 7. Otherwise leave the space blank and send the fee of $10 with your application and deposit.

Correspondence (space 7): This space should contain the name, address, area code, and telephone number of the person to be consulted if correspondence about this application becomes necessary.

Certification (space 8): The application cannot be accepted unless it bears the date and the **handwritten signature** of the author or other copyright claimant, or of the owner of exclusive right(s), or of the duly authorized agent of the author, claimant, or owner of exclusive right(s).

Address for Return of Certificate (space 9): The address box must be completed legibly since the certificate will be returned in a window envelope.

MORE INFORMATION

Form of Deposit for Works of the Visual Arts

Exceptions to General Deposit Requirements: As explained on the reverse side of this page, the statutory deposit requirements (generally one copy for unpublished works and two copies for published works) will vary for particular kinds of works of the visual arts. The copyright law authorizes the Register of Copyrights to issue regulations specifying "the administrative classes into which works are to be placed for purposes of deposit and registration, and the nature of the copies or phonorecords to be deposited in the various classes specified." For particular classes, the regulations may require or permit "the deposit of identifying material instead of copies or phonorecords," or "the deposit of only one copy or phonorecord where two would normally be required."

What Should You Deposit? The detailed requirements with respect to the kind of deposit to accompany an application on Form VA are contained in the Copyright

Office Regulations. The following does not cover all of the deposit requirements, but is intended to give you some general guidance.

For an Unpublished Work, the material deposited should represent the entire copyrightable content of the work for which registration is being sought.

For a Published Work, the material deposited should generally consist of two complete copies of the best edition. Exceptions: (1) For certain types of works, one complete copy may be deposited instead of two. These include greeting cards, postcards, stationery, labels, advertisements, scientific drawings, and globes; (2) For most three-dimensional sculptural works, and for certain two-dimensional works, the Copyright Office Regulations require deposit of identifying material (photographs or drawings in a specified form) rather than copies; and (3) Under certain circumstances, for works published in five copies or less or in limited, numbered editions, the deposit may consist of one copy or of identifying reproductions.

FORM VA

UNITED STATES COPYRIGHT OFFICE

REGISTRATION NUMBER

VA   VAU

EFFECTIVE DATE OF REGISTRATION

Month   Day   Year

DO NOT WRITE ABOVE THIS LINE. IF YOU NEED MORE SPACE, USE A SEPARATE CONTINUATION SHEET.

1

TITLE OF THIS WORK ▼

NATURE OF THIS WORK ▼ See instructions

PREVIOUS OR ALTERNATIVE TITLES ▼

PUBLICATION AS A CONTRIBUTION If this work was published as a contribution to a periodical, serial, or collection, give information about the collective work in which the contribution appeared. **Title of Collective Work ▼**

If published in a periodical or serial give: **Volume ▼**   **Number ▼**   **Issue Date ▼**   **On Pages ▼**

2

a

NAME OF AUTHOR ▼

DATES OF BIRTH AND DEATH
Year Born ▼   Year Died ▼

Was this contribution to the work a "work made for hire"?
☐ Yes
☐ No

AUTHOR'S NATIONALITY OR DOMICILE
Name of Country
OR { Citizen of ▶ _____
Domiciled in ▶ _____

WAS THIS AUTHOR'S CONTRIBUTION TO THE WORK
Anonymous? ☐ Yes ☐ No
Pseudonymous? ☐ Yes ☐ No

If the answer to either of these questions is "Yes," see detailed instructions.

NATURE OF AUTHORSHIP Briefly describe nature of the material created by this author in which copyright is claimed. ▼

NOTE

Under the law, the "author" of a "work made for hire" is generally the employer, not the employee (see instructions). For any part of this work that was "made for hire" check "Yes" in the space provided, give the employer (or other person for whom the work was prepared) as "Author" of that part, and leave the space for dates of birth and death blank.

b

NAME OF AUTHOR ▼

DATES OF BIRTH AND DEATH
Year Born ▼   Year Died ▼

Was this contribution to the work a "work made for hire"?
☐ Yes
☐ No

AUTHOR'S NATIONALITY OR DOMICILE
Name of country
OR { Citizen of ▶ _____
Domiciled in ▶ _____

WAS THIS AUTHOR'S CONTRIBUTION TO THE WORK
Anonymous? ☐ Yes ☐ No
Pseudonymous? ☐ Yes ☐ No

If the answer to either of these questions is "Yes," see detailed instructions.

NATURE OF AUTHORSHIP Briefly describe nature of the material created by this author in which copyright is claimed. ▼

c

NAME OF AUTHOR ▼

DATES OF BIRTH AND DEATH
Year Born ▼   Year Died ▼

Was this contribution to the work a "work made for hire"?
☐ Yes
☐ No

AUTHOR'S NATIONALITY OR DOMICILE
Name of Country
OR { Citizen of ▶ _____
Domiciled in ▶ _____

WAS THIS AUTHOR'S CONTRIBUTION TO THE WORK
Anonymous? ☐ Yes ☐ No
Pseudonymous? ☐ Yes ☐ No

If the answer to either of these questions is "Yes," see detailed instructions.

NATURE OF AUTHORSHIP Briefly describe nature of the material created by this author in which copyright is claimed. ▼

3

YEAR IN WHICH CREATION OF THIS WORK WAS COMPLETED This information must be given in all cases. ◀ Year

DATE AND NATION OF FIRST PUBLICATION OF THIS PARTICULAR WORK
Complete this information ONLY if this work has been published.
Month ▶ _____ Day ▶ _____ Year ▶ _____ ◀ Nation

4

See instructions before completing this space.

COPYRIGHT CLAIMANT(S) Name and address must be given even if the claimant is the same as the author given in space 2.▼

TRANSFER If the claimant(s) named here in space 4 are different from the author(s) named in space 2, give a brief statement of how the claimant(s) obtained ownership of the copyright.▼

APPLICATION RECEIVED

ONE DEPOSIT RECEIVED

TWO DEPOSITS RECEIVED

REMITTANCE NUMBER AND DATE

DO NOT WRITE HERE OFFICE USE ONLY

MORE ON BACK ▶
• Complete all applicable spaces (numbers 5-9) on the reverse side of this page.
• See detailed instructions.
• Sign the form at line 8.

DO NOT WRITE HERE
Page 1 of _____ pages

EXAMINED BY	FORM VA
CHECKED BY	

☐ CORRESPONDENCE
Yes

☐ DEPOSIT ACCOUNT
FUNDS USED

FOR
COPYRIGHT
OFFICE
USE
ONLY

DO NOT WRITE ABOVE THIS LINE. IF YOU NEED MORE SPACE, USE A SEPARATE CONTINUATION SHEET.

PREVIOUS REGISTRATION Has registration for this work, or for an earlier version of this work, already been made in the Copyright Office?
☐ **Yes** ☐ **No** If your answer is "Yes," why is another registration being sought? (Check appropriate box) ▼

☐ This is the first published edition of a work previously registered in unpublished form.

☐ This is the first application submitted by this author as copyright claimant.

☐ This is a changed version of the work, as shown by space 6 on this application.

If your answer is "Yes," give: **Previous Registration Number ▼**   **Year of Registration ▼**

5

DERIVATIVE WORK OR COMPILATION Complete both space 6a & 6b for a derivative work; complete only 6b for a compilation.
a. Preexisting Material Identify any preexisting work or works that this work is based on or incorporates. ▼

b. Material Added to This Work Give a brief, general statement of the material that has been added to this work and in which copyright is claimed. ▼

6

See instructions
before completing
this space.

DEPOSIT ACCOUNT If the registration fee is to be charged to a Deposit Account established in the Copyright Office, give name and number of Account.
Name ▼   **Account Number ▼**

7

CORRESPONDENCE Give name and address to which correspondence about this application should be sent.   Name/Address/Apt/City/State/Zip ▼

Area Code & Telephone Number ▶

Be sure to
give your
daytime phone
◀ number.

CERTIFICATION*   I, the undersigned, hereby certify that I am the
Check only one ▼
☐ author
☐ other copyright claimant
☐ owner of exclusive right(s)
☐ authorized agent of _____
              Name of author or other copyright claimant, or owner of exclusive right(s) ▲

8

of the work identified in this application and that the statements made
by me in this application are correct to the best of my knowledge.

Typed or printed name and date ▼ If this is a published work, this date must be the same as or later than the date of publication given in space 3.

_____ **date ▶** _____

Handwritten signature (X) ▼

**MAIL
CERTIFI-
CATE TO**

Name ▼

Number/Street/Apartment Number ▼

City/State/ZIP ▼

**Certificate
will be
mailed in
window
envelope**

Have you:
● Completed all necessary
  spaces?
● Signed your application in space
  8?
● Enclosed check or money order
  for $10 payable to *Register of
  Copyrights?*
● Enclosed your deposit material
  with the application and fee?
MAIL TO: Register of Copyrights,
Library of Congress, Washington,
D.C. 20559.

9

* 17 U.S.C. § 506(e): Any person who knowingly makes a false representation of a material fact in the application for copyright registration provided for by section 409, or in any written statement filed in
connection with the application, shall be fined not more than $2,500.

☐U.S. GOVERNMENT PRINTING OFFICE: 1987—181—531/40,025

April 1987—60,000

Filling Out Application Form SR

Detach and read these instructions before completing this form. Make sure all applicable spaces have been filled in before you return this form.

BASIC INFORMATION

When to Use This Form: Use Form SR for copyright registration of published or unpublished sound recordings. It should be used where the copyright claim is limited to the sound recording itself, and it may also be used where the same copyright claimant is seeking simultaneous registration of the underlying musical, dramatic, or literary work embodied in the phonorecord.

With one exception, "sound recordings" are works that result from the fixation of a series of musical, spoken, or other sounds. The exception is for the audio portions of audiovisual works, such as a motion picture soundtrack or an audio cassette accompanying a filmstrip; these are considered a part of the audiovisual work as a whole.

Deposit to Accompany Application: An application for copyright registration of a sound recording must be accompanied by a deposit consisting of phonorecords representing the entire work for which registration is to be made.

Unpublished Work: Deposit one complete phonorecord.

Published Work: Deposit two complete phonorecords of the best edition, together with "any printed or other visually perceptible material" published with the phonorecords.

Work First Published Outside the United States: Deposit one complete phonorecord of the first foreign edition.

Contribution to a Collective Work: Deposit one complete phonorecord of the best edition of the collective work.

The Copyright Notice: For published sound recordings, the law provides that a copyright notice in a specified form "shall be placed on all publicly distributed phonorecords of the sound recording." Use of the copyright notice is the responsibility of the copyright owner and does not require advance permission from the Copyright Office. The required form of the notice for phonorecords of sound recordings consists of three elements: (1) the symbol "℗" (the letter "P" in a circle); (2) the year of first publication of the sound recording; and (3) the name of the owner of copyright. For example: "℗ 1981 Rittenhouse Record Co." The notice is to be "placed on the surface of the phonorecord, or on the label or container, in such manner and location as to give reasonable notice of the claim of copyright." For further information about copyright, write:
Information and Publications Section, LM-455
Copyright Office, Library of Congress, Washington, D.C. 20559

LINE-BY-LINE INSTRUCTIONS

1 SPACE 1: Title

Title of This Work: Every work submitted for copyright registration must be given a title to identify that particular work. If the phonorecords or any accompanying printed material bear a title (or an identifying phrase that could serve as a title), transcribe that wording completely and exactly on the application. Indexing of the registration and future identification of the work may depend on the information you give here.

Nature of Material Recorded: Indicate the general type or character of the works or other material embodied in the recording. The box marked "Literary" should be checked for nondramatic spoken material of all sorts, including narration, interviews, panel discussions, and training material. If the material recorded is not musical, dramatic, or literary in nature, check "Other" and briefly describe the type of sounds fixed in the recording. For example: "Sound Effects"; "Bird Calls"; "Crowd Noises."

Previous or Alternative Titles: Complete this space if there are any additional titles for the work under which someone searching for the registration might be likely to look, or under which a document pertaining to the work might be recorded.

2 SPACE 2: Author(s)

General Instructions: After reading these instructions, decide who are the "authors" of this work for copyright purposes. Then, unless the work is a "collective work," give the requested information about every "author" who contributed any appreciable amount of copyrightable matter to this version of the work. If you need further space, request additional Continuation Sheets. In the case of a collective work, such as a collection of previously published or registered sound recordings, give information about the author of the collective work as a whole. If you are submitting this Form SR to cover the recorded musical, dramatic, or literary work as well as the sound recording itself, it is important for space 2 to include full information about the various authors of all of the material covered by the copyright claim, making clear the nature of each author's contribution.

Name of Author: The fullest form of the author's name should be given. Unless the work was "made for hire," the individual who actually created the work is its "author." In the case of a work made for hire, the statute provides that "the employer or other person for whom the work was prepared is considered the author."

What is a "Work Made for Hire"? A "work made for hire" is defined as: (1) "a work prepared by an employee within the scope of his or her employment"; or (2) "a work specially ordered or commissioned for use as a contribution to a collective work, as a part of a motion picture or other audiovisual work, as a translation, as a supplementary work, as a compilation, as an instructional text, as a test, as answer material for a test, or as an atlas, if the parties expressly agree in a written instrument signed by them that the work shall be considered a work made for hire." If you have checked "Yes" to indicate that the work was "made for hire," you must give the full legal name of the employer (or other person for whom the work was prepared). You may also include the name of the employee along with the name of the employer (for example: "Elster Record Co., employer for hire of John Ferguson").

"Anonymous" or "Pseudonymous" Work: An author's contribution to a work is "anonymous" if that author is not identified on the copies or phonorecords of the work. An author's contribution to a work is "pseudonymous" if that author is identified on the copies or phonorecords under a fictitious name. If the work is "anonymous" you may: (1) leave the line blank; or (2) state "anonymous" on the line; or (3) reveal the author's identity. If the work is "pseudonymous" you may: (1) leave the line blank; or (2) give the pseudonym and identify it as such (for example: "Huntley Haverstock, pseudonym"); or (3) reveal the author's name, making clear which is the real name and which is the pseudonym (for example: "Judith Barton, whose pseudonym is Madeline Elster"). However, the citizenship or domicile of the author **must** be given in all cases.

Dates of Birth and Death: If the author is dead, the statute requires that the year of death be included in the application unless the work is anonymous or pseudonymous. The author's birth date is optional, but is useful as a form of identification. Leave this space blank if the author's contribution was a "work made for hire."

Author's Nationality or Domicile: Give the country of which the author is a citizen, or the country in which the author is domiciled. Nationality or domicile **must** be given in all cases.

Nature of Authorship: Give a brief general statement of the nature of this particular author's contribution to the work. If you are submitting this Form SR to cover both the sound recording and the underlying musical, dramatic, or literary work, make sure that the precise nature of each author's contribution is reflected here. Examples where the authorship pertains to the recording: "Sound Recording"; "Performance and Recording"; "Compilation and Remixing of Sounds." Examples where the authorship pertains to both the recording and the underlying work: "Words, Music, Performance, Recording"; "Arrangement of Music and Recording"; "Compilation of Poems and Reading."

3 SPACE 3: Creation and Publication

General Instructions: Do not confuse "creation" with "publication." Every application for copyright registration must state "the year in which creation of the work was completed." Give the date and nation of first publication only if the work has been published.

Creation: Under the statute, a work is "created" when it is fixed in a copy or phonorecord for the first time. Where a work has been prepared over a period of time, the part of the work existing in fixed form on a particular date constitutes the created work on that date. The date you give here should be the year in which the author completed the particular version for which registration is now being sought, even if other versions exist or if further changes or additions are planned.

Publication: The statute defines "publication" as "the distribution of copies or phonorecords of a work to the public by sale or other transfer of ownership, or by rental, lease, or lending"; a work is also "published" if there has been an "offering to distribute copies or phonorecords to a group of persons for purposes of further distribution, public performance, or public display." Give the full date (month, day, year) when, and the country where, publication first occurred. If first publication took place simultaneously in the United States and other countries, it is sufficient to state "U.S.A."

4 SPACE 4: Claimant(s)

Name(s) and Address(es) of Copyright Claimant(s): Give the name(s) and address(es) of the copyright claimant(s) in this work even if the claimant is the same as the author. Copyright in a work belongs initially to the author of the work (including, in the case of a work made for hire, the employer or other person for whom the work was prepared). The copyright claimant is either the author of the work or a person or organization to whom the copyright initially belonging to the author has been transferred.

Transfer: The statute provides that, if the copyright claimant is not the author, the application for registration must contain "a brief statement of how the claimant obtained ownership of the copyright." If any copyright claimant named in space 4 is not an author named in space 2, give a brief, general statement summarizing the means by which that claimant obtained ownership of the copyright. Examples: "By written contract"; "Transfer of all rights by author"; "Assignment"; "By will." Do not attach transfer documents or other attachments or riders.

5 SPACE 5: Previous Registration

General Instructions: The questions in space 5 are intended to find out whether an earlier registration has been made for this work and, if so, whether there is any basis for a new registration. As a rule, only one basic copyright registration can be made for the same version of a particular work.

Same Version: If this version is substantially the same as the work covered by a previous registration, a second registration is not generally possible unless: (1) the work has been registered in unpublished form and a second registration is now being sought to cover this first published edition; or (2) someone other than the author is identified as copyright claimant in the earlier registration, and the author is now seeking registration in his or her own name. If either of these two exceptions apply, check the appropriate box and give the earlier registration number and date. Otherwise, do not submit Form SR; instead, write the Copyright Office for information about supplementary registration or recordation of transfers of copyright ownership.

Changed Version: If the work has been changed, and you are now seeking registration to cover the additions or revisions, check the last box in space 5, give the earlier registration number and date, and complete both parts of space 6 in accordance with the instructions below.

Previous Registration Number and Date: If more than one previous registration has been made for the work, give the number and date of the latest registration.

6 SPACE 6: Derivative Work or Compilation

General Instructions: Complete space 6 if this work is a "changed version," "compilation," or "derivative work," and if it incorporates one or more earlier works that have already been published or registered for copyright, or that have fallen into the public domain, or sound recordings that were fixed before February 15, 1972. A "compilation" is defined as "a work formed by the collection and assembling of preexisting materials or of data that are selected, coordinated, or arranged in such a way that the resulting work as a whole constitutes an original work of authorship." A "derivative work" is "a work based on one or more preexisting works." Examples of derivative works include recordings reissued with substantial editorial revisions or abridgments of the recorded sounds, and recordings republished with new recorded material, or "any other form in which a work may be recast, transformed, or adapted." Derivative works also include works "consisting of editorial revisions, annotations, or other modifications" if these changes, as a whole, represent an original work of authorship.

Preexisting Material (space 6a): Complete this space and space 6b for derivative works. In this space identify the preexisting work that has been recast, transformed, or adapted. For example, the preexisting material might be: "1970 recording by Sperryville Symphony of Bach Double Concerto." Do not complete this space for compilations.

Material Added to This Work (space 6b): Give a brief, general statement of the additional new material covered by the copyright claim for which registration is sought. In the case of a derivative work, identify this new material. Examples: "Recorded performances on bands 1 and 3"; "Remixed sounds from original multitrack sound sources"; "New words, arrangement, and additional sounds." If the work is a compilation, give a brief, general statement describing both the material that has been compiled and the compilation itself. Example: "Compilation of 1938 Recordings by various swing bands."

7,8,9 SPACE 7, 8, 9: Fee, Correspondence, Certification, Return Address

Deposit Account: If you maintain a Deposit Account in the Copyright Office, identify it in space 7. Otherwise leave the space blank and send the fee of $10 with your application and deposit.

Correspondence (space 7): This space should contain the name, address, area code, and telephone number of the person to be consulted if correspondence about this application becomes necessary.

Certification (space 8): The application cannot be accepted unless it bears the date and the **handwritten signature** of the author or other copyright claimant, or of the owner of exclusive right(s), or of the duly authorized agent of the author, claimant, or owner of exclusive right(s).

Address for Return of Certificate (space 9): The address box must be completed legibly since the certificate will be returned in a window envelope.

MORE INFORMATION

"Works": "Works" are the basic subject matter of copyright; they are what authors create and copyright protects. The statute draws a sharp distinction between the "work" and "any material object in which the work is embodied."

"Copies" and "Phonorecords": These are the two types of material objects in which "works" are embodied. In general, **"copies"** are objects from which a work can be read or visually perceived, directly or with the aid of a machine or device, such as manuscripts, books, sheet music, film, and videotape. **"Phonorecords"** are objects embodying fixations of sounds, such as audio tapes and phonograph disks. For example, a song (the "work") can be reproduced in sheet music ("copies") or phonograph disks ("phonorecords"), or both.

"Sound Recordings": These are "works," not "copies" or "phonorecords." "Sound recordings" are "works that result from the fixation of a series of musical, spoken, or other sounds, but not including the sounds accompanying a motion picture or other audiovisual work." Example: When a record company issues a new release, the release will typically involve two distinct "works": the "musical work" that has been recorded, and the "sound recording" as a separate work in itself. The material objects that the record company sends out are "phonorecords": physical reproductions of both the "musical work" and the "sound recording."

Should You File More Than One Application? If your work consists of a recorded musical, dramatic, or literary work, and both that "work," and the sound recording as a separate "work," are eligible for registration, the application form you should file depends on the following:

File Only Form SR if: The copyright claimant is the same for both the musical, dramatic, or literary work and for the sound recording, and you are seeking a single registration to cover both of these "works."

File Only Form PA (or Form TX) if: You are seeking to register only the musical, dramatic, or literary work, not the sound recording. Form PA is appropriate for works of the performing arts; Form TX is for nondramatic literary works.

Separate Applications Should Be Filed on Form PA (or Form TX) and on Form SR if: (1) The copyright claimant for the musical, dramatic, or literary work is different from the copyright claimant for the sound recording; or (2) You prefer to have separate registrations for the musical, dramatic, or literary work and for the sound recording.

FORM SR
UNITED STATES COPYRIGHT OFFICE

REGISTRATION NUMBER

SR	SRU

EFFECTIVE DATE OF REGISTRATION

Month	Day	Year

DO NOT WRITE ABOVE THIS LINE. IF YOU NEED MORE SPACE, USE A SEPARATE CONTINUATION SHEET.

1

TITLE OF THIS WORK ▼

PREVIOUS OR ALTERNATIVE TITLES ▼

NATURE OF MATERIAL RECORDED ▼ See instructions.
☐ Musical   ☐ Musical-Dramatic
☐ Dramatic ☐ Literary
☐ Other _____

2

a

NAME OF AUTHOR▼

DATES OF BIRTH AND DEATH
Year Born ▼   Year Died ▼

Was this contribution to the work a "work made for hire"?
☐ Yes
☐ No

AUTHOR'S NATIONALITY OR DOMICILE
Name of Country
OR { Citizen of ▶ _____
{ Domiciled in ▶ _____

WAS THIS AUTHOR'S CONTRIBUTION TO THE WORK
Anonymous?   ☐ Yes ☐ No
Pseudonymous? ☐ Yes ☐ No

If the answer to either of these questions is "Yes," see detailed instructions.

NATURE OF AUTHORSHIP Briefly describe nature of the material created by this author in which copyright is claimed. ▼

NOTE
Under the law, the "author" of a "work made for hire" is generally the employer, not the employee (see instructions). For any part of this work that was "made for hire" check "Yes" in the space provided, give the employer (or other person for whom the work was prepared) as "Author" of that part, and leave the space for dates of birth and death blank.

b

NAME OF AUTHOR ▼

DATES OF BIRTH AND DEATH
Year Born ▼   Year Died ▼

Was this contribution to the work a "work made for hire"?
☐ Yes
☐ No

AUTHOR'S NATIONALITY OR DOMICILE
Name of country
OR { Citizen of ▶ _____
{ Domiciled in ▶ _____

WAS THIS AUTHOR'S CONTRIBUTION TO THE WORK
Anonymous?   ☐ Yes ☐ No
Pseudonymous? ☐ Yes ☐ No

If the answer to either of these questions is "Yes," see detailed instructions.

NATURE OF AUTHORSHIP Briefly describe nature of the material created by this author in which copyright is claimed. ▼

c

NAME OF AUTHOR▼

DATES OF BIRTH AND DEATH
Year Born ▼   Year Died ▼

Was this contribution to the work a "work made for hire"?
☐ Yes
☐ No

AUTHOR'S NATIONALITY OR DOMICILE
Name of Country
OR { Citizen of ▶ _____
{ Domiciled in ▶ _____

WAS THIS AUTHOR'S CONTRIBUTION TO THE WORK
Anonymous?   ☐ Yes ☐ No
Pseudonymous? ☐ Yes ☐ No

If the answer to either of these questions is "Yes," see detailed instructions.

NATURE OF AUTHORSHIP Briefly describe nature of the material created by this author in which copyright is claimed. ▼

3

YEAR IN WHICH CREATION OF THIS WORK WAS COMPLETED This information must be given in all cases.
◀ Year

DATE AND NATION OF FIRST PUBLICATION OF THIS PARTICULAR WORK
Complete this information ONLY if this work has been published.
Month ▶ _____ Day ▶ _____ Year ▶ _____
◀ Nation

4

See instructions before completing this space.

COPYRIGHT CLAIMANT(S) Name and address must be given even if the claimant is the same as the author given in space 2.▼

APPLICATION RECEIVED

ONE DEPOSIT RECEIVED

TWO DEPOSITS RECEIVED

REMITTANCE NUMBER AND DATE

DO NOT WRITE HERE OFFICE USE ONLY

TRANSFER If the claimant(s) named here in space 4 are different from the author(s) named in space 2, give a brief statement of how the claimant(s) obtained ownership of the copyright.▼

MORE ON BACK ▶
• Complete all applicable spaces (numbers 5-9) on the reverse side of this page.
• See detailed instructions.
• Sign the form at line 8.

DO NOT WRITE HERE

Page 1 of _____ pages

EXAMINED BY	FORM SR
CHECKED BY	

☐ CORRESPONDENCE Yes

☐ DEPOSIT ACCOUNT FUNDS USED

FOR
COPYRIGHT
OFFICE
USE
ONLY

DO NOT WRITE ABOVE THIS LINE. IF YOU NEED MORE SPACE, USE A SEPARATE CONTINUATION SHEET.

PREVIOUS REGISTRATION Has registration for this work, or for an earlier version of this work, already been made in the Copyright Office?

☐ Yes ☐ No   If your answer is "Yes," why is another registration being sought? (Check appropriate box) ▼

☐ This is the first published edition of a work previously registered in unpublished form.

☐ This is the first application submitted by this author as copyright claimant.

☐ This is a changed version of the work, as shown by space 6 on this application.

If your answer is "Yes," give: **Previous Registration Number ▼**   **Year of Registration ▼**

5

DERIVATIVE WORK OR COMPILATION Complete both space 6a & 6b for a derivative work; complete only 6b for a compilation.

a. Preexisting Material Identify any preexisting work or works that this work is based on or incorporates. ▼

b. Material Added to This Work Give a brief, general statement of the material that has been added to this work and in which copyright is claimed. ▼

6

See instructions before completing this space.

DEPOSIT ACCOUNT If the registration fee is to be charged to a Deposit Account established in the Copyright Office, give name and number of Account.

Name ▼   **Account Number ▼**

7

CORRESPONDENCE Give name and address to which correspondence about this application should be sent.   Name/Address/Apt/City/State/Zip ▼

Area Code & Telephone Number ▶

Be sure to give your daytime phone ◀ number.

CERTIFICATION* I, the undersigned, hereby certify that I am the

Check one ▼

☐ author

☐ other copyright claimant

☐ owner of exclusive right(s)

☐ authorized agent of_____
     Name of author or other copyright claimant, or owner of exclusive right(s) ▲

of the work identified in this application and that the statements made
by me in this application are correct to the best of my knowledge.

8

Typed or printed name and date ▼ If this is a published work, this date must be the same as or later than the date of publication given in space 3.

_date ▶ _____

👉 **Handwritten signature (X) ▼**

**MAIL
CERTIFI-
CATE TO**

**Certificate
will be
mailed in
window
envelope**

Name ▼
Number/Street/Apartment Number ▼
City/State/ZIP ▼

Have you:
● Completed all necessary spaces?
● Signed your application in space 8?
● Enclosed check or money order for $10 payable to *Register of Copyrights?*
● Enclosed your deposit material with the application and fee?
MAIL TO: Register of Copyrights, Library of Congress, Washington, D.C. 20559.

9

* 17 U.S.C. § 506(e): Any person who knowingly makes a false representation of a material fact in the application for copyright registration provided for by section 409, or in any written statement filed in connection with the application, shall be fined not more than $2,500.

August 1987—60,000

Filling Out Application Form SE

Detach and read these instructions before completing this form. Make sure all applicable spaces have been filled in before you return this form.

BASIC INFORMATION

When To Use This Form: Use a separate Form SE for registration of each individual issue of a serial, Class SE. A serial is defined as a work issued or intended to be issued in successive parts bearing numerical or chronological designations and intended to be continued indefinitely. This class includes a variety of works: periodicals; newspapers; annuals; the journals, proceedings, transactions, etc., of societies. Do not use Form SE to register an individual contribution to a serial. Request Form TX for such contributions.

Deposit to Accompany Application: An application for copyright registration must be accompanied by a deposit consisting of copies or phonorecords representing the entire work for which registration is to be made. The following are the general deposit requirements as set forth in the statute:

Unpublished Work: Deposit one complete copy (or phonorecord).

Published Work: Deposit two complete copies (or phonorecords) of the best edition.

Work First Published Outside the United States: Deposit one complete copy (or phonorecord) of the first foreign edition.

Mailing Requirements: It is important that you send the application, the deposit copy or copies, and the $10 fee together in the same envelope or package. The Copyright Office cannot process them unless they are received together. Send to: *Register of Copyrights, Library of Congress, Washington, D.C. 20559.*

The Copyright Notice: For published works, the law provides that a copyright notice in a specified form "shall be placed on all publicly distributed copies from which the work can be visually perceived." Use of the copyright notice is the responsibility of the copyright owner and does not require advance permission from the Copyright Office. The required form of the notice for copies generally consists of three elements: (1) the symbol "©"; or the word "Copyright," or the abbreviation "Copr."; (2) the year of first publication; and (3) the name of the owner of copyright. For example: "© 1981 National News Publishers, Inc." The notice is to be affixed to the copies "in such manner and location as to give reasonable notice of the claim of copyright." For further information about copyright registration, notice, or special questions relating to copyright problems, write:

Information and Publications Section, LM-455
Copyright Office, Library of Congress, Washington, D.C. 20559

PRIVACY ACT ADVISORY STATEMENT Required by the Privacy Act of 1974 (P.L. 93-579)
The authority for requesting this information is title 17, U.S.C., secs. 409 and 410. Furnishing the requested information is voluntary. But if the information is not furnished, it may be necessary to delay or refuse registration and you may not be entitled to certain relief, remedies, and benefits provided in chapters 4 and 5 of title 17, U.S.C.
The principal uses of the requested information are the establishment and maintenance of a public record and the examination of the application for compliance with legal requirements.
Other routine uses include public inspection and copying, preparation of public indexes, preparation of public catalogs of copyright registrations, and preparation of search reports upon request.
NOTE: No other advisory statement will be given in connection with this application. Please keep this statement and refer to it if we communicate with you regarding this application.

LINE-BY-LINE INSTRUCTIONS

1 SPACE 1: Title

Title of This Serial: Every work submitted for copyright registration must be given a title to identify that particular work. If the copies or phonorecords of the work bear a title (or an identifying phrase that could serve as a title), copy that wording *completely* and *exactly* on the application. Give the volume and number of the periodical issue for which you are seeking registration. The "Date on copies" in space 1 should be the date appearing on the actual copies (for example: "June 1981," "Winter 1981"). Indexing of the registration and future identification of the work will depend on the information you give here.

Previous or Alternative Titles: Complete this space only if there are any additional titles for the serial under which someone searching for the registration might be likely to look, or under which a document pertaining to the work might be recorded.

2 SPACE 2: Author(s)

General Instructions: After reading these instructions, decide who are the "authors" of this work for copyright purposes. In the case of a serial issue, the organization which directs the creation of the serial issue as a whole is generally considered the author of the "collective work" (see "Nature of Authorship") whether it employs a staff or uses the efforts of volunteers. Where, however, an individual is independently responsible for the serial issue, name that person as author of the "collective work."

Name of Author: The fullest form of the author's name should be given. In the case of a "work made for hire," the statute provides that "the employer or other person for whom the work was prepared is considered the author." If this issue is a "work made for hire," the author's name will be the full legal name of the hiring organization, corporation, or individual. The title of the periodical should not ordinarily be listed as "author" because the title itself does not usually correspond to a legal entity capable of authorship. When an individual creates an issue of a serial independently and not as an "employee" of an organization or corporation, that individual should be listed as the "author."

Author's Nationality or Domicile: Give the country of which the author is a citizen, or the country in which the author is domiciled. Nationality or domicile **must** be given in all cases. The citizenship of an organization formed under United States Federal or state law should be stated as "U.S.A."

What is a "Work Made for Hire"? A "work made for hire" is defined as: (1) "a work prepared by an employee within the scope of his or her employment"; or (2) "a work specially ordered or commissioned for use as a contribution to a collective work, as a part of a motion picture or other audiovisual work, as a translation, as a supplementary work, as a compilation, as an instructional text, as a test, as answer material for a test, or as an atlas, if the parties expressly agree in a written instrument signed by them that the work shall be considered a work made for hire." An organization that uses the efforts of volunteers in the creation of a "collective work" (see "Nature of Authorship") may also be considered the author of a "work made for hire" even though those volunteers were not specifically paid by the organization. In the case of a "work made for hire," give the full legal name of the employer and check "Yes" to indicate that the work was made for hire. You may also include the name of the employee along with the name of the employer (for example: "Elster Publishing Co., employer for hire of John Ferguson").

"Anonymous" or "Pseudonymous" Work: Leave this space **blank** if the serial is a "work made for hire." An author's contribution to a work is "anonymous" if that author is not identified on the copies or phonorecords of the work. An author's contribution to a work is "pseudonymous" if that author is identified on the copies or phonorecords under a fictitious name. If the work is "anonymous" you may: (1) leave the line blank; or (2) state "anonymous" on the line; or (3) reveal the author's identity. If the work is "pseudonymous" you may: (1) leave the line blank; or (2) give the pseudonym and identify it as such (for example: "Huntley Haverstock, pseudonym"); or (3) reveal the author's name, making clear which is the real name and which is the pseudonym (for example: "Judith Barton, whose pseudonym is Madeline Elster"). However, the citizenship or domicile of the author **must** be given in all cases.

Dates of Birth and Death: Leave this space blank if the author's contribution was a "work made for hire." If the author is dead, the statute requires that the year of death be included in the application unless the work is anonymous or pseudonymous. The author's birth date is optional, but is useful as a form of identification.

Nature of Authorship: Give a brief statement of the nature of the particular author's contribution to the work. If an organization directed, controlled, and supervised the creation of the serial issue as a whole, check the box "collective work." The term "collective work" means that the author is responsible for compilation and editorial revision, and may also be responsible for certain individual contributions to the serial issue. Further examples of "Authorship" which may apply both to organizational and to individual authors are "Entire text"; "Entire text and/or illustrations"; "Editorial revision, compilation, plus additional new material."

3 SPACE 3: Creation and Publication

General Instructions: Do not confuse "creation" with "publication." Every application for copyright registration must state "the year in which creation of the work was completed." Give the date and nation of first publication only if the work has been published.

Creation: Under the statute, a work is "created" when it is fixed in a copy or phonorecord for the first time. Where a work has been prepared over a period of time, the part of the work existing in fixed form on a particular date constitutes the created work on that date. The date you give here should be the year in which this particular issue was completed.

Publication: The statute defines "publication" as "the distribution of copies or phonorecords of a work to the public by sale or other transfer of ownership, or by rental, lease, or lending"; a work is also "published" if there has been an "offering to distribute copies or phonorecords to a group of persons for purposes of further distribution, public performance, or public display." Give the full date (month, day, year) when, and the country where, publication of this particular issue first occurred. If first publication took place simultaneously in the United States and other countries, it is sufficient to state "U.S.A."

4 SPACE 4: Claimant(s)

Name(s) and Address(es) of Copyright Claimant(s): This space must be completed. Give the name(s) and address(es) of the copyright claimant(s) of this work even if the claimant is the same as the author named in space 2. Copyright in a work belongs initially to the author of the work (including, in the case of a work made for hire, the employer or other person for whom the work was prepared). The copyright claimant is either the author of the work or a person or organization to whom the copyright initially belonging to the author has been transferred.

Transfer: The statute provides that, if the copyright claimant is not the author, the application for registration must contain "a brief statement of how the claimant obtained ownership of the copyright." A transfer of copyright ownership (other than one brought about by operation of law) must be in writing. If any copyright claimant named in space 4 is not an author named in space 2, give a brief, general statement describing the means by which that claimant obtained ownership of the copyright from the original author. Examples: "By written contract"; "Written transfer of all rights by author"; "Assignment"; "Inherited by will." Do not attach the actual document of transfer or other attachments or riders.

5 SPACE 5: Previous Registration

General Instructions: This space applies only rarely to serials. Complete space 5 if this particular issue has been registered earlier or if it contains a substantial amount of material that has been previously registered. Do not complete this space if the previous registrations are simply those made for earlier issues.

Previous Registration:
a. Check this box if this issue has been registered in unpublished form and a second registration is now sought to cover the first published edition.

b. Check this box if someone other than the author is identified as copyright claimant in the earlier registration and the author is now seeking registration in his or her own name. If the work in question is a contribution to a collective work, as opposed to the issue as a whole, file Form TX, not Form SE.

c. Check this box (and complete space 6) if this particular issue, or a substantial portion of the material in it, has been previously registered and you are now seeking registration for the additions and revisions which appear in this issue for the first time.

Previous Registration Number and Date: Complete this line if you checked one of the boxes above. If more than one previous registration has been made for the issue or for material in it, give only the number and year date for the latest registration.

6 SPACE 6: Derivative Work or Compilation

General Instructions: Complete space 6 if this issue is a "changed version," "compilation," or "derivative work," which incorporates one or more earlier works that have already been published or registered for copyright, or that have fallen into the public domain. Do not complete space 6 for an issue consisting of entirely new material appearing for the first time, such as a new issue of a continuing serial. A "compilation" is defined as "a work formed by the collection and assembling of preexisting materials or of data that are se-

lected, coordinated, or arranged in such a way that the resulting work as a whole constitutes an original work of authorship." A "derivative work" is "a work based on one or more preexisting works." Examples of derivative works include translations, fictionalizations, abridgments, condensations, or "any other form in which a work may be recast, transformed, or adapted." Derivative works also include works "consisting of editorial revisions, annotations, or other modifications" if these changes, as a whole, represent an original work of authorship.

Preexisting Material (space 6a): For derivative works, complete this space and space 6b. In space 6a identify the preexisting work that has been recast, transformed, adapted, or updated. Example: "1978 Morgan Co. Sales Catalog." Do not complete space 6a for compilations.

Material Added to This Work (space 6b): Give a brief, general statement of the new material covered by the copyright claim for which registration is sought. **Derivative work** examples include: "Editorial revisions and additions to the Catalog"; "Translation"; "Additional material." If a periodical issue is a **compilation**, describe both the compilation itself and the material that has been compiled. Examples: "Compilation of previously published journal articles"; "Compilation of previously published data." An issue may be both a derivative work and a compilation, in which case a sample statement might be: "Compilation of [describe] and additional new material."

7 SPACE 7: Manufacturing Provisions

General Instructions: The copyright statute currently provides, as a general rule, that the copies of a published work "consisting preponderantly of nondramatic literary material in the English language" be manufactured in the United States or Canada in order to be lawfully imported and publicly distributed in the United States. If the work being registered is unpublished or not in English, leave this space blank. Complete this space if registration is sought for a published work "consisting preponderantly of nondramatic literary material that is in the English language." Identify those who manufactured the copies and where those manufacturing processes were performed. As an exception to the manufacturing provisions, the statute prescribes that, where manufacture has taken place outside the United States or Canada, a maximum of 2000 copies of the foreign edition may be imported into the United States without affecting the copyright owners' rights. For this purpose, the Copyright Office will issue an Import Statement upon request and payment of a fee of $3 at the time of registration or at any later time. For further information about import statements, write for Form IS.

8 SPACE 8: Reproduction for Use of Blind or Physically Handicapped Individuals

General Instructions: One of the major programs of the Library of Congress is to provide Braille editions and special recordings of works for the exclusive use of the blind and physically handicapped. In an effort to simplify and speed up the copyright licensing procedures that are a necessary part of this program, section 710 of the copyright statute provides for the establishment of a voluntary licensing system to be tied in with copyright registration. Copyright Office regulations provide that you may grant a license for such reproduction and distribution solely for the use of persons who are certified by competent authority as unable to read normal printed material as a result of physical limitations. The license is entirely voluntary, nonexclusive, and may be terminated upon 90 days notice.

How to Grant the License: If you wish to grant it, check one of the three boxes in space 8. Your check in one of these boxes, together with your signature in space 10, will mean that the Library of Congress can proceed to reproduce and distribute under the license without further paperwork. For further information, write for Circular R63.

9,10,11 SPACE 9, 10, 11: Fee, Correspondence, Certification, Return Address

Deposit Account: If you maintain a Deposit Account in the Copyright Office, identify it in space 9. Otherwise leave the space blank and send the fee of $10 with your application and deposit.

Correspondence (space 9): This space should contain the name, address, area code, and telephone number of the person to be consulted if correspondence about this application becomes necessary.

Certification (space 10): The application cannot be accepted unless it bears the date and the **handwritten signature** of the author or other copyright claimant, or of the owner of exclusive right(s), or of the duly authorized agent of the author, claimant, or owner of exclusive right(s).

Address for Return of Certificate (space 11): The address box must be completed legibly since the certificate will be returned in a window envelope.

FORM SE
UNITED STATES COPYRIGHT OFFICE

REGISTRATION NUMBER

U

EFFECTIVE DATE OF REGISTRATION

Month	Day	Year

DO NOT WRITE ABOVE THIS LINE. IF YOU NEED MORE SPACE, USE A SEPARATE CONTINUATION SHEET.

1

TITLE OF THIS SERIAL ▼

Volume ▼   Number ▼   Date on Copies ▼   Frequency of Publication ▼

PREVIOUS OR ALTERNATIVE TITLES ▼

2

a

NAME OF AUTHOR ▼

DATES OF BIRTH AND DEATH
Year Born ▼   Year Died ▼

Was this contribution to the work a "work made for hire"?
☐ Yes
☐ No

AUTHOR'S NATIONALITY OR DOMICILE
Name of Country
OR { Citizen of ▶
     Domiciled in ▶

WAS THIS AUTHOR'S CONTRIBUTION TO THE WORK
Anonymous?   ☐ Yes ☐ No
Pseudonymous? ☐ Yes ☐ No

If the answer to either of these questions is "Yes," see detailed instructions.

NATURE OF AUTHORSHIP   Briefly describe nature of the material created by this author in which copyright is claimed. ▼
☐ Collective Work   Other:

NOTE

Under the law, the "author" of a "work made for hire" is generally the employer, not the employee (see instructions). For any part of this work that was "made for hire" check "Yes" in the space provided, give the employer (or other person for whom the work was prepared) as "Author" of that part, and leave the space for dates of birth and death blank.

b

NAME OF AUTHOR ▼

DATES OF BIRTH AND DEATH
Year Born ▼   Year Died ▼

Was this contribution to the work a "work made for hire"?
☐ Yes
☐ No

AUTHOR'S NATIONALITY OR DOMICILE
Name of country
OR { Citizen of ▶
     Domiciled in ▶

WAS THIS AUTHOR'S CONTRIBUTION TO THE WORK
Anonymous?   ☐ Yes ☐ No
Pseudonymous? ☐ Yes ☐ No

If the answer to either of these questions is "Yes," see detailed instructions.

NATURE OF AUTHORSHIP   Briefly describe nature of the material created by this author in which copyright is claimed. ▼
☐ Collective Work   Other:

c

NAME OF AUTHOR ▼

DATES OF BIRTH AND DEATH
Year Born ▼   Year Died ▼

Was this contribution to the work a "work made for hire"?
☐ Yes
☐ No

AUTHOR'S NATIONALITY OR DOMICILE
Name of Country
OR { Citizen of ▶
     Domiciled in ▶

WAS THIS AUTHOR'S CONTRIBUTION TO THE WORK
Anonymous?   ☐ Yes ☐ No
Pseudonymous? ☐ Yes ☐ No

If the answer to either of these questions is "Yes," see detailed instructions.

NATURE OF AUTHORSHIP   Briefly describe nature of the material created by this author in which copyright is claimed. ▼
☐ Collective Work   Other:

3

YEAR IN WHICH CREATION OF THIS ISSUE WAS COMPLETED This information must be given in all cases.
◀ Year

DATE AND NATION OF FIRST PUBLICATION OF THIS PARTICULAR ISSUE Complete this information ONLY if this work has been published.
Month ▶   Day ▶   Year ▶
◀ Nation

4

See instructions before completing this space.

COPYRIGHT CLAIMANT(S) Name and address must be given even if the claimant is the same as the author given in space 2.▼

TRANSFER If the claimant(s) named here in space 4 are different from the author(s) named in space 2, give a brief statement of how the claimant(s) obtained ownership of the copyright.▼

APPLICATION RECEIVED

ONE DEPOSIT RECEIVED

TWO DEPOSITS RECEIVED

REMITTANCE NUMBER AND DATE

MORE ON BACK ▶
• Complete all applicable spaces (numbers 5-11) on the reverse side of this page
• See detailed instructions.
• Sign the form at line 10.

DO NOT WRITE HERE

Page 1 of _____ pages

EXAMINED BY	FORM SE
CHECKED BY	
☐ CORRESPONDENCE Yes	FOR COPYRIGHT OFFICE USE ONLY
☐ DEPOSIT ACCOUNT FUNDS USED	

DO NOT WRITE ABOVE THIS LINE. IF YOU NEED MORE SPACE, USE A SEPARATE CONTINUATION SHEET.

PREVIOUS REGISTRATION Has registration for this issue, or for an earlier version of this particular issue, already been made in the Copyright Office?

☐ Yes ☐ No If your answer is "Yes," why is another registration being sought? (Check appropriate box) ▼

a. ☐ This is the first published version of an issue previously registered in unpublished form.

b. ☐ This is the first application submitted by this author as copyright claimant.

c. ☐ This is a changed version of this issue, as shown by space 6 on this application.

If your answer is "Yes," give: **Previous Registration Number** ▼   **Year of Registration** ▼

5

DERIVATIVE WORK OR COMPILATION Complete both space 6a & 6b for a derivative work; complete only 6b for a compilation.

a. **Preexisting Material** Identify any preexisting work or works that this work is based on or incorporates. ▼

b. **Material Added to This Work** Give a brief, general statement of the material that has been added to this work and in which copyright is claimed.▼

6

See instructions before completing this space.

MANUFACTURERS AND LOCATIONS If this is a published work consisting preponderantly of nondramatic literary material in English, the law may require that the copies be manufactured in the United States or Canada for full protection. If so, the names of the manufacturers who performed certain processes, and the places where these processes were performed **must** be given. See instructions for details.

Names of Manufacturers ▼   **Places of Manufacture** ▼

7

REPRODUCTION FOR USE OF BLIND OR PHYSICALLY HANDICAPPED INDIVIDUALS   A signature on this form at space 10, and a check in one of the boxes here in space 8, constitutes a non-exclusive grant of permission to the Library of Congress to reproduce and distribute solely for the blind and physically handicapped and under the conditions and limitations prescribed by the regulations of the Copyright Office: (1) copies of the work identified in space 1 of this application in Braille (or similar tactile symbols); or (2) phonorecords embodying a fixation of a reading of that work; or (3) both.

a ☐ Copies and Phonorecords   **b** ☐ Copies Only   **c** ☐ Phonorecords Only

8

See instructions.

DEPOSIT ACCOUNT If the registration fee is to be charged to a Deposit Account established in the Copyright Office, give name and number of Account.

Name ▼   **Account Number** ▼

CORRESPONDENCE Give name and address to which correspondence about this application should be sent.   Name/Address/Apt/City/State/Zip ▼

Area Code & Telephone Number ▶

9

Be sure to give your daytime phone ◀ number.

CERTIFICATION* I, the undersigned, hereby certify that I am the

Check one ▶

☐ author
☐ other copyright claimant
☐ owner of exclusive right(s)
☐ authorized agent of _____

of the work identified in this application and that the statements made by me in this application are correct to the best of my knowledge.

Name of author or other copyright claimant, or owner of exclusive right(s) ▲

Typed or printed name and date ▼ If this is a published work, this date must be the same as or later than the date of publication given in space 3.

_____ date ▶ _____

Handwritten signature (X) ▼

10

MAIL CERTIFI-CATE TO

Certificate will be mailed in window envelope

Name ▼

Number/Street/Apartment Number ▼

City/State/ZIP ▼

Have you:
- Completed all necessary spaces?
- Signed your application in space 10?
- Enclosed check or money order for $10 payable to *Register of Copyrights*?
- Enclosed your deposit material with the application and fee?

MAIL TO: Register of Copyrights, Library of Congress, Washington, D.C. 20559.

11

* 17 U.S.C. § 506(e): Any person who knowingly makes a false representation of a material fact in the application for copyright registration provided for by section 409, or in any written statement filed in connection with the application, shall be fined not more than $2,500.

U.S. GOVERNMENT PRINTING OFFICE: 1988–202–133/60,012   January 1988–10,000

Part 2
Patents

INTRODUCTION

A patent is grant for a term of 17 years and conveys the ''right to exclude others from making, using or selling'' an invention.

The authority to protect authors and inventors was conferred in Article 1, Section 8, Item 8 of the United States Constitution, which states: ''The Congress shall have power . . . to promote the progress of science and the useful acts by securing the authors and inventors the exclusive right to their respective writings and discovers.'' In 1790, Congress enacted the first patent laws for ''Any useful art, manufacture, engine, machine, or device, or any improvement therein, not before known or used.''

The patent system has a rich history. Its development over the past two centuries is a fascinating study. July 31, 1990, marks the bicentennial of the first invention patented in the United States. George Washington, Thomas Jefferson and Edmund Randolph signed the patent which granted Samuel Hopkins, a resident of Vermont, ''the right to exclude others from making, using or selling'' his invention for pot and pearl ashes.

Today, patent laws are administered by the Patent and Trademark Office (PTO) in Washington, D.C. These laws are intended to stimulate progress and benefit mankind. Between 1790 and 1836, the year the Patent Office was destroyed by fire, a total of 9,957 patents were issued. By 1893, the figure rose substantially to 500,000. In 1986, the PTO granted 76,993 patents, a 2.2 percent increase over the previous year. The actual number of patent applications received that year was 131,403. The ratio of applications to grants has remained fairly constant in this century. About half of all applications lead to patented inventions.

Generally speaking, an invention can be patented if it incorporates novel details, whether or not the main idea is new. Only the change or improvement is patentable, not the known principle or previously patented invention on which it's built. The mere fact that an inventor is able to obtain a patent doesn't mean it has commercial value, real novelty, or that it's even practical. These are important areas which should be considered prior to spending time and money to obtain a patent.

The patent law requires that the subject matter of the invention have a ''useful'' purpose. This concept includes operativeness, which means the invention must be able to perform its intended purpose. In other words, it must be more than a nice idea on paper; it has to actually work as stated in the patent application. Otherwise, it's not patentable.

There are several categories patents fall under: utility, design, and plant.

Plant patents are granted to anyone who has invented or discovered and asexually reproduced any distinct and new variety of plant, including cultivated sports, mutants, hybrids, and newly found seedlings, other than a tuber-propagated plant or a plant found in an uncultivated state. Asexually produced plants are created from seeds, not propagated by means of cuttings, layering, budding, grafting, inarching, etc. The word ''asexually'' means without requiring sex to reproduce (asexual reproduction). The definition of plant patents has been broadened to include living cells or combinations of cells, such as are produced in gene splitting and biochemistry.

"The Plant Variety Act (Public Law 91-557), approved Dec. 24, 1970, provides for a system of protection for asexually reproduced varieties, for which protection was not previously provided, under the administration of a Plant Variety Protection Office within the Department of Agriculture." Requests for information regarding the protection of asexually reproduced varieties should be addressed to:

COMMISSIONERS, PLANT VARIETY PROTECTION OFFICE
Consumer and Marketing Service, Grain Division
6525 Bellcrest Rd
Hyattsville, MD 20782.

Design patents are concerned with the appearance of an article rather than its structure or utilitarian features. The design must appear to be novel. A design patent is usually created to satisfy a certain purpose and isn't as readily marketable as its counterparts. A design and utility patent may be held on the same invention, but will cover different aspects.

Utility patents include all other patentable inventions that aren't covered by the previous categories. These include structural or mechanical patents; process, method, and systems patents; and patents on materials or combinations of materials.

An invention doesn't have to be complicated to be patentable. Some of the most successful patents have been for relatively trivial inventions. What might appear simple and unpatentable may be quite the contrary. Often, the simplest improvements are patentable and prove commercially successful.

WHAT IS NOT PATENTABLE?

- An idea alone is not patentable. An idea can only be patented once it is in a tangible form which is reached by a process known as "reduction to practice."

- A scientific principle is not patentable. A property of matter or a law of nature, for example, is public domain.

- A result cannot be patented; only the device that creates the result may be patented. Heat, light and running water are examples of things that can't be patented, but a heater, a light fixture, and a faucet are all patentable.

- A patent can't be obtained by aggregation. Combining two independent things which do not cofunction or duplicating things to create one item is not acceptable.

- Something that is not useful cannot be patented. An invention that can't operate to perform its intended purpose won't be granted a patent.

- A device that infringes on the rights of others can't be patented.

- A patent can't be obtained by adaptation, such as the use of a razor to sharpen pencils. A pencil sharpener, however, is patentable.
- Changing the form, size, material, proportions, or arrangement alone of an existing invention doesn't warrant patentability. If something new is achieved however, a patent might be obtained.
- An invention that doesn't possess novelty and utility isn't patentable.
- If a device or its improvements are obvious, then it cannot be patented. It must be unobvious to "a person having ordinary skill in the art to which said subject matter pertains."
- An invention which might be injurious to public morals cannot be patented.

NOVELTY

The subject matter sought to be patented must be sufficiently different from what has been used or described before, so that it can be said to be unobvious to a person having ordinary skill in the area of technology related to the invention. For example, the substitution of one material for another, or changes in size, are ordinarily not patentable. Also, the effect of a combination of ingredients, such as chemicals, isn't enough to warrant a patent.

An invention must be new and cannot be patented if

"(a) The invention was known or used by others in this country, or patented or described in a printed publication in this or a foreign country, before the invention thereof by the applicant for patent, or

(b) The invention was patented or described in a printed publication in this or a foreign country or in public use or on sale in this country more than one year prior to the application for patent in the United States . . ."

The fields of invention have been divided into 400 classes and 115,000 subclasses. The Patent and Trademark Office provides publications concerning classifications. These include *The Manual of Classification, Index to the U.S. Patent Classification,* and *Classification Definitions.* Other PTO and government publications are listed in Part 5 of this book.

A patent search, also known as a prior art search, will reveal inventions which may be like or similar to another invention. (Refer to "The Patent Search" below.) A preliminary search will disclose if features of a "new" invention are genuinely novel.

REDUCTION TO PRACTICE

A person seeking to protect an invention idea should diligently reduce the idea to practice. Once an idea is put into practical form, it becomes tangible; an idea or suggestion alone cannot be patented. The person who develops and tests the idea first is entitled to patent protection.

By properly recording the invention process, the inventor will always be able to provide proof, if necessary, that he is the first or actual inventor. If properly recorded, a court of law will recognize the actual inventor by the development of the invention. This documentation will afford protection to the inventor prior to the invention being patented. It's important to establish your claim to an invention as early as possible to prove that you are the first inventor. This will give you a decided legal advantage over subsequent persons who may come along with the same or similar invention and try to challenge it.

An excellent case in point is the story of Alexander Graham Bell, who invented the telephone. He was convinced that his new invention wasn't patentable. Fortunately, friends of his changed his mind. Within an hour of filing his patent application, an interfering application was submitted by another inventor, a man named Gray. Bell's fame and fortune had nearly been lost!

An invention which hasn't been reduced to practice first, but has received a patent, is considered "constructive" reduction to practice and carries the same weight. Although the preliminary steps are bypassed, the granting of a patent is equivalent to "reduction to practice." The disadvantage to this method is that, until the invention is actually patented, the inventor is leaving himself wide open, since the process of reducing the idea to practice has been circumvented or just wasn't recorded. The better prepared the inventor is, the more chance he has of successfully defending a legal contest.

The "date of invention" can be earlier than the date on which the patent application was filed. How? By simply proving when the invention was reduced to practice. On what date did the invention complete the development and test phase? The day of conception can also be the date of invention if it an be proved that diligence was exhibited to develop and test the invention.

The invention might be immediately worked out in detail, or only the general principles might be defined. A model or a full-scale prototype can be built at any time. It doesn't matter if the model works. What *does* matter is the method employed in the reduction to practice and that diligence was applied to disclose the completed invention to the public at the earliest possible time after its original conception.

THE INVENTION RECORD

The single best proof of priority and reduction to practice is to keep a permanent written record. An invention notebook should be maintained from the conception of an idea to the filing of the patent application. A laboratory notebook is frequently used to record this kind of information. The notebook should be permanently bound (i.e., spiral bound, stitched, etc.) with consecutively numbered pages and durable covers. After use, the bottom of each page should be signed, dated and witnessed.

The entire invention process should be logged as it evolves. The notebook must be diligently maintained to be of value. If each step is recorded, the book will provide a certified and incontestable history of events. Record the invention's progress in minute detail—be factual and explicit!

Following are some important areas to cover. If you think of others that are relevant, add them when appropriate.

Begin the invention notebook by providing a complete picture of your invention and what you propose it will do. Your name and address, the date should be entered first. Then, give the name of the invention, its purpose, conception, background, complete description, known prior art, novelty, alternatives, and sketches. This will reflect the basis of what you plan to achieve, how you perceive it, your present knowledge, etc.

Each time a development occurs, it might be necessary to cover several or all of the following areas. Date each development as it is recorded. When a page has been completed, sign and date it and have someone witness it by doing the same. Identify the development along with a thorough description followed by:

- Changes
- Improvements/modifications
- Test description and results
- Problem areas/drawbacks
- Conclusion
- Photos, sketches, drawings, diagrams
- Other contributors
- People you've discussed the invention with

A few additional tips:

- Keep all bills of sale, receipts, canceled checks, etc.
- Keep copies of all agreements, records, etc.
- Photograph models, tests, etc.
- Date each prototype when completed.
- Save all supplier and other related correspondence.
- Have different people witness the invention notebook.
- Use other forms of documentation that may be suitable.

Sketches help explain your thoughts. Putting your ideas on paper is a great way to think out the development process. Anyone who reads your invention notebook will better understand what you were trying to accomplish. Several types of drawings may be employed as needed. Engineering, perspective, and schematic drawings all have their use when trying to visually convey ideas. It's a good habit to make a sketch of every idea and step and include it in the invention notebook.

THE PROTOTYPE

A prototype should eventually be made of the proposed invention. This is an important process which will help reveal problems and provide an opportunity to make vital improvements. Preferably, you should build the model yourself, but if necessary, seek appropriate help. The diary will protect the invention from outsiders who will become exposed to your ideas.

If feasible, it's best to construct a full-scale prototype using actual materials. If this is impractical, a scaled-down version is suitable if all conditions are kept the same and if the balanced ratio of the model doesn't change.

The materials and supplies necessary to build the prototype can probably be located from a manufacturer or supplier listed in the Thomas Register of American Manufacturers. The reference sections of most libraries will have this set. Other sources can be uncovered in your local Yellow Pages. A well-equipped hardware store or supply house might be all you need. On the other hand, you may have your home-work cut out for you, but tracking down the desired materials will be worth the effort. You should remain open-minded to alternative materials and possibilities during the search—something better may arise.

Undetected flaws in the invention can later be expensive. Another inventor might try to capitalize on your errors or negligence by patenting an improvement on your device. Unless the invention is built to its maximum effectiveness, it might never realize its full commercial value. The patent should provide broad protection, thereby preventing others from making easy modifications.

Once a prototype has been completed, it is equally important to test and evaluate the findings. Problem areas should be recognized and corrected.

ATTORNEYS AND AGENTS

There are basically three ways to obtain a patent: hire a lawyer, hire a patent agent, or prepare and file the application yourself.

The Patent and Trademark Office allows both attorneys and nonattorneys to practice before them. Anyone can execute a patent application and handle the patent procedures without the services of a patent attorney or patent agent.

Certain qualifications must be met for a lawyer to become a recognized patent attorney, one of which is a college degree in engineering, physical science, or the equivalent. The same requirements, qualifications, and examination are also required of agents; however, agents do not possess a law degree. Although a patent agent isn't a lawyer, he may be just as qualified as a patent attorney for the purpose of executing patent applications. Patent agents include engineers, chemists, scientists and others, but they can't practice law.

Attorneys and agents who meet the requirements are registered and licensed to practice before the Patent and Trademark Office. The PTO publishes an official roster entitled *Patent Attorneys and Agents Registered to Practice Before the U.S. Patent and Trademark Office*. It's listed in the back of this book under "Government Publications" and can be ordered directly from the Patent and Trademark Office.

If a patent attorney or agent is employed, all PTO communications are transmitted through that person on behalf of the inventor. A power of attorney is necessary to authorize legal representation. This power may be revoked by the inventor at his discretion. The inventor can also correspond directly with the PTO to learn of the progress of the application without going through the attorney or agent.

Patent agents, like patent attorneys, can be very useful, and like most professionals, both receive excellent compensation for their efforts. Undoubtedly, these individuals provide a valuable service to their clients. Unfortunately, however, not all inventors can afford the expense. This is probably the single biggest factor inventors face when deciding whether to retain a lawyer. An active inventor might find the legal expenses completely prohibitive because of the frequent necessity to patent. So he may decide to handle the patent procedure himself.

Aside from the cost savings, do-it-yourself patenting allows the inventor more control, a better understanding of patent procedures, and a thorough understanding of his own invention. The inventor will learn each detail and step necessary to secure a patent. Thereby, no one will be more qualified to fully describe the ideas and principles incorporated in the invention.

THE PATENT SEARCH

The patent search is also known as a prior art search. "Prior art" is previous works by others related to your invention. Prior art can include other patented devices or published information on the subject. A qualified person can be hired to conduct the search or you can do it yourself. If a patent searcher is retained to perform this function, it's important that he be experienced. A patent attorney or registered agent is also qualified to handle searches.

Without a doubt, inventors understand their creations better than anyone. That's why it is best for the inventor to conduct his own patent search. It will also save him money. The only drawback is that the inventor is less familiar with the practice of searching.

The patent classification system covers over 400 classes and over 115,000 subclasses. Any pertinent classification should be examined that might show highly relevant prior art. The subclassifications are further divided into the many different areas of each classification. This helps make the search easier. This search will also show you into which classifications and subclassifications your invention falls. PTO publications concerning the U.S. Patent Classification System include *The Manual of Classification, Index to the U.S. Patent Classification,* and *Classification Definitions.*

Understanding the prior art will help you, as the patent applicant, to better understand your own invention. Is your idea patentable? If not, what is obstructing it? Is it possible to design around the prior art? Is the invention more commercially valuable than what's presently available? A search prior to preparing the patent application might save you unnecessary time and expense. It might prove that your idea is really not worth trying to patent, or it might be that, as your invention stands, changes in the application would be necessary before filing, thus requiring additional time and possibly expense.

Occasionally, an inventor knows an industry so well, or is at the threshold of an industry's development, that a patent search would be fruitless. Ordinarily, though, a search is advantageous and will assist the inventor in refining the invention, understanding its place in relation to other inventions, and simplifying completion of the application.

A search can be conducted at the Search Room at the Patent and Trademark Office in Arlington, Virginia, or at one of the Patent Depository Libraries listed in this section. Each search room contains a set of U.S. patents arranged in numerical order since 1836 and a complete set of the Official Gazette. Hours are 8:00 A.M. to 8:30 P.M., Monday through Friday, except federal holidays.

The Scientific Library is also located at the PTO. It contains over 120,000 volumes of scientific and technical books in different languages, about 90,000 bound volumes of periodicals devoted to science and technology, the official journals of 77 foreign patent organizations, and over 12 million foreign patents.

The Scientific Library and the Search Room are located at:

PATENT AND TRADEMARK OFFICE
Crystal Plaza 3
2021 Jefferson Davis Hwy.
Arlington, VA 22202

The PTO and Patent Depository Libraries (PDLs) also provide technical staff assistance to aid the public in gaining effective access to information contained in patents. PDLs provide an online computer database known as CASSIS, Classification and Search Support Information System. It permits for the effective identification of appropriate classifications for a search, provides the numbers of patents assigned to a classification to permit finding the patents in a numerical file of patents, provides the current classification of all patents, and permits word-searching in classification titles, abstracts, and the index. Each PDL has a collection of patent publications, documents, and forms. Photocopy and microfilm capabilities are generally available at each location for a fee. Call in advance of a visit for the extent of a PDLs collection and services.

PATENT DEPOSITORY LIBRARIES

State	Name of Library
Alabama	Auburn University Libraries
	Birmingham Public Library
Alaska	Anchorage Municipal Libraries
Arizona	Tempe: Science Library, Arizona State University
Arkansas	Little Rock: Arkansas State Library
California	Los Angeles Public Library
	Sacramento: California State Library
	San Diego Public Library
	Sunnyvale: Patent Information Clearinghouse
Colorado	Denver Public Library

State	Name of Library
Delaware	Newark: University of Delaware
Florida	Fort Lauderdale: Broward County Main Library
	Miami: Dade Public Library
Georgia	Atlanta: Price Gilbert Memorial Library, Georgia Institute of Technology
Idaho	Moscow: University of Idaho Library
Illinois	Chicago Public Library
	Springfield: Illinois State Library
Indiana	Indianapolis: Marion County Public Library
Louisiana	Baton Rouge: Troy H. Middleton Library, Louisiana State University
Maryland	College Park: Engineering and Physical Sciences Library, University of Maryland
Massachusetts	Amherst: Physical Sciences Library, University of Massachusetts
	Boston Public Library
Michigan	Ann Arbor: Engineering Transportation Library, University of Michigan
	Detroit Public Library
Minnesota	Minneapolis Public Library & Information Center
Missouri	Kansas City: Linda Hall Library
	St. Louis Public Library
Montana	Butte: Montana College of Mineral Science & Technology Library
Nebraska	Lincoln: University of Nebraska, Engineering Library
Nevada	Reno: University of Nevada Library
New Hampshire	Durham: University of New Hampshire Library
New Jersey	Newark Public Library
New Mexico	Albuquerque: University of New Mexico Library
New York	Albany: New York State Library
	Buffalo and Erie County Library
	New York Public Library (The Research Libraries)
North Carolina	Raleigh: D.H. Hill Library, N.C. State University
Ohio	Cincinnati & Hamilton County, Public Library of
	Cleveland Public Library
	Columbus: Ohio State University Libraries
	Toledo/Lucas County Public Library
Oklahoma	Stillwater: Oklahoma State University Library
Oregon	Salem: Oregon State Library
Pennsylvania	Cambridge Springs: Alliance College Library
	Philadelphia: Franklin Institute Library
	Pittsburgh: Carnegie Library of Pittsburgh
	University Park: Pattee Library, Pennsylvania State University

State	Name of Library
Rhode Island	Providence Public Library
South Carolina	Charleston: Medical University of South Carolina
Tennessee	Memphis & Shelby County Public and Information Center
	Nashville: Vanderbilt University Library
Texas	Austin: Mckinney Engineering Library, University of Texas
	College Station: Sterling C. Evans Library, Texas A & M University
	Dallas Public Library
	Houston: The Foundren Library, Rice University
Utah	Salt Lake City: Marriott Library, University of Utah
Washington	Seattle: Engineering Library, University of Washington
Wisconsin	Madison: Kurt F. Wendt Engineering Library, University of Wisconsin
	Milwaukee Public Library

PATENT SEARCHERS

AMERICAN INVENTORS CORPORATION
1-800-367-0737

AMERICAN PATENT R & D
2155 Queens Chapel Rd., NE
Washington, D.C.
(202) 636-4332

CVG INTERNATIONAL AMERICA, INC.
555 5th Ave.
New York, NY
(212) 557-2869

GEORGE SPECTOR, PROFESSIONAL
  PATENT ENGINEER
233 Broadway, Room 3815
Woolworth Building
New York, NY
(212) 267-8989

PATENTVESTMENTS INTERNATIONAL
1050 Connecticut Ave., NW
Washington, D.C.
(202) 429-6645

STAN STANTON'S SEARCH SERVICE
1511 "K" NW
Washington, D.C.
(202) 638-1210

WASHINGTON PATENT OFFICE
  SEARCHERS
927 S. Walter Reed Dr.
Arlington, VA
(703) 522-6304

WOOLCOTT & COMPANY
1911 Jefferson Davis Hwy.
Arlington, VA 22202
(703) 998-5505

AFFILIATED INVENTORS FOUNDATION
1-800-525-5885

AMERICAN PATENT SEARCHES
Litman Law Offices Ltd.
1725 S. Jefferson Davis Hwy.
Arlington, VA
(301) 920-6000

CHENPATENTS
3013 Birchtree Lane
Silver Springs, MD
(301) 460-8921

CRYSTAL PATENT RESEARCH, INC.
14529 Woodcrest Dr.
Rockville, MD
(301) 460-5726

INVENTION, INC.
2001 Jefferson Davis Hwy.
Arlington, VA
(301) 521-1200

PTR SPECIALTIES
727 23rd St., South
Arlington, VA
(301) 892-8218

PATENT OFFICE SERVICES, INC.
8305 Larchwood St.
New Carrollton, VA
(301) 577-6797

ROBERTS & ASSOCIATES PATENT
   SERVICES CO.
13103 Brittany Dr.
Silver Springs, MD
(301) 421-1949

SINGLA ASSOCIATES
7632 Mandan Rd.
Greenbelt, VA
(301) 345-5586

WASHINGTON PATENT OFFICE
   SEARCHERS
(301) 522-6304

THE SPECIFICATION

The invention process is a journey from the mind which then proceeds through several phases of development before it faces its final challenge at the hands of the patent examiner. It begins as an idea, gradually changing form, until it evolves into a tangible object which must then be analyzed, enhanced, understood, and finally described so that others can understand it.

The specification explains in detail the elements which comprise the invention. It's an official communique of your novel creation. This document must fully and completely disclose the invention. It must be clear, concise, and expressed in terms which would ''enable any person skilled in the technological area to which the invention pertains, or with which it is most nearly connected, to make and use the same.'' The specification must:

- Reveal the complete invention for which a patent is sought and show its distinct and novel features.
- Fully describe the process, machine, manufacture, composition of matter of the invention or improvement, and, when appropriate, explain the mode of operation or principle.
- Show the inventor's preferred method of executing the invention.

In return for complete disclosure of an invention, the inventor is granted a monopoly for the term of the patent. The monopoly is limited by the scope of the inventor's disclosures and claims.

The specification is a complete disclosure of the invention to the public. It consists of seven distinct parts:

1. The title
2. Background
3. Brief summary of the invention
4. Brief description of the drawing(s), if any
5. Detailed description
6. Claim(s)
7. Abstract of the disclosure

Let's examine each one:

1. The Title. The title should accurately describe and suggest the subject matter. It should be as short and specific as possible and it should appear as the heading on the first page of the specification.

2. The Background.

a) Briefly state the field of invention in accurate, technical language, including its intended purpose, the origin of the idea, and its place in the field.

b) Identify any patent application(s) related to your own when appropriate, for example, a copending application by the applicant. Give the serial number and filing date and indicate the relationship of the applicants.

c) Point out prior art, including drawbacks, disadvantages, or defects, and how your invention predominates. This applies to prior art that appears in publications as well. (The results of the patent search are very helpful here.) Give patent numbers.

3. A Brief Summary. This is a general statement of the nature and substance of the invention. It should include the object(s) of the invention and its adaptability as intended and claimed. Now is the time to also explain the advantages of the invention.

4. A Brief Description. When drawings are used, a brief description of the nature of each one is necessary. Separate photographs of the drawings can be used in lieu of actual illustrations. A figure or reference number should identify the different parts and views, for example, "Fig. 1 is a plan view of my invention . . .," "Fig. 2 is a perspective view of the part . . .," "Fig. 3 is a section view . . .," etc.

5. A Detailed Description. Utility and design patents require a detailed description of the invention. This part should be complete, providing the best mode for construction, the best compounds and materials, and the best mode for operating it. It must fully describe the specific embodiment of the process, machine, manufacture, composition of matter, or improvement invented. In the case of an improvement, the description should be confined to the specific improvement and only the parts necessary to understand how it functions. Include a list of reference numbers and identify each with a title and purpose. Reference numbers must correspond to the text.

6. Claims. The claim(s) constitute the essence of the patent. It clearly defines what it is that the inventor has invented and the protection he seeks. The inventor acquires a patent only on what he claims and forfeits the right to what is not claimed, even if it has been completely described or shown in the drawings and other parts of the specification.

The claims are brief descriptions which detail all essential features that distinguish the invention from prior art. Novelty and patentability are determined by the claims. Courts of law judge infringement on the basis of the claims.

- "When more than one claim is presented, they may be placed in dependent form in which a claim may refer back to and further restrict one or more preceding claims.

- "A claim in multiple dependent form shall contain a reference, in the alternative only, to more than one claim previously set forth and then specify a further limitation of the subject matter claimed. A multiple dependent claim shall not serve as a basis for any other multiple dependent claims. A multiple dependent claim shall be construed to incorporate by reference all the limitations of the particular claim in relation to which it is being considered.

- "The claim or claims must conform to the invention as set forth in the remainder of the specification and the terms and phrases used in the claims must find clear support or antecedent basis in the description so that the meaning of the terms in the claims may be ascertainable by reference to the description."

Writing the claims requires careful attention to details. A patent search is very helpful and will assist the inventor when drafting the claims. Reviewing a copy of the Official Patent Gazette and copies of patents will better illustrate how claims are written and the language commonly used to allow the broadest protection. Keep in mind, however, that not all of the applications can be said to be good examples. Don't rush to complete the specifications, and particularly the claims. Give special attention to how you're going to construct the claims. Begin with a claim that distinctly claims the subject matter which the inventor regards as his invention or discovery. Remember, the claim(s) are the operative part of the patent and they cover only what is stated.

The claim must be written in accordance with the data provided in the specification and with reference to prior art as it is understood. It's constructed with regard to proper practice, possible equivalents, and potential infringement. The claim should also make reference to the avoidance of interference with prior art and reference to possible future attack.

A group of claims serve to ensure the validity and scope of the patent. It's a protective means for preventing infringement and avoidance of the patent. One or more claims can be declared invalid without invalidating the entire patent. Any number of patent claims can be infringed upon and the patent will still be protected.

There is some latitude in wording the claim. Claims should always be stated in the most concise and clear manner possible without using unnecessary connectives, clauses, phrases, modifiers, etc. Have a clear understanding of words being used to construct a claim. If necessary, check the meaning of a word in the dictionary. A word might not be the best choice or allow the broadest definition of what it is you want to say. If that's the case, get out your thesaurus and find the ideal term.

There are numerous points of caution when constructing claims. Repeated reference to the same element in a claim isn't allowed. Indefinite, vague, or abstract claims are also refused. Claims for both an article and the process for making it or similar combinations generally require separate applications. Functional claims are disallowed (these concentrate on the function, result, or effect of an invention rather than its composition of matter or structure).

The benefits of studying other patent specifications and claims can't be emphasized enough. You can start by purchasing a single copy of the Official Patent Gazette from the Patent and Trademark Office, and then order copies of patents that interest you. A printed copy of a patent may be ordered from the PTO for only $1.50. The Gazette publishes the patent number which will be necessary when ordering a copy of a printed patent, or visit a nearby Patent Depository Library to study copies of the Gazette, patents, and other PTO publications. A serious study and dedicated inventor should want to learn the ins and outs of the patent business.

7. A Brief Abstract. Once again, review the patents of others to help you in writing your abstract. The abstract is a brief technical disclosure of the invention. On a separate page (in the specification) with the heading, ''Abstract of the Disclosure,'' write 200 to 300 words that summarize your invention in clear, complete, and concise terms. It can be only one paragraph.

The invention record will be a valuable aid when writing the specification. The inventor should be able to convey the invention to others better than anyone. A thorough understanding of specifications will enable you to successfully construct and draft your own specification. In addition to saving money, this all-important document can favorably influence the examiner's decision if properly prepared.

The specification should be neatly typewritten on legal-size paper (8 to $8^1/_2$ × $10^1/_2$ to 13 inches), $1^1/_2$- or double-spaced lines with 1-inch margins on the left side and at the top of the pages. The PTO will also accept specifications that are legibly written or printed in permanent ink on one side of the paper. All papers must be correct, legible, neat, and clearly written; otherwise, the PTO may require typewritten or printed pages. Write your name at the top of each sheet.

A design specification is normally short and consists of only one claim.

For a plant patent specification, ''The specification should include a complete detailed description of the plant and its characteristics which distinguish it from other related known varieties, and its antecedents, expressed in botanical terms in the general form followed in standard botanical text books or publications dealing with the varieties of the kind of plant involved, rather than a mere a broad nonbotanical characterization such as commonly found in nursery or seed catalogs. The specification should also include the origin or percentage of the plant variety sought to be patented and must particularly point out where and in what manner the variety of plant has been asexually reproduced. Where color is a distinctive feature of the plant, the color should be positively identified in the specification by reference to a desig-

nated color as given by a recognized color dictionary. Where the plant variety origi-
nated as a newly found seedling, the specification must fully describe the conditions
(cultivation, environment, etc.) under which the seedling was found growing to
establish that it was not found in an uncultivated state.''

A plant patent is granted for the whole plant. Therefore, only one claim is permitted.

THE DRAWING

All applications must be accompanied by a drawing of the invention except compositions of matter and sometimes processes. It must illustrate every feature of the
invention specified in the claim(s).

The Patent and Trademark Office has specific rules that govern the standards
for drawings. This information is contained in Code 37 of the Federal Regulations.
The requirements are included here and are strictly enforced by the PTO. Informal
drawings or ones that don't comply with the rules will be acceptable for examination.
A correct drawing of the invention can be registered at a later time.

A draftsperson may be employed or you can do it yourself. If using a draftsperson, be sure to inform him that the drawing is for submission to the Patent Office,
and so to follow the PTO's standards for drawings.

If you choose to do the drawing yourself, there are some aids which will make
the task easier and more professional. The necessary tools and supplies can be
found at local art and drafting stores. One of these is transfer lettering which is manufactured by several companies, one of the largest being Letraset. This company
publishes a comprehensive catalog of its products entitled, ''Graphic Art Materials
Reference Manual.'' A copy can be purchased at most art supply stores that sell
Letraset or you can contact the company directly:

LETRASET USA
40 Eisenhower Dr.
Paramus, NJ 07653

Transfer lettering eliminates the need for drawing freehand. A wide range of
type styles and point sizes are available. The transfer system is very diverse and
includes letters, numbers, designs, shapes, lines, borders, punctuation, motifs,
signage, flags, and the following symbols: architectural, data processing, technical,
music, demographics, and sports and leisure. Persons who have never worked with
transfer lettering may find The LetraGraphix Lettering System handy to use.

Several companies also manufacture templates. These are fairly inexpensive and
come in a wide variety of designs. There are house plan templates, spring and screw
templates, electrical symbol templates, etc. Brands include Rapidesign, Pickett,
Timely, Timesaver, and Lietz. Drawing instruments and drafting accessories are also

available at drafting supply stores. A local store might have a drafting catalog you can take, or contact:

THE ART SUPPLY CATALOG CO.
13916 Cordary Ave.
Hawthorne, CA 90251

Request the latest copy of Art & Drafting Materials.

Another recommended source for art and drafting materials is Dick Blick with warehouses and retail outlets across the U.S. Call for a copy of the Dick Blick Art Materials catalog. A large selection of templates and drawing instruments are available. One precision lettering device which this company sells is the Letterguide Adjustable Scriber, it allows anyone to produce professional lettering. A separate template catalog can be obtained on request. The main location is:

DICK BLICK CENTRAL
Rt. 150 East
Galesburg, IL
(309) 343-6181

For the nearest location, call 1(800) 447-8192 outside Illinois; in Illinois, call 1(800) 322-8183.

When you are ready to begin the drawings, adhere to the following drawing rules.

No names or other identification is permitted within the "sight" of the drawing, and applicants are expected to use the space above and below the hole locations to identify each sheet of drawings. The identification may consist of the attorney's name and docket number or the inventor's name and case number and may include the sheet number and the total number filed (i.e., "sheet 204").

1.84 Standards for Drawings

This section is derived from the U.S. Patent and Trademark Office's "Rules of Practice."

a) *Paper and Ink*. Drawings must be made upon paper which is flexible, strong, white, smooth, nonshiny and durable. Two-ply or three-ply bristol board is preferred. The surface of the paper should be calendered and of a quality which will permit erasures and corrections with India ink. India ink, or its equivalent in quality, is preferred for pen drawings to secure perfectly black solid lines. The use of white pigment to cover lines is not normally acceptable.

b) *Size of sheet and margins*. The size of the sheets on which drawings are made may either be exactly $8^1/2 \times 14$ inches (21.6×35.6 cm) or exactly 21.0×29.7 cm (DIN size A4). All drawing sheets in a particular application must be the same size. One of the shorter sizes of the sheet is regarded as its top.

On $8^{1}/_{2}$- × -14-inch drawing sheets, the drawings must include a top margin of 2 inches (5.1 cm) and bottom and side margins of $^{1}/_{4}$ inch (6.4 mm) from the edges, thereby leaving a "sight" precisely 8 × $11^{3}/_{4}$ inches (20.3 × 29.8 cm). Margin border lines are not permitted. All work must be included within the "sight." The sheets may be provided with two $^{1}/_{4}$-inch (6.4 cm) holes, having their centerlines spaced $^{11}/_{16}$ inch (17.5 mm) below the top edge and $2^{3}/_{4}$ inches (7.0 cm) apart, said holes being equally spaced from the respective side edges.

On 21.0- × -29.7-cm drawing sheets, the drawing must include a top margin of at least 2.5 cm, a left side margin 2.5 cm, a right side margin of 1.5 cm, and a bottom margin of 1.0 cm. Margin border lines are not permitted. All work must be contained within a sight size not to exceed 17 × 26.2 cm.

c) *Character of lines*. All drawings must be made with drafting instruments or by a process that will give them satisfactory reproduction characteristics. Every line and letter must be durable, black, sufficiently dense and dark, uniformly thick and well defined; the weight of all lines and letters must be heavy enough to permit adequate reproduction. This direction applies to all lines, however fine, to shading, and to lines representing cut surfaces in sectional views. All lines must be clean, sharp, and solid. Fine or crowded lines should be avoided. Solid black should not be used for sectional or surface shading. Freehand work should be avoided wherever it is possible to do so.

d) *Hatching and shading*. Hatching should be made by oblique parallel lines spaced sufficiently apart to enable the lines to be distinguished without difficulty. Heavy lines on the shaded side of objects should be preferably used except where they tend to thicken the work and obscure reference characters. The light should come from the upper left-hand corner at an angle of 45°. Surface deliniations should preferably be shown by proper shading, which should be open.

e) *Scale*. The scale to which a drawing is made ought to be large enough to show the mechanism without crowding when the drawing is reduced by two-thirds in size when reproduced, and views of portions of the mechanism on a larger scale should be used when necessary to show details clearly. Two or more sheets should be used if one does not give sufficient room to accomplish this end, but the number of sheets should not be more than is necessary.

f) *Reference characters*. The different views should be consecutively numbered figures. Reference numerals (and letters, but numerals are preferred) must be plain, legible, and carefully formed, and must not be encircled. They should, if possible, measure at least $^{1}/_{8}$ inch (3.2 mm) in height so that they may bear reduction to $^{1}/_{24}$ inch (1.1 mm) and they may be slightly larger when there is sufficient room. They should not be so placed in the close and complex parts of the drawing as to interfere with a thorough comprehension of the same, and therefore should rarely cross or mingle with the lines. When necessarily grouped around a certain part, they should be placed at a little distance, at the closest point where there is available space, and connected by lines with the parts to which they refer. They should not be placed upon hatched or shaded surfaces, but when necessary, a blank space may be left in the hatching or shading where the character occurs so that it shall appear perfectly distinct and separate from the work. The same part of an invention appearing in more than one view of the drawing must always be designated by the same character, and the same character must never be used to designate different parts. Reference signs not mentioned in the description shall not appear in the drawing, and vice versa.

g) *Symbols, legends.* Graphic drawing symbols and other labeled representations may be used for conventional elements when appropriate, subject to approval by the Office. The elements for which such symbols and representations are used must be adequately identified in the specification. While descriptive matter on drawings is not permitted, suitable legends may be used, or may be required in proper cases, as in diagrammatic views and flow sheets, to show materials, and where labeled representations are employed to illustrate conventional elements. Arrows may be required, in proper cases, to show the direction of movement. The lettering should be as large as, or larger than, the reference characters.

h) (Reserved.)

i) *Views.* The drawing must contain as many figures as may be necessary to show the invention; the figures should be consecutively numbered if possible in the order in which they appear. The figures may be plain, elevation, section, or perspective views, and detail views of portions of elements, or a larger scale if necessary, can also be used. Exploded views, with separated parts of the same figure embraced by a bracket, to show the relationship or order of assembly of various parts, are permissible. When necessary, a view of a large machine or device may be broken down in its entirety, and extended over several sheets if there is no loss in the facility of understanding the view.

Where figures on two or more sheets form in effect a single complete figure, the figures on the several sheets should be so arranged that the complete figure can be understood by laying the sheets adjacent to one another. The arrangement should be such that no part of any of the figures appearing on the various sheets is concealed and that the complete figure can be understood even though spaces will occur in the complete figure because of the margins on the drawing sheets. The plane upon which a sectional view is taken should be indicated on the general view by a broken line, the ends of which should be designated by numerals corresponding to the figure number of the sectional view, and have arrows applied to indicate the direction in which the view is taken. A moved position may be shown by a broken line superimposed upon a suitable figure if this can be done without crowding; otherwise, a separate figure must be used for this purpose. Modified forms of construction can only be shown in separate figures. Views should not be connected by projection lines nor should centerlines be used.

j) *Arrangement of views.* All views on the same sheet should stand in the same direction and, if possible, stand so that they can be read with the sheet held in an upright position. If views longer than the width of the sheet are necessary for the clearest illustration of the invention, the sheet may be turned on its side that the top of the sheet with the appropriate top margin is on the right-hand side. One figure must not be placed upon another or within the outline of another.

k) *Figure for Official Gazette.* The drawing should, as far as possible, be so planned that one of the views will be suitable for publication in the Official Gazette as the illustration of the invention.

l) *Extraneous matter.* Identifying indicia (such as the attorney's docket number, inventor's name, number of sheets, etc.) not to exceed 2³/₄ inches (7.0 cm) in width may be placed in a centered location between the side edges within ³/₄ inch (19.1 mm) of the top edge. Authorized security markings may be placed on the drawings provided they are outside of the illustrations and are removed when the material is declassified. Other extraneous matter will not be permitted upon the face of a drawing.

m) *Transmission of drawings.* Drawings transmitted to the Office should be sent flat, protected by a sheet of heavy binder's board, or may be rolled for transmission in a suitable mailing tube, but must never be folded. If received creased or mutilated, new drawings will be required.

Plant Patent Drawing

The PTO's "Rules of Practice" states that "Plant patent drawings are not mechanical drawings and should be artistically and competently executed. The drawing must disclose all the characteristics of the plant capable of visual representation.

"When color is a distinguishing characteristic of the new variety, the drawing must be in color. Two duplicate copies of color drawings must be submitted. Color drawings can be made either in permanent watercolor or oil, or in lieu thereof, can be photographs made by color photography or properly colored on sensitized paper. The paper, in any case, must correspond in size, weight, and quality to the paper required for other drawings. Mounted photographs are acceptable."

MODELS, EXHIBITS, AND SPECIMENS

A model is not permitted unless specifically requested by the examiner. The specification and drawing must fully disclose the invention and must be understandable without the use of a model.

Specimens might be required for inventions involving the composition of matter or its ingredients or intermediates. If it is microbiological invention, a deposit of the microorganism is required.

DOING BUSINESS WITH THE PATENT OFFICE

Patents are granted by the Patent and Trademark Office in Washington, D.C. All correspondence and applications concerning U.S. patents are handled by this office.

Applicants do not need to personally visit the PTO. All filings can be handled by mail or through a registered patent attorney or agent. Correspondence and papers must adhere to the custom and policy of "decorum and courtesy." This also applies to patent attorneys and agents.

When writing the Patent Office, use separate letters for each area of inquiry. More than one letter may be sent in a single envelope. Each question, request, payment, order, etc. requires a different cover letter; however, none of these should be included with letters concerning Office actions in applications.

All correspondence regarding patents should include the serial number, filing date, and Group Art Unit number. The applicant's name and address must be included along with the title of the invention, the patent number, and the date of issue.

Patent applications are not public information until a patent is granted.

THE APPLICANT

The actual inventor is the only person who may apply for a patent. If two or more persons did the inventing, then they may must apply as joint inventors.

A person who falsely claims to be the inventor on a patent application is subject to criminal penalties. Even a financial backer is not allowed to be included as an inventor unless that person actually contributed to the creation of the invention.

There are a few exceptions to this rule:

- If the inventor is dead, then the legal representatives can file the patent application.
- If the inventor is legally insane, then the legal guardian can file the application.
- A patent application can be filed by a joint inventor if the other inventor can't be located or refuses to comply.

A citizen of any country can apply for a U.S. patent. However, the inventor cannot have patented the invention more than 12 months before filing in the U.S. If filed within the previous 12-month period, the patent may receive "right of priority" and the official U.S. filing date will be the same as the first foreign filing date. In the case of a design patent, the period is the preceding six months. A copy of the foreign application must be certified by the foreign patent office and submitted at the same time that the U.S. patent application is filed.

An applicant must make an oath or declaration with every application. If a foreign application has been filed prior to the U.S. application in any foreign country, then the following information must be contained in the oath or declaration and accompany the application:

- State the country of the earliest filing.
- Give the filing date of the application.
- State all applications filed more than 12 months before the U.S. application.

If the applicant resides in a foreign country at the time of filing, the oath may be administered by a diplomat in consular offices of the U.S., or by any U.S. officer authorized to administer oaths in a foreign country under an official seal. Evidence of the officer's authority must be provided by a certificate of a diplomatic or consular office of the United States.

The application papers must then be attached together by a ribbon passed through all pages of the application (except the drawing) one or more times. The ends of the ribbons are brought together and affixed by the seal. Otherwise, each page must be individually impressed by the officer's official seal.

A declaration eliminates the necessity of the oath and its formalities, including the need to personally appear before the official.

Foreign applicants can be represented by a registered U.S. patent attorney or agent.

APPLICATION FOR PATENT

After careful and proper completion of all parts of the specification, you're ready to prepare the application. Follow the steps outlined here to save unnecessary delay and expense.

The application should include:

1. The specification
2. The drawing(s)
3. A Declaration for Patent Application
4. A transmittal letter
5. A Small-Entity Declaration
6. Payment
7. Return receipt postcard

Optional at time of filing:

8. An Information Disclosure Statement
9. Assignment

All documents requiring a signature must be signed in ink. After final preparation, photocopy all documents for your records. You might want to make a couple of extra copies.

The exact requirements for submitting the specification can be found in "The Specification" section. The guidelines for filing the specification must be closely observed or else the PTO will return the papers.

All required parts of the patent application should be filed together. All documents must be neat and complete. If parts of the application are submitted separately, then each part must be signed and accompanied by a cover letter with a clear explanation. Reference must be made to the original filing.

Upon receipt of the application, the PTO will issue a serial number. The applicant will then be informed of this number and the filing date. Subsequent correspondence concerning the application should bear the correct serial number and filing date.

All forms required for the patent filing are included in this section for your convenience. Other patent and trademark forms are available for various purposes; a few are included in this book. A list of PTO forms and their respective form numbers are shown in this part.

FORM P.O.-103(a) (REV. 10/69)	341	06/13/74	479.041
	GROUP NO.	FILING DATE	SERIAL NO. (SERIES OF 1970)

U. S. DEPT. OF COMMERCE PATENT OFFICE

Receipt is acknowledged of the patent application identified at right. It will be considered in its order and you will be notified as to the examination thereof.

Commissioner

(Over)

MAHER, WILLIAM A., SEPULVEDA, CALIF.,

APPLICANT — INVENTION

STEAM PROPULSION SYSTEM

DRAWINGS	TOTAL CL'S		FILING FEE REC	TRANSACTION	ATT'Y DK.
3	5	2	$75		50084

SANFORD ASTOR,
9036 RESEDA BLVD.,
NORTHRIDGE, CALIF. 91324

FORM P.O.-103(a) (REV. 10/69)	342	06/13/74	479.042
	GROUP NO.	FILING DATE	SERIAL NO. (SERIES OF 1970)

U. S. DEPT. OF COMMERCE PATENT OFFICE

Receipt is acknowledged of the patent application identified at right. It will be considered in its order and you will be notified as to the examination thereof.

Commissioner

(Over)

MAHER, WILLIAM A., SEPULVEDA, CALIF.,

APPLICANT — INVENTION

STEAM PROPULSION SYSTEM

DRAWINGS	TOTAL CL'S		FILING FEE REC	TRANSACTION	ATT'Y DK.
3	4	2	$75		50084

SANFORD ASTOR,
9036 RESEDA BLVD.,
NORTHRIDGE, CALIF. 91324

Application Process

Let's summarize the application process:

1. *The Specification*. The specification includes: a) title, b) background, c) brief summary, d) brief description of the drawing(s), e) detailed description, f) claim(s), and g) brief abstract. The specification should be typewritten on

legal-size paper (8 to $8^{1}/_{2} \times 10^{1}/_{2}$ to 13 inches), $1^{1}/_{2}$ spacing or double-spaced with 1-inch margins on the left side and on the top. All papers must be correct, legible, neat, and clearly written. Refer to "The Specification" section for more details and requirements.

2. *The Drawing(s)*. Submit three photocopies of your original drawings. If the PTO requires any changes, you will then be able to do them on the original art. Formal or informal drawings must follow the PTO rules for the "Standard for Drawings" which can be found in the "The Drawing" in this section. If an informal drawing accompanies the application, the PTO will eventually require a formalized version. Formal, informal drawings and photocopies of drawings must all be on $8^{1}/_{2}$-$\times$-14-inch paper or the international size, 21.0×29.7 cm (A4 size). These are exact dimensions. See the "The Drawing" section for additional drawing requirements. If you anticipate filing a foreign patent application, use only the A4 size.

3. *A Declaration for Patent Application*. This form is the actual patent application. It must be accurately completed in full and signed by the true inventor(s). Let's explore in order each point of this important form.

   a) Give the title of the invention exactly as stated in the specification.
   b) Will the specification be enclosed with the application? Check the appropriate box. The application and specification should be submitted together. If not, give the date, application serial number, and amendment date (if applicable) when the specification was filed.
   c) You agree that you have reviewed and understand the specification, the claim(s), and any amendments.
   d) You agree to disclose any pertinent information relevant to the PTO's examination of the application.
   e) Claim foreign priorities here and list all prior foreign application(s) including the number, country, complete date, and whether you are claiming priority by circling the appropriate box.
   f) List any previous patent(s) by applicant(s), pending applications(s), or abandoned application(s) by including the serial number, filing date, and status.
   g) Appointment of a registered patent attorney or patent agent. Give name(s), address, and telephone.
   h) You acknowledge that all information and statements contained in the application and regarding the patent filing are true. False statements are punishable by law.
   i) Give full inventors name(s), mailing and residential address(es), citizenship, date of application, and finally your signature.

4. *A Transmittal Letter.* A copy of the Patent Application Transmittal Letter

must be dated and submitted at the same time as the Declaration for Patent Application. It requests:

a) The title of the invention.
b) Inventor's name(s).
c) Are formal or informal sheets of the drawing enclosed?
d) Name an assignee, if any, and enclose a copy of the assignment form.
e) Type of application enclosed.
f) Is a copy of the power of attorney authorization, if any, enclosed?
g) Are you claiming small entity status? If so, enclose a Verified Statement Claiming Small-Entity Status form for independent inventors.
h) Calculate filing fees based on the number of claims. The filing fee is $370 for a large entity or $185 for a small entity. These fees permit a maximum total of 20 claims that include up to three independent claims.
i) If you have a deposit account with the PTO and you wish to charge the account, indicate this and give the account number.
j) Enclose a duplicate copy of the Transmittal Letter with filing.
k) Enclose a check for the full amount of the filing fees.
l) This authorizes the PTO to charge or credit your deposit account if there is an overpayment or underpayment.
m) Additional authorization for PTO to charge or credit a deposit account.
n) Date and sign the bottom of the letter. The date should be the same as the patent application date.

5. *A Small-Entity Declaration.* Completion of this form by an independent inventor allows payment of half the basic $370 patent-filing fee. Most individual inventors, small businesses, and nonprofit organizations qualify as small entities and are entitled to file this form. On the Patent Application Transmittal Letter, be sure to indicate that you are filing as a small entity, which only requires a basic fee of $185. Read the Small-Entity Status form carefully and give all information requested. Sign and date the bottom of the form.

6. *Payment.* If payment is not charged to a deposit account, then a check or money order must accompany the application. Deposit accounts are generally maintained by persons or organizations that do a large volume of business with the Patent and Trademark Office.

7. *Return Receipt Postcard.* This is a postcard addressed with your name and address for the PTO to return to you after it has received the patent application. On this card, list all items submitted in the application package. In addition, include the invention title, the number of pages submitted, and the check number and amount. When the postcard is returned, you will know that your application has been received by the PTO. File the return receipt with your other patent information. Separate correspondence should also include a return receipt postcard listing appropriate information.

If these seven steps have been completed, you are ready to mail your application package. Address the envelope to:

COMMISSIONER OF PATENTS AND TRADEMARKS
Washington, D.C. 20231
Contents: Patent Application

The two following steps are optional at this time. They can be included with the application or can be filed later.

8. *An Information Disclosure Statement.* The PTO requires all applicants to furnish an Information Disclosure Statement. This consists of a List of Prior Art Cited by Applicant form and an explanation and pertinent facts of each reference cited. The IDS must be filed with the application or within three months of filing. The extra period will allow you plenty of time to accurately finish the necessary information.

The form for List of Prior Art Cited by Applicant is included in this section. If you have completed a patent search, the IDS won't be difficult to do, but it will require careful execution. The form asks for the document number, date, inventor's name, class, subclass, and filing date of each piece of prior art. All known prior art must be disclosed in this list. In addition, on a separate piece of paper, explain each reference made, and include pertinent information on how the prior art relates to your invention. If you file the Information Disclosure Statement separately, include the following information at the top of it:

IN THE UNITED STATES PATENT AND TRADEMARK OFFICE
Application number:
Application filed: (*date*)
Applicant(s):
Application title: (*invention name and title*)
Mailed: (*date*)   at   (*city, state*)

Now, here's the statement:

INFORMATION DISCLOSURE STATEMENT

(Your name,
address,
and telephone here)

Commissioner of Patents and Trademarks
Washington, D.C. 20231

Dear Sir:

The following are references to prior art cited in the attached PTO 1449 form.

(List each reference here beginning with the inventor's last name
of the prior art and followed by a discussion of its relevant parts)

Sincerely,

(Your name)

9. *Assignments.* An assignment is a legal instrument that transfers ownership in a patent. A patent is personal property, just like household furniture. It may be licensed, mortgaged, sold, or willed to any person, partnership, or corporation. It might be for a temporary period, as in the case of a mortgage, or it might be permanent, as in the case of an outright sale of all interests in the patent.

All rights or a percentage of your ownership might be assigned to another party. The assigned rights can also be limited to a specific region of the country.

Let's pretend that you've decided to set up your own manufacturing operation. You've chosen to incorporate the business after speaking with the family lawyer. To capitalize the new corporation, you trade 100 percent interest in your patent in lieu of 51 percent of the proposed outstanding stock or authorized stock. The remaining 49 percent of the shares you sell to family and friends to raise the necessary start-up capital. Instead of owning a patent, you now own shares in a new corporation.

Several months pass when along comes Whizkids, Inc., a dynamic team of marketing experts who propose to distribute your new firm's patented product through their established sales channels in the 13 western states.

You are thoroughly impressed by their presentation and track record. So, overwhelmed with enthusiasm and as president of the corporation, you exercise your power and agree to their terms. You grant them 25 percent interest in the patent in exchange for a five-year marketing agreement.

However, during the crucial negotiations, your attorney was skiing the Swiss Alps. Upon his return, he informs you that it would have been better to grant an exclusive license to market the product in the western United States than to give up 25 percent of the corporation's most valuable asset.

Here are three points:

- A patent can also be licensed; it doesn't have to be assigned.
- Territorial rights can be assigned or licensed.
- Serious consideration should always be given before consummating a transfer of part or all of your rights in a patent. If necessary, consult a competent lawyer first.

Once an assignment is made, your rights to the patent might be irreversible. An example where ownership would revert back to the inventor is in the case of a mortgage. The patented property would temporarily pass hands to the mortgagee or lender until the mortgage is satisfied.

The PTO records assignments and grants that serve as constructive notice. "If an assignment, grant, or conveyance of a patent or an interest in a patent (or an application for patent) is not recorded in the Office within 3 months from its date, it is void against a subsequent purchaser for a valuable consideration without notice, unless it is recorded prior to the subsequent purchaser."

The assignment should include the patent number, filing date, name of the inventor, and the title of the invention.

An assignment can be executed at the same time that the application is prepared. It is then filed with all other patent papers (a $7 recording fee should be added to the filing fee). Include the extra amount in the same check or money order as the basic fee. Be sure to add to the patent application that an assignment is included, and list the assignment on the return receipt postcard. If the assignment is recorded by the time the issue fee is paid, then the assignee will be issued the patent as the owner.

Two or more persons can be joint owners of a patent. "Any joint owner of a patent, no matter how small the part interest, may make, use, and sell the invention for his or her own profit, without regard to the other owner, and may sell the interest or any part of it, or grant licenses to others, without regard to the other joint owner, *unless* the joint owners have made a contract governing their relation to each other." Being a joint owner of a patent is very similar to being a general partner in a partnership. The best precaution against inherent risks is a written agreement between the joint owners that clearly outlines the rights and obligations of each party.

Assignments and joint owner's agreements are usually drafted by an attorney. You might find a simple agreement of this nature in a library.

Types of Patents

Now, here is pertinent information concerning types of patents. This is useful when preparing the patent application.

Utility Patent. The term of the patent is 17 years. The basic filing fee for each application of an original patent—except for design or plant patents—is $370, unless you claim "small-entity status," and then it's $185.

A maintenance fee is due $3^1/_2$, $7^1/_2$, and $11^1/_2$ years after the original grant, and must be paid at the stipulated times to keep the patent in full force. Fees can be paid without a surcharge during the "window period," six months preceding each due date (refer to the fee schedule). The amounts are subject to change every three years. The current fees are effective from April, 1989 to March, 1992.

Design Patent. The term of the patent is 14 years. The basic filing fee for each design application is $150, the issue fee is $220. These fees are halved for qualifying small entities and for individuals. No maintenance fees are required.

Two design patent applications are included in this book. One contains a declaration and the other an oath. Determine from prior discussions of oaths and declarations which is appropriate for your purpose. Both applications include a power of attorney. If none, state "No power of attorney given."

Here are the items that should accompany your design application mailing.

1. Design application with declaration or oath (power of attorney is optional)
2. Small-entity status
3. Payment ($75 for small entities)
4. Return receipt postcard

Plant Patent. A plant patent application contains essentially the same elements as a utility patent application. The application must be filed in duplicate, but only one copy has to be signed. The second copy is forwarded by the PTO to the Department of Agriculture for an advisory report on the plant variety.

The filing fee for each plant application is $250. The issue fee is $310. A small entity pays $125.

The oath or declaration required for the application must also state that the applicant asexually reproduced the new plant variety. This statement is included in both plant patent applications furnished here.

All inquiries related to plant patents and pending applications should be directed to the Patent and Trademark Office and not the department of Agriculture.

ENGLISH LANGUAGE FORMS

Form No.	Form Title
3.12	Oath to Accompany Application for Patent, by an Administrator (or Executor)
3.12a	Declaration to Accompany Application for Patent, by an Administrator (or Executor)
3.13	Oath Not Accompanying Application
3.13a	Declaration Not Accompanying Application
3.14	Supplemental Oath for Amendment Presenting Claims for Matter Disclosed But Not Originally Claimed
3.14a	Supplemental Declaration for Amendment Presenting Claims for Matter Disclosed But Not Originally Claimed
3.16	Combined Oath and Power of Attorney in Original Application
3.16a	Combined Declaration and Power of Attorney in Original Application
3.17	Oath in Division or Continuation Application
3.17a	Declaration in Division or Continuation Application
3.18	Oath in Copending Application Containing Additional Subject Matter
3.18a	Declaration in Copending Application Containing Additional Subject Matter
3.23	Design Patent Application; Oath
3.23a	Design Patent Application; Declaration
3.26	Plant Patent Application; Oath
3.26a	Plant Patent Application; Declaration
3.28	Reissue Application by the Inventor, Offer to Surrender
3.29	Reissue Application by the Assignee, Offer to Surrender
3.31	Reissue Application, Oath; by the Inventor
3.31a	Reissue Application, Declaration; by Inventor
3.32	Reissue Application, Oath; by Assignee
3.32a	Reissue Application, Declaration; by Assignee
3.33	Oath as to Loss of Letters Patent
3.33a	Declaration as to Loss of Letters Patent
3.36	Power of Attorney or Authorization of Agent, Not Accompanying Application
3.37	Revocation of Power of Attorney or Authorization of Agent
3.41	Notice of Appeal from the Primary Examiner to the Board of Appeals
3.43	Disclaimer in Patent
3.46	Disclaimer During Interference
3.50	Waiver of Patent Rights Under Section 1.139
3.51	Application Transmittal Letter
3.52	Amendment Transmittal Letter
3.53	Terminal Disclaimer in Application
3.54	Division-Continuation Program Application Transmittal Form
3.55	Format for Certificate of Mailing-Included with Correspondence
3.55a	Certificate of Mailing-Separate Paper
3.56	Oath to be Filed with U.S. Designated Office Under 35 USC 371(C)(4)

Form No.	Form Title
3.57	Declaration to be Filed with U.S. Designated Office Under 35 USC 371(C)(4)
3.70	Reissue Application Fee Determination Record
3.71	Certificate of Correction
3.72	List of Prior Art Cited by Applicant
3.73	Oath Second Page
3.73a	Declaration Second Page
3.74	Disclosure Document Deposit Form
3.75	Coupon Order Request
3.76	Deposit Account Order Form
3.77	Cash Order Form
3.78	Assignment of Application
3.79	Assignment of Patent
1360	Multiple Dependent Claim Fee Calculation Sheet

FOREIGN LANGUAGE FORMS
(Oaths and Declarations Including Power of Attorney)

3.16(ARA)	Arabic Oath in Original Application
3.16a(ARA)	Arabic Declaration in Original Application
3.16(BUL)	Bulgarian Oath in Original Application
3.16a(BUL)	Bulgarian Declaration in Original Application
3.16(CHI)	Chinese Oath in Original Application
3.16a(CHI)	Chinese Declaration in Original Application
3.16(CZE)	Czech Oath in Original Application
3.16a(CZE)	Czech Declaration in Original Application
3.16(DAN)	Danish Oath in Original Application
3.16a(DAN)	Danish Declaration in Original Application
3.17a(DAN)	Danish Declaration in Division or Continuation Application
3.23a(DAN)	Danish Declaration in Design Application
3.16(DUT)	Dutch Oath in Original Application
316a(DUT)	Dutch Declaration in Original Application
3.17a(DUT)	Dutch Declaration in Division or Continuation Application
3.23a(DUT)	Dutch Declaration in Design Application
3.16(FIN)	Finnish Oath in Original Application
3.16a(FIN)	Finnish Declaration in Original Application
3.17a(FIN)	Finnish Declaration in Division or Continuation Application
3.23a(FIN)	Finnish Declaration in Design Application
3.16(FRE)	French Oath in Original Application
3.16a(FRE)	French Declaration in Original Application
3.17a(FRE)	French Declaration in Division or Continuation Application
3.23a(FRE)	French Declaration in Design Application
3.16(GER)	German Oath in Original Application

3.16a(GER)	German Declaration in Original Application
3.17a(GER)	German Declaration in Division or Continuation Application
3.23a(GER)	German Declaration in Design Application
3.16(GRE)	Greek Oath in Original Application
3.16a(GRE)	Greek Declaration in Original Application
3.16(HUN)	Hungarian Oath in Original Application
3.16a(HUN)	Hungarian Declaration in Original Application
3.18a(HUN)	Hungarian Declaration in Continuation-in-Part Application
3.16(IND)	Indonesian Oath in Original Application
3.16a(IND)	Indonesian Declaration in Original Application
3.16(ITA)	Italian Oath in Original Application
3.16a(ITA)	Italian Declaration in Original Application
3.17a(ITA)	Italian Declaration in Division or Continuation Application
3.23a(ITA)	Italian Declaration in Design Application
3.16(JAP)	Japanese Oath in Original Application
3.16a(JAP)	Japanese Declaration in Original Application
3.17a(JAP)	Japanese Declaration in Division or Continuation Application
3.23a(JAP)	Japanese Declaration in Design Application
3.16(KOR)	Korean Oath in Original Application
3.16a(KOR)	Korean Declaration in Original Application
3.16(NOR)	Norwegian Oath in Original Application
3.16a(NOR)	Norwegian Declaration in Original Application
3.17a(NOR)	Norwegian Declaration in Division or Continuation Application
3.23a(NOR)	Norwegian Declaration in Design Application
3.16(POL)	Polish Oath in Original Application
3.16a(POL)	Polish Declaration in Original Application
3.16(POR)	Portugese Oath in Original Application
3.16a(POR)	Portugese Declaration in Original Application
3.16(ROM)	Romanian Oath in Original Application
3.16a(ROM)	Romanian Declaration in Original Application
3.16(RUS)	Russian Oath in Original Application
3.16a(RUS)	Russian Declaration in Original Application
3.17a(RUS)	Russian Declaration in Division or Continuation Application
3.23a(RUS)	Russian Declaration in Design Application
3.16(SER)	Serbo-Croation Oath in Original Application
3.16a(SER)	Serbo-Croation Declaration in Original Application
3.16(SPA)	Spanish Oath in Original Application
3.16a(SPA)	Spanish Declaration in Original Application
3.17a(SPA)	Spanish Declaration in Division or Continuation Application
3.23a(SPA)	Spanish Declaration in Design Application
3.16(SWE)	Swedish Oath in Original Application
3.16a(SWE)	Swedish Declaration in Original Application
3.17a(SWE)	Swedish Declaration in Division or Continuation Application
3.23a(SWE)	Swedish Declaration in Design Application

OATH – ORIGINAL APPLICATION	ATTORNEY'S DOCKET NO.

As a below-named inventor, I hereby swear or affirm that:

my residence, post office address and citizenship are as stated below next to my name;

I verily believe I am the original, first and sole inventor (if only one name is listed below at 201) or a joint inventor (if plural inventors are named below at 201-203) of the invention entitled _____

_____

which is described and claimed in the attached specification;

I do not know and do not believe that the invention was ever known or used in the United States of America before my or our invention thereof;

I do not know and do not believe that the invention was ever patented or described in any printed publication in any country before my or our invention thereof or more than one year prior to this application;

I do not know and do not believe that the invention was in public use or on sale in the United States of America more than one year prior to this application;

I acknowledge my duty to disclose information of which I am aware which is material to the examination of this application;

the invention has not been patented or made the subject of an inventor's certificate issued before the date of this application in any country foreign to the United States of America on an application filed by me or my legal representatives or assigns more than twelve months prior to this application; and

as to applications for patents or inventor's certificate on the invention filed in any country foreign to the United States of America prior to this application by me or my legal representatives or assigns,

☐ no such applications have been filed, or

☐ such applications have been filed as follows:

EARLIEST FOREIGN APPLICATION(S), IF ANY, FILED WITHIN 12 MONTHS PRIOR TO THIS APPLICATION

COUNTRY	APPLICATION NO.	DATE OF FILING (DAY, MO., YR.)	DATE OF ISSUE (DAY, MO., YR.)	PRIORITY CLAIMED UNDER 35 U.S.C. 119
				YES ☐ NO ☐
				YES ☐ NO ☐

ALL FOREIGN APPLICATIONS, IF ANY, FILED MORE THAN 12 MONTHS PRIOR TO THIS APPLICATION

SEND CORRESPONDENCE TO:	DIRECT TELEPHONE CALLS TO: *(name and telephone number)*

		FAMILY NAME	FIRST GIVEN NAME	SECOND GIVEN NAME
201	FULL NAME OF INVENTOR	FAMILY NAME	FIRST GIVEN NAME	SECOND GIVEN NAME
	RESIDENCE CITIZENSHIP	CITY	STATE OR FOREIGN COUNTRY	COUNTRY OF CITIZENSHIP
	POST OFFICE ADDRESS	POST OFFICE ADDRESS / CITY	CITY	STATE & ZIP CODE/COUNTRY
202	FULL NAME OF INVENTOR	FAMILY NAME	FIRST GIVEN NAME	SECOND GIVEN NAME
	RESIDENCE CITIZENSHIP	CITY	STATE OR FOREIGN COUNTRY	COUNTRY OF CITIZENSHIP
	POST OFFICE ADDRESS	POST OFFICE ADDRESS / CITY	CITY	STATE & ZIP CODE/COUNTRY
203	FULL NAME OF INVENTOR	FAMILY NAME	FIRST GIVEN NAME	SECOND GIVEN NAME
	RESIDENCE CITIZENSHIP	CITY	STATE OR FOREIGN COUNTRY	COUNTRY OF CITIZENSHIP
	POST OFFICE ADDRESS	POST OFFICE ADDRESS / CITY	CITY	STATE & ZIP CODE/COUNTRY

(continued)

SIGNATURE OF INVENTOR 201	SIGNATURE OF INVENTOR 202	SIGNATURE OF INVENTOR 203
DATE	DATE	DATE

State of _____)

SS

County of _____)

Sworn to and subscribed before me this _____ day of _____ , 19 _____ .

_____

(signature of notary or officer)

(SEAL)

_____

(official character)

OMB No. 0851-0011 (12/31/86)

DECLARATION FOR PATENT APPLICATION

Docket No. _____

As a below named inventor, I hereby declare that:

My residence, post office address and citizenship are as stated below next to my name.

I believe I am the original, first and sole inventor (if only one name is listed below) or an original, first and joint inventor (if plural names are listed below) of the subject matter which is claimed and for which a patent is sought on the invention entitled _____, the specification of which

(check one) ☐ is attached hereto.
        ☐ was filed on _____ as
        Application Serial No. _____
        and was amended on _____ (if applicable).

I hereby state that I have reviewed and understand the contents of the above identified specification, including the claims, as amended by any amendment referred to above.

I acknowledge the duty to disclose information which is material to the examination of this application in accordance with Title 37, Code of Federal Regulations, §1.56(a).

I hereby claim foreign priority benefits under Title 35, United States Code, §119 of any foreign application(s) for patent or inventor's certificate listed below and have also identified below any foreign application for patent or inventor's certificate having a filing date before that of the application on which priority is claimed:

Prior Foreign Application(s)   Priority Claimed

(Number)	(Country)	(Day/Month/Year Filed)	Yes	No
(Number)	(Country)	(Day/Month/Year Filed)	Yes	No
(Number)	(Country)	(Day/Month/Year Filed)	Yes	No

I hereby claim the benefit under Title 35, United States Code, §120 of any United States application(s) listed below and, insofar as the subject matter of each of the claims of this application is not disclosed in the prior United States application in the manner provided by the first paragraph of Title 35, United States Code, §112, I acknowledge the duty to disclose material information as defined in Title 37, Code of Federal Regulations, §1.56(a) which occurred between the filing date of the prior application and the national or PCT international filing date of this application:

(Application Serial No.)	(Filing Date)	(Status—patented, pending, abandoned)
(Application Serial No.)	(Filing Date)	(Status—patented, pending, abandoned)

I hereby appoint the following attorney(s) and/or agent(s) to prosecute this application and to transact all business in the Patent and Trademark Office connected therewith:

Address all telephone calls to _____ at telephone no. _____
Address all correspondence to _____

I hereby declare that all statements made herein of my own knowledge are true and that all statements made on information and belief are believed to be true; and further that these statements were made with the knowledge that willful false statements and the like so made are punishable by fine or imprisonment, or both, under Section 1001 of Title 18 of the United States Code and that such willful false statements may jeopardize the validity of the application or any patent issued thereon.

Full name of sole or first inventor _____
Inventor's signature _____ Date _____
Residence _____ Citizenship _____
Post Office Address _____

Full name of second joint inventor, if any _____
Second Inventor's signature _____ Date _____
Residence _____ Citizenship _____
Post Office Address _____

(Supply similar information and signature for third and subsequent joint inventors.)

Form PTO-FB-A110 (8-83)

OMB No. 0651-0011 (12/31/86)

DECLARATION FOR PATENT APPLICATION

Docket No. _____

As a below named inventor, I hereby declare that:

My residence, post office address and citizenship are as stated below next to my name.

a) I believe I am the original, first and sole inventor (if only one name is listed below) or an original, first and joint inventor (if plural names are listed below) of the subject matter which is claimed and for which a patent is sought on the invention entitled _____, the specification of which

b) (check one) ☐ is attached hereto.
☐ was filed on _____ as
Application Serial No. _____
and was amended on _____ (if applicable).

c) I hereby state that I have reviewed and understand the contents of the above identified specification, including the claims, as amended by any amendment referred to above.

d) I acknowledge the duty to disclose information which is material to the examination of this application in accordance with Title 37, Code of Federal Regulations, §1.56(a).

e) I hereby claim foreign priority benefits under Title 35, United States Code, §119 of any foreign application(s) for patent or inventor's certificate listed below and have also identified below any foreign application for patent or inventor's certificate having a filing date before that of the application on which priority is claimed:

Prior Foreign Application(s)   Priority Claimed

(Number)	(Country)	(Day/Month/Year Filed)	Yes	No
(Number)	(Country)	(Day/Month/Year Filed)	Yes	No
(Number)	(Country)	(Day/Month/Year Filed)	Yes	No

f) I hereby claim the benefit under Title 35, United States Code, §120 of any United States application(s) listed below and, insofar as the subject matter of each of the claims of this application is not disclosed in the prior United States application in the manner provided by the first paragraph of Title 35, United States Code, §112, I acknowledge the duty to disclose material information as defined in Title 37, Code of Federal Regulations, §1.56(a) which occurred between the filing date of the prior application and the national or PCT international filing date of this application:

(Application Serial No.)	(Filing Date)	(Status—patented, pending, abandoned)
(Application Serial No.)	(Filing Date)	(Status—patented, pending, abandoned)

g) I hereby appoint the following attorney(s) and/or agent(s) to prosecute this application and to transact all business in the Patent and Trademark Office connected therewith:

_____

Address all telephone calls to _____ at telephone no. _____

Address all correspondence to _____

_____

_____

_____

h) I hereby declare that all statements made herein of my own knowledge are true and that all statements made on information and belief are believed to be true; and further that these statements were made with the knowledge that willful false statements and the like so made are punishable by fine or imprisonment, or both, under Section 1001 of Title 18 of the United States Code and that such willful false statements may jeopardize the validity of the application or any patent issued thereon.

i) Full name of sole or first inventor _____

Inventor's signature _____ Date _____

Residence _____ Citizenship _____

Post Office Address _____

Full name of second joint inventor, if any _____

Second Inventor's signature _____ Date _____

Residence _____ Citizenship _____

Post Office Address _____

(Supply similar information and signature for third and subsequent joint inventors.)

Form PTO-FB-A110 (8-83)

OMB No. 0651-0011 (12/31/86)

Applicant or Patentee: _____ Attorney's
Serial or Patent No.: _____ Docket No.: _____
Filed or Issued: _____
For: _____

VERIFIED STATEMENT (DECLARATION) CLAIMING SMALL ENTITY
STATUS (37 CFR 1.9 (f) and 1.27 (b)) — INDEPENDENT INVENTOR

As a below named inventor, I hereby declare that I qualify as an independent inventor as defined in 37 CFR 1.9 (c) for purposes of paying reduced fees under section 41 (a) and (b) of Title 35, United States Code, to the Patent and Trademark
Office with regard to the invention entitled _____
described in

    [ ] the specification filed herewith
    [ ] application serial no. _____ , filed _____ .
    [ ] patent no. _____ , issued _____ .

I have not assigned, granted, conveyed or licensed and am under no obligation under contract or law to assign, grant, convey
or license, any rights in the invention to any person who could not be classified as an independent inventor under 37 CFR
1.9 (c) if that person had made the invention, or to any concern which would not qualify as a small business concern under
37 CFR 1.9 (d) or a nonprofit organization under 37 CFR 1.9 (e).

Each person, concern or organization to which I have assigned, granted, conveyed, or licensed or am under an obligation
under contract or law to assign, grant, convey, or license any rights in the invention is listed below:

    [ ] no such person, concern, or organization
    [ ] persons, concerns or organizations listed below*

        *NOTE: Separate verified statements are required from each named person, concern or organiza-
        tion having rights to the invention averring to their status as small entities. (37 CFR 1.27)

FULL NAME _____
ADDRESS _____
        [ ] INDIVIDUAL   [ ] SMALL BUSINESS CONCERN   [ ] NONPROFIT ORGANIZATION

FULL NAME _____
ADDRESS _____
        [ ] INDIVIDUAL   [ ] SMALL BUSINESS CONCERN   [ ] NONPROFIT ORGANIZATION

FULL NAME _____
ADDRESS _____
        [ ] INDIVIDUAL   [ ] SMALL BUSINESS CONCERN   [ ] NONPROFIT ORGANIZATION

I acknowledge the duty to file, in this application or patent, notification of any change in status resulting in loss of entitle-
ment to small entity status prior to paying, or at the time of paying, the earliest of the issue fee or any maintenance fee
due after the date on which status as a small entity is no longer appropriate. (37 CFR 1.28 (b))

I hereby declare that all statements made herein of my own knowledge are true and that all statements made on information
and belief are believed to be true; and further that these statements were made with the knowledge that willful false statements
and the like so made are punishable by fine or imprisonment, or both, under section 1001 of Title 18 of the United States
Code, and that such willful false statements may jeopardize the validity of the application, any patent issuing thereon, or
any patent to which this verified statement is directed.

NAME OF INVENTOR _____   NAME OF INVENTOR _____   NAME OF INVENTOR _____

_____   _____   _____
Signature of Inventor   Signature of Inventor   Signature of Inventor

_____   _____   _____
Date   Date   Date

Form PTO-FB-A410 (8-83)

SUPPLEMENTAL OATH FOR AMENDMENT PRESENTING CLAIMS FOR MATTER DISCLOSED BUT NOT ORIGINALLY CLAIMED	ATTORNEY'S DOCKET NO.

I, _____

_____ , as an inventor named in the application for letters

patent for an improvement in _____

_____ Serial No. _____ ,

filed in the United States Patent and Trademark Office on about the _____ day of _____ ,

19 ____ , hereby swear or affirm that the subject matter of the ☐ attached amendment, ☐ amendment filed

on about _____ , 19 _____ , was part of my or our invention and was invented
before the filing of the original application, above identified, for such invention; that I do not know and do not
believe that the invention was ever known or used in the United States of America before my invention thereof,
or was ever patented or described in any printed publication in any country before my or our invention thereof,
or more than one year before said application, or was in public use or on sale in the United States of America
more than one year before the date of said application, that said invention has not been patented or made the
subject of an inventor's certificate issued before the date of said application in any country foreign to the
United States of America on an application filed by me or my legal representatives or assigns more than twelve
months prior to said application in the United States of America, and has not been abandoned.

_____
(signature)

_____
(signature)

_____
(signature)

State of _____)
) SS
County of _____)

Sworn to and subscribed before me this _____ day of _____ 19 _____ .

_____
(signature of notary or officer)

(SEAL)

_____
(official character)

Patent and Trademark Office - U.S. DEPT. of COMMERCE

SUPPLEMENTAL DECLARATION FOR AMENDMENT PRESENTING CLAIMS FOR MATTER DISCLOSED BUT NOT ORIGINALLY CLAIMED	ATTORNEY'S DOCKET NO.

I, _____

_____ , as an inventor named in the application for letters

patent for an improvement in _____

_____ Serial No. _____ ,

filed in the United States Patent and Trademark Office on about the _____ day of _____ ,

19_____ , hereby swear or affirm that the subject matter of the ☐ attached amendment, ☐ amendment filed

on about _____ , 19 _____ , was part of my or our invention and was invented before the filing of the original application, above identified, for such invention; that I do not know and do not believe that the invention was ever known or used in the United States of America before my invention thereof, or was ever patented or described in any printed publication in any country before my or our invention thereof, or more than one year before said application, or was in public use or on sale in the United States of America more than one year before the date of said application, that said invention has not been patented or made the subject of an inventor's certificate issued before the date of said application in any country foreign to the United States of America on an application filed by me or my legal representatives or assigns more than twelve months prior to said application in the United States of America, and has not been abandoned.

I hereby declare that all statements made herein of my own knowledge are true and that all statements made on information and belief are believed to be true; and further that these statements were made with the knowledge that willfull false statements and the like so made are punishable by fine or imprisonment, or both, under section 1001 of Title 18 of the United States Code, and that such wilful false statements may jeopardize the validity of the application or any patent issuing thereon.

_____ _____
(signature)   (date)

_____ _____
(signature)   (date)

_____ _____
(signature)   (date)

DECLARATION AND POWER OF ATTORNEY – ORIGINAL APPLICATION	ATTORNEY'S DOCKET NO.

As a below named inventor, I hereby declare that:

My residence, post office address and citizenship are as stated below next to my name;

I verily believe I am the original, first and sole inventor (if only one name is listed below at 201) or a joint inventor (if plural

inventors are named below at 201-203) of the invention entitled _____

_____

which is described and claimed in the attached specification;

I do not know and do not believe that the invention was ever known or used in the United States of America before my or our invention thereof;

I do not know and do not believe that the invention was ever patented or described in any printed publication in any country before my or our invention thereof or more than one year prior to this application;

I do not know and do not believe that the invention was in public use or on sale in the United States of America more than one year prior to this application;

I acknowledge my duty to disclose information of which I am aware which is material to the examination of this application;

the invention has not been patented or made the subject of an inventor's certificate issued before the date of this application in any country foreign to the United States of America on an application filed by me or my legal representatives or assigns more than twelve months prior to this application; and

as to applications for patents or inventor's certificate on the invention filed in any country foreign to the United States of America, prior to this application by me or my legal representatives or assigns,

☐ no such applications have been filed, or

☐ such applications have been filed as follows:

EARLIEST FOREIGN APPLICATION(S), IF ANY, FILED WITHIN 12 MONTHS PRIOR TO THIS APPLICATION

COUNTRY	APPLICATION NUMBER	DATE OF FILING (day, month, year)	DATE OF ISSUE (day, month, year)	PRIORITY CLAIMED UNDER 35 USC 119
				☐ YES ☐ NO
				☐ YES ☐ NO

ALL FOREIGN APPLICATIONS, IF ANY, FILED MORE THAN 12 MONTHS PRIOR TO THIS APPLICATION

POWER OF ATTORNEY: As a named inventor, I hereby appoint the following attorney(s) and/or agent(s) to prosecute this application and transact all business in the Patent and Trademark Office connected therewith. *(list name and registration number)*

SEND CORRESPONDENCE TO:

DIRECT TELEPHONE CALLS TO: *(name and telephone number)*

		FAMILY NAME	FIRST GIVEN NAME	SECOND GIVEN NAME
201	FULL NAME OF INVENTOR			
	RESIDENCE & CITIZENSHIP	CITY	STATE OR FOREIGN COUNTRY	COUNTRY OF CITIZENSHIP
	POST OFFICE ADDRESS	POST OFFICE ADDRESS	CITY	STATE & ZIP CODE/COUNTRY
202	FULL NAME OF INVENTOR	FAMILY NAME	FIRST GIVEN NAME	SECOND GIVEN NAME
	RESIDENCE & CITIZENSHIP	CITY	STATE OR FOREIGN COUNTRY	COUNTRY OF CITIZENSHIP
	POST OFFICE ADDRESS	POST OFFICE ADDRESS	CITY	STATE & ZIP CODE/COUNTRY

PTO Form 3.16(a)   Patent and Trademark Office - U.S. DEPARTMENT of COMMERCE

(continued)

	FULL NAME OF INVENTOR	FAMILY NAME	FIRST GIVEN NAME	SECOND GIVEN NAME
203	RESIDENCE & CITIZENSHIP	CITY	STATE OR FOREIGN COUNTRY	COUNTRY OF CITIZENSHIP
	POST OFFICE ADDRESS	POST OFFICE ADDRESS	CITY	STATE & ZIP CODE/COUNTRY

I hereby declare that all statements made herein of my own knowledge are true and that all statements made on information and belief are believed to be true; and further that these statements were made with the knowledge that willful false statements and the like so made are punishable by fine or imprisonment, or both, under section 1001 of Title 18 of the United States Code, and that such willful false statements may jeopardize the validity of the application or any patent issuing thereon.

SIGNATURE OF INVENTOR 201	SIGNATURE OF INVENTOR 202	SIGNATURE OF INVENTOR 203
DATE	DATE	DATE

OATH AND POWER OF ATTORNEY — ORIGINAL APPLICATION	ATTORNEY'S DOCKET NO.

As a below named inventor, I hereby declare that:

My residence, post office address and citizenship are as stated below next to my name;

I verily believe I am the original, first and sole inventor (if only one name is listed below at 201) or a joint inventor (if plural

inventors are named below at 201-203) of the invention entitled _____

_____

which is described and claimed in the attached specification;

I do not know and do not believe that the invention was ever known or used in the United States of America before my or our invention thereof;

I do not know and do not believe that the invention was ever patented or described in any printed publication in any country before my or our invention thereof or more than one year prior to this application;

I do not know and do not believe that the invention was in public use or on sale in the United States of America more than one year prior to this application;

I acknowledge my duty to disclose information of which I am aware which is material to the examination of this application;

the invention has not been patented or made the subject of an inventor's certificate issued before the date of this application in any country foreign to the United States of America on an application filed by me or my legal representatives or assigns more than twelve months prior to this application; and

as to applications for patents or inventor's certificate on the invention filed in any country foreign to the United States of America, prior to this application by me or my legal representatives or assigns,

☐ no such applications have been filed, or

☐ such applications have been filed as follows:

EARLIEST FOREIGN APPLICATION(S), IF ANY, FILED WITHIN 12 MONTHS PRIOR TO THIS APPLICATION

COUNTRY	APPLICATION NUMBER	DATE OF FILING (day, month, year)	DATE OF ISSUE (day, month, year)	PRIORITY CLAIMED UNDER 35 USC 119	
				☐ YES	☐ NO
				☐ YES	☐ NO

ALL FOREIGN APPLICATIONS, IF ANY, FILED MORE THAN 12 MONTHS PRIOR TO THIS APPLICATION

POWER OF ATTORNEY: As a named inventor, I hereby appoint the following attorney(s) and/or agent(s) to prosecute this application and transact all business in the Patent and Trademark Office connected therewith. *(list name and registration number)*

SEND CORRESPONDENCE TO:

DIRECT TELEPHONE CALLS TO: *(name and telephone number)*

		FAMILY NAME	FIRST GIVEN NAME	SECOND GIVEN NAME
201	FULL NAME OF INVENTOR	FAMILY NAME	FIRST GIVEN NAME	SECOND GIVEN NAME
	RESIDENCE & CITIZENSHIP	CITY	STATE OR FOREIGN COUNTRY	COUNTRY OF CITIZENSHIP
	POST OFFICE ADDRESS	POST OFFICE ADDRESS	CITY	STATE & ZIP CODE/COUNTRY
202	FULL NAME OF INVENTOR	FAMILY NAME	FIRST GIVEN NAME	SECOND GIVEN NAME
	RESIDENCE & CITIZENSHIP	CITY	STATE OR FOREIGN COUNTRY	COUNTRY OF CITIZENSHIP
	POST OFFICE ADDRESS	POST OFFICE ADDRESS	CITY	STATE & ZIP CODE/COUNTRY

PTO Form 3.16   Patent and Trademark Office - U.S. DEPARTMENT of COMMERCE

(continued)

FULL NAME OF INVENTOR	FAMILY NAME		FIRST GIVEN NAME	SECOND GIVEN NAME
RESIDENCE & CITIZENSHIP	CITY		STATE OR FOREIGN COUNTRY	COUNTRY OF CITIZENSHIP
POST OFFICE ADDRESS	POST OFFICE ADDRESS		CITY	STATE & ZIP CODE/COUNTRY

(203)

SIGNATURE OF INVENTOR 201	SIGNATURE OF INVENTOR 202	SIGNATURE OF INVENTOR 203
DATE	DATE	DATE

State of _____)

County of _____) SS

Sworn to and subscribed before me this _____ day of _____ , 19 ____.

_____
(signature of notary or officer)

(SEAL)

_____
(official character)

DECLARATION AND POWER OF ATTORNEY DESIGN PATENT APPLICATION	ATTORNEY'S DOCKET NO.

As a below-named inventor, I hereby swear or affirm that:
my residence, post office address and citizenship are as stated below next to my name;
I verily believe I am the original, first and sole inventor (if only one name is listed below at 201) or a joint inventor (if plural

inventors are named below at 201-203) of the design entitled _____

_____

which is described and claimed in the attached specification;
I do not know and do not believe that the design was ever known or used in the United States of America before my or our invention thereof;
I do not know and do not believe that the design was ever patented or described in any printed publication in any country before my or our invention thereof or more than one year prior to this application;
I do not know and do not believe that the design was in public use or on sale in the United States of America more than one year prior to this application;
I acknowledge my duty to disclose information of which I am aware which is material to the examination of this application;
the invention has not been patented or made the subject of an inventor's certificate issued before the date of this application in any country foreign to the United States of America on an application filed by me or my legal representatives or assigns more than six m o nths prior to this application; and
as to applications for patents or inventor's certificate on the design filed in any country foreign to the United States of America prior to this application by me or my legal representatives or assigns,

☐ no such applications have been filed, or
☐ such applications have been filed as follows:

EARLIEST FOREIGN APPLICATION(S), IF ANY, FILED WITHIN 6 MONTHS PRIOR TO THIS APPLICATION

COUNTRY	APPLICATION NO.	DATE OF FILING (DAY, MO., YR.)	DATE OF ISSUE (DAY, MO., YR.)	PRIORITY CLAIMED UNDER 35 U.S.C. 119
				YES ☐ NO ☐
				YES ☐ NO ☐

ALL FOREIGN APPLICATIONS, IF ANY, FILED MORE THAN 6 MONTHS PRIOR TO THIS APPLICATION

POWER OF ATTORNEY: As a named inventor, I hereby appoint the following attorney(s) and/or agent(s) to prosecute this application and transact all business in the Patent and Trademark Office connected therewith. *(list name and registration no.)*

SEND CORRESPONDENCE TO:

DIRECT TELEPHONE CALLS TO:
(name and telephone number)

		FAMILY NAME	FIRST GIVEN NAME	SECOND GIVEN NAME
201	FULL NAME OF INVENTOR			
	RESIDENCE & CITIZENSHIP	CITY	STATE OR FOREIGN COUNTRY	COUNTRY OF CITIZENSHIP
	POST OFFICE ADDRESS	POST OFFICE ADDRESS — CITY		STATE & ZIP CODE/COUNTRY
202	FULL NAME OF INVENTOR	FAMILY NAME	FIRST GIVEN NAME	SECOND GIVEN NAME
	RESIDENCE & CITIZENSHIP	CITY	STATE OR FOREIGN COUNTRY	COUNTRY OF CITIZENSHIP
	POST OFFICE ADDRESS	POST OFFICE ADDRESS — CITY		STATE & ZIP CODE/COUNTRY
203	FULL NAME OF INVENTOR	FAMILY NAME	FIRST GIVEN NAME	SECOND GIVEN NAME
	RESIDENCE & CITIZENSHIP	CITY	STATE OR FOREIGN COUNTRY	COUNTRY OF CITIZENSHIP
	POST OFFICE ADDRESS	POST OFFICE ADDRESS — CITY		STATE & ZIP CODE/COUNTRY

PTO Form 3.23(a) Patent and Trademark Office - U.S. DEPARTMENT of COMMERCE

(continued)

I hereby declare that all statements made herein of my own knowledge are true and that all statements made on information and belief are believed to be true; and further that these statements were made with the knowledge that willful false statements and the like so made are punishable by fine or imprisonment, or both, under section 1001 of Title 18 of the United States Code, and that such willful false statements may jeopardize the validity of the application or any patent issuing thereon.

SIGNATURE OF INVENTOR 201	SIGNATURE OF INVENTOR 202	SIGNATURE OF INVENTOR 203
DATE	DATE	DATE

	ATTORNEY'S DOCKET NO.
OATH AND POWER OF ATTORNEY – DESIGN PATENT APPLICATION	

As a below-named inventor, I hereby swear or affirm that:
my residence, post office address and citizenship are as stated below next to my name;
I verily believe I am the original, first and sole inventor (if only one name is listed below at 201) or a joint inventor (if plural

inventors are named below at 201-203) of the design entitled _____

_____
which is described and claimed in the attached specification;
I do not know and do not believe that the design was ever known or used in the United States of America before my or our
  invention thereof;
I do not know and do not believe that the design was ever patented or described in any printed publication in any country before
  my or our invention thereof or more than one year prior to this application;
I do not know and do not believe that the design was in public use or on sale in the United States of America more than one year
  prior to this application;
I acknowledge my duty to disclose information of which I am aware which is material to the examination of this application;
the invention has not been patented or made the subject of an inventor's certificate issued before the date of this application
  in any country foreign to the United States of America on an application filed by me or my legal representatives or assigns more
  than six mo nths prior to this application; and
as to applications for patents or inventor's certificate on the design filed in any country foreign to the United States of America
  prior to this application by me or my legal representatives or assigns,

☐ no such applications have been filed, or
☐ such applications have been filed as follows:

EARLIEST FOREIGN APPLICATION(S), IF ANY, FILED WITHIN 6 MONTHS PRIOR TO THIS APPLICATION				
COUNTRY	APPLICATION NO.	DATE OF FILING (DAY, MO., YR.)	DATE OF ISSUE (DAY, MO., YR.)	PRIORITY CLAIMED UNDER 35 U.S.C. 119
				YES ☐ NO ☐
				YES ☐ NO ☐
ALL FOREIGN APPLICATIONS, IF ANY, FILED MORE THAN 6 MONTHS PRIOR TO THIS APPLICATION				

POWER OF ATTORNEY: As a named inventor, I hereby appoint the following attorney(s) and/or agent(s) to prosecute this
application and transact all business in the Patent and Trademark Office connected therewith. *(list name and registration no.)*

SEND CORRESPONDENCE TO:

DIRECT TELEPHONE CALLS TO:
(name and telephone number)

201	FULL NAME OF INVENTOR	FAMILY NAME	FIRST GIVEN NAME	SECOND GIVEN NAME
	RESIDENCE & CITIZENSHIP	CITY	STATE OR FOREIGN COUNTRY	COUNTRY OF CITIZENSHIP
	POST OFFICE ADDRESS	POST OFFICE ADDRESS	CITY	STATE & ZIP CODE/COUNTRY
202	FULL NAME OF INVENTOR	FAMILY NAME	FIRST GIVEN NAME	SECOND GIVEN NAME
	RESIDENCE & CITIZENSHIP	CITY	STATE OR FOREIGN COUNTRY	COUNTRY OF CITIZENSHIP
	POST OFFICE ADDRESS	POST OFFICE ADDRESS	CITY	STATE & ZIP CODE/COUNTRY
203	FULL NAME OF INVENTOR	FAMILY NAME	FIRST GIVEN NAME	SECOND GIVEN NAME
	RESIDENCE & CITIZENSHIP	CITY	STATE OR FOREIGN COUNTRY	COUNTRY OF CITIZENSHIP
	POST OFFICE ADDRESS	POST OFFICE ADDRESS	CITY	STATE & ZIP CODE/COUNTRY

PTO Form 3.23   Patent and Trademark Office - U.S. DEPARTMENT of COMMERCE

(continued)

80   PATENTS

SIGNATURE OF INVENTOR 201	SIGNATURE OF INVENTOR 202	SIGNATURE OF INVENTOR 203
DATE	DATE	DATE

State of _____)

County of _____) SS

Sworn to and subscribed before me this _____ day of _____ , 19 _____.

_____
(signature of notary or officer)

(SEAL)

_____
(official character)

OATH AND POWER OF ATTORNEY – PLANT PATENT APPLICATION	ATTORNEY'S DOCKET NO.

As a below named inventor, I hereby swear or affirm that:

My residence, post office address and citizenship are as stated below next to my name;

I verily believe I am the original, first and sole inventor (if only one name is listed below at 201) or a joint inventor (if plural inventors are named below at 201-203) of the new and distinct variety of _____

_____ which is described and claimed in the attached specification;

I have asexually reproduced the new and distinct variety;

I do not know and do not believe that the new and distinct variety was ever known or used in the United States of America before my or our invention thereof;

I do not know and do not believe that the new and distinct variety was ever patented or described in any printed publication in any country before my or our invention thereof or more than one year prior to this application;

I do not know and do not believe that the new and distinct variety was in public use or on sale in the United States of America more than one year prior to this application;

I acknowledge my duty to disclose information of which I am aware which is material to the examination of this application;

the invention has not been patented or made the subject of an inventor's certificate issued before the date of this application; and

as to applications for patents or inventor's certificate on said new and distinct variety of plant filed in any country foreign to the United States of America, prior to this application by me or my legal representatives or assigns,

☐ no such applications have been filed, or

☐ such applications have been filed as follows:

EARLIEST FOREIGN APPLICATION(S), IF ANY, FILED WITHIN 12 MONTHS PRIOR TO THIS APPLICATION

COUNTRY	APPLICATION NUMBER	DATE OF FILING (day, month, year)	DATE OF ISSUE (day, month, year)	PRIORITY CLAIMED UNDER 35 U.S.C. 119
				YES ☐ NO ☐
				YES ☐ NO ☐

ALL FOREIGN APPLICATIONS, IF ANY, FILED MORE THAN 12 MONTHS PRIOR TO THIS APPLICATION

POWER OF ATTORNEY: As a named inventor, I hereby appoint the following attorney(s) and/or agent(s) to prosecute this application and transact all business in the Patent and Trademark Office connected therewith. *(list name and registration no.)*

SEND CORRESPONDENCE TO:	DIRECT TELEPHONE CALLS TO: *(name and telephone number)*

	FULL NAME OF INVENTOR	FAMILY NAME	FIRST GIVEN NAME	SECOND GIVEN NAME
201	RESIDENCE & CITIZENSHIP	CITY	STATE OR FOREIGN COUNTRY	COUNTRY OF CITIZENSHIP
	POST OFFICE ADDRESS	POST OFFICE ADDRESS	CITY	STATE & ZIP CODE/COUNTRY
	FULL NAME OF INVENTOR	FAMILY NAME	FIRST GIVEN NAME	SECOND GIVEN NAME
202	RESIDENCE & CITIZENSHIP	CITY	STATE OR FOREIGN COUNTRY	COUNTRY OF CITIZENSHIP
	POST OFFICE ADDRESS	POST OFFICE ADDRESS	CITY	STATE & ZIP CODE/COUNTRY
	FULL NAME OF INVENTOR	FAMILY NAME	FIRST GIVEN NAME	SECOND GIVEN NAME
203	RESIDENCE & CITIZENSHIP	CITY	STATE OR FOREIGN COUNTRY	COUNTRY OF CITIZENSHIP
	POST OFFICE ADDRESS	POST OFFICE ADDRESS	CITY	STATE & ZIP CODE/COUNTRY

PTO Form 3.26   Patent and Trademark Office - U.S. DEPARTMENT of COMMERCE

(continued)

SIGNATURE OF INVENTOR 201	SIGNATURE OF INVENTOR 202	SIGNATURE OF INVENTOR 203
DATE	DATE	DATE

State of _____)

County of _____) SS

Sworn to and subscribed before me this _____ day of _____ , 19 _____ .

(SEAL)

_____
(signature of notary or officer)

_____
(official character)

Patent and Trademark Office - U.S. DEPARTMENT of COMMERCE

POWER OF ATTORNEY OR AUTHORIZATION OF AGENT, NOT ACCOMPANYING APPLICATION	ATTORNEY'S DOCKET NO.

To the Commissioner of Patents and Trademarks:

I, the undersigned, having on or about the _____ day of _____ , 19 ____, made application for

letters patent for an improvement in _____ ,

Serial Number _____ , hereby appoint _____

of _____ , State of _____ ,

Registration Number _____ and telephone number _____ ,
as my attorney or agent to prosecute said application, and to transact all business in the Patent and Trademark
Office connected therewith.

_____
(signature)

_____
(date)

REVOCATION OF POWER OF ATTORNEY OR AUTHORIZATION OF AGENT	ATTORNEY'S DOCKET NO.

To the Commissioner of Patents and Trademarks:

I, the undersigned, having on or about the _____ day of _____ , 19 _____ , appointed

_____ , of _____ ,

State of _____ , as my attorney or agent to prosecute an application for

letters patent, which application was filed on or about the _____ day of _____ , 19 ___ ,

for an improvement in _____ ,

Serial Number _____ , hereby revoke the power of attorney or authorization of agent then
given.

_____
(signature)

_____
(date)

   Patent and Trademark Office - U.S. DEPT. of COMMERCE

A suggested format for the certificate of mailing under 37 CFR 1.8(a)
to be included on the correspondence.

I hereby certify that this correspondence is being deposited with the United States Postal Service as first
class mail in an envelope addressed to: Commissioner of Patents and Trademarks, Washington, D. C. 20231,

on _____ .
       (date)

_____
(name of person making deposit)

_____
(signature)

_____
(date)

CERTIFICATE OF MAILING – SEPARATE PAPER	ATTORNEY'S DOCKET NO.

IN RE APPLICATION OF

SERIAL NUMBER	FILED

FOR

GRP. ART UNIT	EXAMINER

I hereby certify that the _____
(identify type of correspondence)

is being deposited with the United States Postal Service as first class mail in an envelope addressed to:

Commissioner of Patents and Trademarks, Washington, D. C. 20231, on _____.
(date of deposit)

_____
(name of person making deposit)

_____
(signature)

_____
(date)

U.S. DEPARTMENT OF COMMERCE   Patent and Trademark Office

INSTRUCTIONS: This form is for use in preparing Certificate of Correction copy for printing by the Patent and Trademark Office.

- Return both parts of this form. DO NOT FURNISH PHOTOCOPIES FOR PRINTING.
- Type within the borders printed on the form.
- Use a typewriter that will give clean, clear impressions. Unsuitable copy will have to be retyped and therefore delay printing. Use a typewriter with a carbon ribbon if possible. If a fabric ribbon typewriter is used, the ribbon should be medium inked and in good condition. Changes are best made with white correction fluid.
- If necessary, staple in the area indicated in the left margin, ONLY.
- Type mailing address and patent number below within the perforated area.
- Indicate additional printed copies requested at 30¢ per page.
- A two-inch blank space should be left at the bottom of the last page of the form for the placement of the signature of the Attesting Officer.

┌─── DETACH HERE BEFORE MAILING BOTH COPIES OF THE TYPED CERTIFICATE TO THE PATENT AND TRADEMARK OFFICE ───┐

Staple Here Only !

PRINTER'S TRIM LINE

UNITED STATES PATENT AND TRADEMARK OFFICE
CERTIFICATE OF CORRECTION

PATENT NO.   :

DATED   :

INVENTOR(S) :

It is certified that error appears in the above-identified patent and that said Letters Patent is hereby corrected as shown below:

MAILING ADDRESS OF SENDER:

PATENT NO. _____

No. of add'l. copies @ 30¢ per page

 _____

FORM PTO 1050 (REV. 3-82)

88 PATENTS

Sheet _____ of _____

Form PTO-1449 (REV. 8-83)	U.S. DEPARTMENT OF COMMERCE PATENT AND TRADEMARK OFFICE	ATTY. DOCKET NO.		SERIAL NO.	
INFORMATION DISCLOSURE CITATION *(Use several sheets if necessary)*		APPLICANT			
		FILING DATE		GROUP	

U.S. PATENT DOCUMENTS

*EXAMINER INITIAL		DOCUMENT NUMBER	DATE	NAME	CLASS	SUBCLASS	FILING DATE IF APPROPRIATE

FOREIGN PATENT DOCUMENTS

	DOCUMENT NUMBER	DATE	COUNTRY	CLASS	SUBCLASS	TRANSLATION YES	NO

OTHER DOCUMENTS *(Including Author, Title, Date, Pertinent Pages, Etc.)*

EXAMINER	DATE CONSIDERED

*EXAMINER: Initial if citation considered, whether or not citation is in conformance with MPEP 609; Draw line through citation if not in conformance and not considered. Include copy of this form with next communication to applicant.

DISCLOSURE DOCUMENT DEPOSIT

	FOR OFFICE USE ONLY
	DATE DEPOSITED
	DEPOSIT NUMBER

To the Commissioner of Patents and Trademarks:

The undersigned, being the inventor of the disclosed invention, requests that the enclosed papers be accepted under the Disclosure Document Program, and that they be preserved for a period of two years.

☐ The $10.00 fee is enclosed.

Mail receipt to: _____

_____

_____

_____
(signature)

_____
(date)

WARNING TO INVENTORS

The two-year retention period should not be considered to be a "grace period" during which the inventor can wait to file his/her patent application without possible loss of benefits. It must be recognized that in establishing priority of invention an affidavit of testimony referring to a Disclosure Documents must usually also establish diligence in completing the invention or in filing the patent application since the filing of the Disclosure Document.

Inventors are also reminded that any public use or sale in the United States or publication of the invention anywhere in the world more than one year prior to the filing of a patent application on that invention will prohibit the granting of a patent on it.

If the inventor is not familiar with what is considered to be "diligence in completing the invention" or "reduction to practice" under the patent law, or if he/she has other questions about patent matters, the Patent and Trademark Office advises him/her to consult an attorney or agent registered to practice before the Patent and Trademark Office. A "Directory of Registered Patent Attorneys and Agents Arranged by States and Counties" is available from the Superintendent of Documents, U.S. Government Printing Office, Washington, D.C. 20402. Patent attorneys and agents may be found in the telephone directories of most major cities. Also, many large cities have associations of patent attorneys which may be consulted.

PTO Form 3.74   **Patent and Trademark Office - U.S. DEPT. of COMMERCE**

PATENT FEES AND PAYMENT

Filing Fees

Basic fee for filing each application of an original patent, except design or plant applications:

By a small entity	$185.00
By other than a small entity	$370.00

In addition to the basic fee in an original application, for filing or for the later presentation of each independent claim in excess of three:

By a small entity	$18.00
By other than a small entity	$36.00

In addition to the basic fee in an original application, if the application contains, or is amended to contain, a multiple dependent claim(s), per application:

By a small entity	$60.00
By other than a small entity	$120.00

Surcharge for filing the basic filing fee, oath, or declaration on a date later than the filing date of the application:

By a small entity	$60.00
By other than a small entity	$120.00

For filing each design application:

By a small entity	$75.00
By other than a small entity	$150.00

Basic fee for filing each plant application:

By a small entity	$125.00
By other than a small entity	$250.00

Basic fee for filing each reissue application:

By a small entity	$185.00
By other than a small entity	$370.00

In addition to the basic filing fee in a reissue application, for filing or for the later presentation of each claim in excess of the number of independent claims in the original patent:

By a small entity	$18.00
By other than a small entity	$36.00

Patent Issue Fees

Issue fee for issuing each original or reissue patent, except a design or plant patent:

By a small entity	$310.00
By other than a small entity	$620.00

Issue fee for issuing a design patent:

By a small entity	$110.00
By other than a small entity	$220.00

Issue fee for issuing a plant patent:

By a small entity	$155.00
By other than a small entity	$310.00

Post-Issuance Fees

For providing a certificate of correction of an applicant's mistake:

$60.00

Petition for correction of inventionship in patent:

$120.00

For filing a request for reexamination:

$2,000.00

For filing each statutory disclaimer:

By a small entity	$31.00
By other than a small entity	$62.00

For maintaining an original or reissue patent, except a design or plant patent, based on an application filed on or after December 12, 1980, and before August 27, 1982, in force beyond four years; the fee is due by three years and six months after the original grant:

$245.00

For maintaining an original or reissue patent, except a design or plant patent, based on an application filed on or after December 12, 1980, and before August 27, 1982, in force beyond eight years; the fee is due by seven years and six months after the original grant:

$495.00

For maintaining an original or reissue patent, except a design or plant patent, based on an application filed on or after December 12, 1980, and before August 27, 1982, in force beyond 12 years; the fee is due by 11 years and six months after the original grant:

$740.00

For maintaining an original or reissue patent, except a design or plant patent, based on an application filed on or after August 27, 1982, in force beyond four years; the fee is due by three years and six months after the original grant:

| By a small entity | $245.00 |
| By other than a small entity | $490.00 |

For maintaining an original or reissue patent, except a design or plant patent, based on an application filed on or after August 27, 1982, in force beyond eight years; the fee is due by seven years and six months after the original grant:

| By a small entity | $495.00 |
| By other than a small entity | $990.00 |

For maintaining an original or reissue patent, except a design or plant patent, based on an application filed on or after August 27, 1982, in force beyond 12 years; the fee is due by 11 years and six months after the original grant:

| By a small entity | $740.00 |
| By other than a small entity | $1,480.00 |

Surcharge for paying a maintenance fee during the six-month grace period following the expiration of three years and six months, seven years and six months, and 11 years and six months after the date of the original grant of a patent based on an application filed on or after December 12, 1980, and before August 27, 1982:

$120.00

Surcharge for paying a maintenance fee during the six-month grace period following the expiration of three years and six months, seven years and six months, and 11 years and six months after the date of the original grant of a patent based on an application filed on or after August 27, 1982:

| By a small entity | $60.00 |
| By other than a small entity | $120.00 |

Surcharge for accepting a maintenance fee after expiration of a patent for nontimely payment of a maintenance fee where the delay in payment is shown to the satisfaction of the Commissioner to have been unavoidable:

$550.00

Patent Application Processing Fees

Extension fee for response within the first month:

By a small entity	$31.00
By other than a small entity	$62.00

Extension fee for response within second month:

By a small entity	$90.00
By other than a small entity	$180.00

Extension fee for response within third month:

By a small entity	$215.00
By other than a small entity	$430.00

Extension fee for response within fourth month:

By a small entity	$340.00
By other than a small entity	$680.00

For filing a notice of appeal from the examiner to the Board of Patent Appeals and Interferences:

By a small entity	$70.00
By other than a small entity	$140.00

In addition to the fee for filing a notice of appeal, for filing a brief in support of the appeal:

By a small entity	$70.00
By other than a small entity	$140.00

For filing a request for an oral hearing before the Board of Patent Appeals and Interferences:

By a small entity	$60.00
By other than a small entity	$120.00

For filing a petition to the Commission under a section of this part listed below which refers to 37 CFR 1.17(h):

$120.00

- For filing by other than all the inventors or a person who is not the inventor
- For correction inventorship
- For a decision on questions not specifically provided for
- To suspend the rules
- For a review of a refusal to publish a statutory invention registration
- For a review of a decision refusing to accept and record payment of a maintenance fee filed prior to the expiration of a patent

- For reconsideration of a decision on a petition refusing to accept delayed payment of a maintenance fee in an expired patent
- For a petition in an interference
- For a request for reconsideration of a decision on petition in an interference
- For late filing of an interference settlement agreement
- For expediting the handling of a foreign filing license
- For changing the scope of a license
- For a retroactive license

For filing a petition to the Commissioner under a section of this part listed below which refers to 37 CFR 1.17 (i) $120.00

- For access to an assignment record
- For access to an application
- For entry of late priority papers
- To make an application special
- To suspend action in an application
- For divisional reissues to be issued separately
- For access to an interference settlement agreement
- For an amendment after payment of an issue fee
- To withdraw an application from issue
- To defer issuance of a patent
- For a patent to be issued to an assignee (assignment recorded late)

For filing a petition to institute a public use proceeding:

$1,200.00

For processing an application filed with a specification in a non-English language:

$30.00

For filing a petition (1) for the revival of an unavoidably abandoned application under 35 USC 133 or 371, or (2) for delayed payment of the issue fee under 35 USC 151:

By a small entity	$31.00
By other than a small entity	$62.00

For filing a petition (1) for revival of an unintentionally abandoned application or (2) for the unintentionally delayed payment of the fee for issuing a patent:

By a small entity	$310.00
By other than a small entity	$620.00

International Application Filing and Processing Fees

The following fees and charges are established by the Patent and Trademark Office under the authority of 35 USC 376:

A transmittal fee: $170.00

A search fee where:

No corresponding prior United States national application with fees has been filed:

$55.00

Corresponding prior United States national application with fees has been filed:

$380.00

The European Patent Office is the international authority:

$1,160.00

A supplemental search fee when required by the United States Patent and Trademark Office :

$150.00

(Any supplemental search fee required by the European Patent Office must be paid directly to that Office.)

The national fee, that is, the amount set forth as the filing fee under "Filing Fees" above credited is requested at the time of filing by an amount of $170.00 where an international search fee has been paid on the corresponding international application to the United States Patent and Trademark Office as an International Searching Authority.

Surcharge for filing the patents fee, oath, or declaration later than 20 months from the priority date:

By a small entity	$60.00
By other than a small entity	$120.00

For filing an English translation of an international application later than 20 months after the priority date:

$30.00

Service Fees

The Patent and Trademark Office will provide the following services upon payment of the fees indicated:
Printed copy of a patent, including a design patent, statutory invention registration, or defensive publication document, except for a color plant patent or color statutory invention registration:

$1.50

Printed copy of a plant patent or statutory invention registration in color:

$106.00

Copy of patent application as filed:

$109.00

Copy of patent file wrapper and contents per 200 pages or a fraction thereof:

$170.00

Copy of Office records, except as otherwise provided in the section per page:

$10.00

For certifying Office records, per certificate:

$3.00

For a search of assignment records, abstract of title and certification, per patent:

$15.00

To compare and certify copies made from Patent and Trademark Office records but not prepared by the Patent and Trademark Office, per copy of document:

$10.00

For filing a disclosure document:

$6.00

For conducting an inventor search of Office records for a 10-year period:

$10.00

For recording each assignment, agreement or other paper relating to the property in a patent or application:

$8.00

For publication in the Official Gazette of a notice of the availability of an application or a patent for licensing or sale, each application or patent:

$20.00

For a duplicate or replacement of a permanent Office-user pass. (There is no charge for the first permanent user pass.)

$10.00

Local delivery box rental, per annum:

$50.00

CopiShare card: Cost per copy:

$.15

For preparing an international-type search report of an international-type search made at the time of the first action on the merits in a national patent application:

$30.00

For processing and retaining any application abandoned pursuant to §1.53(d) unless the required basic filing fee has been paid:

$120.00

Handling fee for application filed without the specification or drawing required by §1.53(b) and the omission is not corrected within the time period set:

$20.00

Handling fee for withdrawal of Statutory Invention Registration:

120.00

Uncertified copy of an non-United States patent document, per document:

$10.00

Copy of patent assignment, certified:

$5.00

Additional filing receipts

Duplicate

$15.00

Corrected due to applicant error

$15.00

For establishing or reinstating a deposit account:

$10.00

Registration of attorneys and agents:

1. For admission to an examination for registration to practice, fee payable upon application

$270.00

2. On registration to practice $90.00
3. For reinstatement to practice $109.00
4. For a certificate of good standing as an attorney or agent

$10.00

Suitable for framing $100.00

5. For review of a decision of the Director of Enrollment and Discipline under §10.2(c)

$100.00

6. For requesting an examination under §10.7(c)

$100.00

For processing each check returned "unpaid" by a bank

$50.00

Note: PCT fees controlled by WIPO & EPO will fluctuate with exchange rates.

The following publications are sold, and the prices for them are fixed, by the Superintendent of Documents, Government Printing Office, Washington, DC 20402, to whom all communications respecting the same should be addressed:

Official Gazette of the United States Patent Office:
Annual subscription, domestic (nonpriority)

$347.00

Annual subscription (priority) $523.00

Single issues $21.00
Annual Index Relating to Patents, price varies
Attorneys and Agents Registered to Practice Before the
    U.S. Patent Office $21.00

The above prices are subject to change without notice.

SPECIAL BOXES FOR MAIL

Special PTO mailbox numbers should be used to allow for forwarding particular types of mail to the appropriate areas as quickly as possible. Such mail is forwarded directly to the appropriate area without being opened. Only the specified type of document should be placed in an envelop addressed to one of these special boxes. If any documents other than those specified for each box are addressed to that box, they will be delayed in reaching the appropriate area for which they are intended.

The following special boxes should be used only for their specified purpose. Address mail as follows:

Box _____
Commissioner of Patents and Trademarks
Washington, DC 20231

Box 3   Mail for the Office of Personnel from NFC
Box 4   Mail for the Office of Legislation and International Affairs
Box 5   "No fee" mail related to trademarks (e.g., amendments to

applications and requests for extensions of time to file an opposition)

Mail direct to the Trademark Trial and Appeal Board should have "Attention TTAB" on the envelope in addition to "Box 5"

Box 6	Mail for the Office of Procurement
Box 7	Reissue applications for patents involved in litigation and any subsequently filed papers for those applications.
Box 8	All papers for the Office of the Solicitor
Box 9	Coupon orders for the U.S. patent and trademark applications
Box 10	Orders for certified copies of patent and trademark applications
Box 11	Electronic Ordering Service (EOS)
Box 12	Contributions to the Examiner Education Program
Box AF	Amendments or responses to final rejections in patent applications submitted under the expedited processing program
Box FWC	Mail related to File Wrapper and Continuations
Box Interference	Communications related to interferences and applications and patents involved in interferences
Box M. Fee	Correspondence related to a patent that is subject to the payment of a maintenance fee
Box Pat. Ext.	Applications for patent term extensions
Box PCT	Mail related to applications filed under the Patent Cooperation Treaty.
Box Reexam	Mail related to a reexamintaion application

DISCLOSURE DOCUMENT PROGRAM

The Disclosure Document Program is administered by the Patent and Trademark Office. This is *not* an alternative to obtaining a patent; this program doesn't eliminate or dilute the value of conventional witnessed or notarized records, as we shall see. The purpose of the program is to preserve Disclosure Documents as evidence of the dates of the conception of inventions.

The disclosure program is a credible form of evidence in conjunction with other common precautions. A signed statement by the inventor(s) revealing the invention is retained in strict confidence for two years. After two years, the document is destroyed unless it's referred to in a separate letter in a related patent application filed within the designated period.

Diligence must be exercised during the two-year period to complete the invention or in filing the patent application after the filing of the Disclosure Document.

The Disclosure Document must contain a clear and complete explanation of the manner and process of making and using the invention. A person with ordinary knowledge in the field of the invention should be able to understand the document well enough to make and use the invention.

Follow the four procedures outlined here when submitting the Disclosure Document:

1. • Only a written disclosure and drawing are acceptable.
   • Use only paper or another thin, flexible material, such as linen or plastic drafting material.
   • The document may be folded, but the dimensions must not exceed 8$\frac{1}{2}$-by-13 inches.
   • Number each page consecutively.
   • Text and drawings must be dark enough to allow good photocopy reproductions.
   • Photographs are acceptable.

2. Use a separate cover letter (in duplicate) signed by the inventor. Address the letter to the Patent and Trademark Office. It should follow this suggested form:

   "The undersigned, being the inventor of the disclosed invention, requests that the enclosed papers be accepted under the Disclosure Document Program, and that they be preserved for a period of two years."

3. Include a self-addressed stamped envelope. The duplicate copy of the papers will be returned to the inventor bearing an identifying number and date of receipt.

4. Make a check or money order payable for $6.00 to the "Commissioner of Patents and Trademarks." Enclose all items in an envelope addressed to:

COMMISSIONER OF PATENTS AND TRADEMARKS
Washington, D.C. 20231

TRADE SECRETS

Trade secrets are alternative to patents. Both have their advantages and disadvantages. However, trade secrets constitute knowledge that affords the possessor advantages in the marketplace.

As with any secret, a trade secret is not always easy to keep. Certain trusted parties must share such a secret in order to exercise it for the benefit of its rightful owner.

Once it is decided that the trade secret approach is the best choice, a policy for controlling the knowledge should be established and adhered to rigorously. Fiduciary relationships should be defined in writing with anyone entrusted with the priveleged information. A clear understanding should exist with all concerned persons prior to disclosure. (Competitors have a natural inclination to want to unravel the next guys well-laid plans, if not to the competitor's advantage, at the least to the disadvantage of the one possessing the secrets.)

Trade secrets are:

- Less expensive to implement than patents
- Not made public (however, if in public use for more than a year, they can't be patented)
- Of unlimited duration
- Not exclusive rights

Trade secrets cover many areas of manufacture and trade. They include compositions, designs, formulas, information, methods, processes, and techniques. After it has been determined that the trade secret can be kept confidential, ask yourself if it can be "reverse engineered."

There are very sophisticated "pirates" lurking in laboratories, factories, and corporate offices around the world. Foreign governments have also been known to be culprits. The more important the secret, the more time and money will the opposition expend.

It would be difficult to keep a machine or manufactured article a secret, such as a specially designed machine invented for the sole purpose of manufacturing a product vs. the sale of the machine. The end product wouldn't reveal much about the method of manufacture. If the employees working with the equipment could be trusted, or weren't aware of its uniqueness or importance, or couldn't ascertain its component structure, then the secret would remain a secret. However, if a knowledgeable industrial spy were to be planted in a position of employment, which could give him access to the unpatented invention, then the advantages of the trade secret could be lost.

These are considerations that must be made in advance of determining whether to proceed with a trade secret which can be protected and which can be more valuable than a patent. A thorough understanding of your industry and its direction will help. Make a point of learning about each manufacturer's products, track record, approach, resources, etc. This area of industrial property protection cannot be adequately evaluated from a naive viewpoint; consider all of the possibilities.

PATENT PENDING

Patented articles must display the word "Patent" and the patent number. Failure in this regard leaves the patent holder open to potential infringement and the loss of his legal right to recover damages.

"Patent Pending" and "Patent Applied For" have no legal basis, but rather give notice that a patent application has been filed with the Patent and Trademark Office. Patent protection doesn't begin, however, until a patent has been allowed.

It's illegal to mark goods stating that they are patented or to indicate that a patent is pending, when in fact it's not true.

Examination Procedures

The Patent and Trademark Office handles patent applications in the order they are received. The applications are then processed as follows:

1. Complete applications are accepted and assigned to the appropriate examining group for further examination.
2. The examiners check for compliance with legal requirements.
3. A search is conducted through U.S. patents, prior foreign patent documents, and the literature to determine that the invention exhibits novelty.
4. A decision is reached by the examiner based on the results of the search.
5. The applicant is notified in writing of the examiner's decision by an "action." Usually, the attorney or agent is contacted. Reasons for adverse action or objection are stated in the action and pertinent references are given. This information will assist the applicant in deciding whether to continue prosecution of the application.
6. If the invention is not considered patentable, the claim(s) will be rejected. An invention that lacks novelty or is slightly different from what is found to be obvious will be rejected. Frequently, some or all of the claims are rejected by the examiner on the first action.
7. If the applicant wishes to continue prosecution of the application, a written response must be submitted that points out supposed errors in the examiner's action. The response must distinctly and specifically address each objection and rejection stated in the action, and must be a legitimate attempt to advance the case to a final action. The maximum period for a response is six months. Simply complaining that the examiner is wrong is insufficient, you have to be prepared to argue and support your position.
8. To amend the application, the applicant must clearly point out why the amended claims are patentable in light of the state of the art disclosed by prior references cited or by the objections made. The applicant must also show how the amendments avoid such references or objections.
9. Once this has been accomplished, the applicant's response may be returned to the PTO for reconsideration, where it will once again undergo the same scrutiny. The second Office action is usually final.
10. Once the PTO has made the action final, the only other alternative available to the applicant is to file an appeal. This can be done in the case of the rejection of any claim and of a further-amendment restriction.

AMENDMENTS TO AN APPLICATION

The preceding section referred to amendments to the application. Following are some details concerning amendments.

The applicant may amend before or after the first examination and action as specified in the rules, or when and as specifically required by the examiner.

After the final rejection or action, amendments may be made that cancel claims or that comply with any requirement of form which has been made, but the admission of any such amendment or its refusal, and any proceedings relative thereto, shall not operate to relieve the application from its condition as subject to appeal or to save it from abandonment.

If amendments touching the merits of the application are presented after, the final rejection, or after the appeal has been taken, or when such an amendment might not otherwise be proper, they may be admitted upon a showing of good and sufficient reason(s) why they are necessary and were not earlier presented.

No amendment can be made as a matter of right in appealed cases. After a decision on appeal, amendments can only be made as provided for in the rules.

The specifications, claims, and drawing(s) must be amended and revised when required to correct inaccuracies of description and definition of unnecessary words and to secure correspondence between the claims, the description, and the drawings.

All amendments of the drawings or specifications, and all additions thereto, must conform to at least one of them as it was at the time of the filing of the application. Matter not found in either, involving a departure from or an addition to the original disclosure, cannot be added to the application even though supported by a supplemental oath or declaration, and can be shown or claimed only in a separate or ground rejection of record which may be pertinent.

Erasures, additions, insertions, or alterations of the papers and records must not be made by the applicant. Amendments are made by filing a paper that directs or requests specific changes. The exact word or words to be deleted or inserted in the application must be specified and the precise point indicated where the deletion or insertion is to be made.

Amendments are "entered" by the Office by drawing a line in red ink through the word or words cancelled and by making the proposed substitutions or insertions in red ink, small insertions being written in at the designated place and larger insertions being indicated by reference.

No change in the drawing may be made except by permission of the Office. Permissible changes in the constuction shown in any drawing may be made only by the bonded draftsman. A sketch in permanent ink showing proposed changes, to become part of the record, must be filed for approval by the Office before the corrections are made. The paper requesting amendments to the drawing should be separate from other papers.

If the number or nature of the amendments render it difficult to consider the case, or to arrange the papers for printing or copying, the examiner may require the entire specification or claims, or any part thereof, to be rewritten.

The original numbering of the claims must be preserved throughout the prosecution. When claims are canceled, the remaining claims must not be renumbered. When claims are added by amendment or substituted for canceled claims, they must be numbered by the applicant consecutively beginning with the number next following the highest numbered claim previously presented. When the application is ready for allowance, the examiner, if necessary, will renumber the claims consecutively in the order in which they appear or in such order as may have been requested by the applicant.

APPEALS

An appeal is made to the The Board of Patent Appeals and Interferences. A brief must be filed which supports the applicant's position along with the required appeal fee. An oral hearing will be held if requested upon payment of the specified fee.

If the decision by the The Board of Appeals is still unfavorable, an appeal can be taken to the Court of Appeals for the Federal District, or a civil action can be filed against the Commissioner in the United States District Court for the District of Columbia. The Court of Appeals will review the record and may affirm or reverse the Office's action. In a civil action, the applicant can present testimony to the court, and the court will make a decision.

ALLOWANCE AND ISSUE OF PATENT

A notice of allowance will be sent to the applicant if the examiners—either upon initial examination or upon reconsideration—determine the patent to be allowable. A fee for issuing the patent is due within three months of the notice. The issue fee is $620 except for design and plant patents; small entities pay half of this amount. If payment isn't made promptly within the allotted period of time, the application will be considered abandoned.

PATENT FORMS

U.S. DEPARTMENT OF COMMERCE
Patent Office

Address Only: COMMISSIONER OF PATENTS
Washington, D.C. 20231

```
Sprague, L.
S. N.  479,042  6/13/74
William A. Maher
Art Unit  344
```

Sanford Astor
9036 Reseda Blvd.,
Northridge, Calif.
          91324

Paper No _____5_____

Mailed ....

This is a communication from the Examiner in
charge of your application.

Commissioner of Patents

☑ This application has been examined.

☐ Responsive to communication filed _____.   ☐ This action is **made final.**

A SHORTENED STATUTORY PERIOD FOR RESPONSE TO THIS ACTION IS SET TO EXPIRE

____*Three*____ MONTH(S) ____DAYS FROM THE DATE OF THIS LETTER.

PART I

The following attachments(s) are part of this action:

a. ☑ Notice of References Cited, Form PO-892.   b. ☐ Notice of Informal Patent Drawing, PO-948.

c. ☐ Notice of Informal Patent Application,   d. ☐
Form PO-152.

PART II

Summary of Action

1. ☑ Claims __1 to 4__ _____are presented for examination.

2. ☐ Claims _____are allowed.

3. ☐ Claims _____would be allowable if amended as indicated.

4. ☑ Claims __1 to 4__ _____are rejected.

5. ☐ Claims _____are objected to.

6. ☐ Claims _____are subject to restriction or election requirement.

7. ☐ Claims _____ are withdrawn from consideration.

8. ☐ Since this application appears to be in condition for allowance except for formal matters, prosecution as to the merits is closed in accordance with the practice under Ex parte Quayle, 1935 C.D. 11; 453 OG. 213.

9. ☐ Since it appears that a discussion with applicant's representative may result in agreements whereby the application may be placed in condition for allowance, the examiner will telephone the representative within about 2 weeks from the date of this letter.

10. ☐ Receipt is acknowledged of papers under 35 USC 119, which papers have been placed of record in the file.

11. ☐ Applicant's claim for priority based on an application filed in _____ on_____ is acknowledged. It is noted, however, that a certified copy as required by 35 USC 119 has not been received.

12. ☐ Other

POL 326 (10 -70)   —1—

FORM PO—1142 (Rev. 6—72)				U.S. DEPT. of COMMERCE Patent Office

PART III   SERIAL NUMBER 479042   GROUP ART UNIT 344

NOTIFICATION OF REJECTION(S) AND/OR OBJECTION(S) (35 USC 132)

	CLAIMS (1)	REASONS FOR REJECTION (2)	REFERENCES * (3)	INFORMATION IDENTIFICATION AND COMMENTS (4)
1	1 to 4	35 USC 112		The claims fail to properly define the invention because in claim 1, as an example, the various elements of the claim are set forth as a mere catalog of parts. The claim fails to define structure which would interrelate the various elements.
2	1 + 3	35 USC 103	A v B	To substitute the jacket of B for the element 24 of A would be obvious.
3	2	35 USC 103	A v B + C	A + B are applied as set forth in ¶ 2 To provide A with burner means such as shown by C would be obvious
4	4	35 USC 103	A v B + D	A + B are applied as set forth in ¶ 2 To provide A with controls for fuel, air + water such as shown by D would be obvious
5				Patents E + F are cited to show the state of the art.

* Capital letters representing references are identified on accompanying Form PO—892.
The symbol "v" between letters represents — in view of —.
The symbol "+" or "&" between letters represents — and —.
A slash "/" between letters represents the alternative — or —.

NOTE: Sections 100, 101, 102, 103 and 112 of the Patent Statute (Title 35 of the United States Code) are reproduced on the back of this sheet.

EXAMINER   TEL. NO. (703) –557 – 3467

Kenneth W. Sprague

KENNETH W. SPRAGUE
EXAMINER
GROUP ART UNIT 344

—2—

```
 1                    IN THE UNITED STATES PATENT OFFICE

 2

 3    In re the application of

 4    WILLIAM A. MAHER

 5    Serial Number 165,987

 6    Filed:  July 26, 1971

 7    For:  Steam Propulsion System

 8                         AMENDMENT

 9    Honorable Commissioner of Patents

10    Washington D.C.

11    Sir:

12           This is in response to the office action dated October

13    17, 1972.

14    Cancel claims 10, 11 & 12.

15    Add the following new claims:

16           13.  A propulsion system comprising a vapor heat

17    transfer generator comprising a pump to introduce water to the

18    generator, a fog nozzle to change the water to water vapor, a

19    fuel supply line to introduce fuel to the generator to convert

20    the water vapor to steam, means to carry the steam produced, a

21    rotary cylinder positive displacement motor, actuated by said

22    steam.

23           14.  The system of Claim 13 comprising a throttle valve

24    and a four-way reverse valve for control of the steam flow from

25    the generator to the motor.

26           15.  The system of Claim 14 wherein four motors are oper-

27    ated by the steam, each motor mounted within a wheel.

28           16.  A propulsion system comprising:

29           (a)  A burner motor.

30           (b)  A fuel solenoid to control introduction of fuel.

31           (c)  A water solenoid to control introduction of water.

32           (d)  A pump to pump water to the generator.

             (e)  Fog nozzles to convert the water to water vapor.

             (f)  A spiral jacket for passage of the water vapor.
```

(g)   An inner radiant tube and an outer radiant tube to provide heat transfer to the spiral jacket to convert the water vapor to steam.

(h)   Means to carry the steam to,

(i)   a rotary cylinder positive displacement motor.

17.   A propulsion system comprising a vapor heat transfer steam generator and a rotary cylinder motor comprising multiple rotor blades, a rotating carrier adapted to hold said rotor blades, a motor shaft attached to said rotating carrier, ports for the introduction of steam and the removing of steam adapted so as to cause rotation of the rotor blades.

18.   A propulsion system comprising a vapor heat transfer steam generator and a rotary cylinder positive displacement motor comprising:

(a)   an outer cylindrical shell

(b)   an inner rotating cylinder positioned in said outer shell between

(c)   radial and thrust bearings reducing, to a minimum, friction from the entire rotating assembly.

(d)   a carrier adapted to receive

(e)   rotor blades which slide in said carrier

(f)   a rotating disc to position said rotor blades

(g)   a motor shaft attached to said carrier

(h)   Ports for the introduction and release of steam adapted to cause said rotors to rotate within said outer shell.

19.   A propulsion system comprising a vapor heat transfer generator comprising a pump to introduce water to the generator, a fog nozzle to change the water to water vapor, a spiral jacket for passage of the water vapor, a fuel supply line to introduce fuel to the generator to convert the water vapor to steam, lines to carry the steam produced to a rotary cylinder

1 positive displacement motor comprising an outer cylindrical

2 shell, an inner rotating cylinder entirely positioned in said

3 outer shell between bearings, multiple rotor blades, a rotating

4 carrier adapted to hold said blades, a motor shaft attached to

5 said carrier, ports for the introduction of steam and removing

6 of steam adapted to cause said blades to rotate.

7 REMARKS

8 The Examiner has rejected claims 10 & 11 over Hipple and

9 12 over Hipple in view of Kennedy or Keldrauk. Hipple's patent

10 is related to a new valve and only generally discloses a source

11 of hydraulic fluid and a rotary hydraulic motor. Claims 10-12

12 have been cancelled and new claims 13 to 18 added which more clear-

13 ly define applicant's system which comprises a new steam gener-

14 ation system and a new rotary motor.

15 None of the references cited show the steam generation

16 system claimed by applicants utilizing a fog nozzle to convert

17 the water to water vapor prior to its conversion to steam, and

18 both inner and outer radiant tubes to provide heat transfer.

19 This enables the heat transfer surfaces to operate at 550° F

20 which gives a tremendous increase in heat transfer as compared

21 to a water tube boiler.

22 In addition, none of the patents show the rotary motor

23 as claimed by applicant. Applicant's motor is designed so that

24 the entire inner rotating assembly of rotary cylinder, rotor and

25 veins is entirely supported by thrust and radial bearings. This

26 allows the motor to rotate virtually friction free and achieve

27 an r.p.m. much higher than any previous rotary motor.

28 Kennedy and Keldrauch fail to show the carrier, the

29 rotating blades within said carrier and the disc posistioning

30 the carrier, as well as the entire bearing support.

31 Woerner and Close fail to add anything to the other

32

-3-

references to anticipate applicant's system.

The claims as amended are now clearly patentable over the references cited and early allowance is respectfully requested.

In addition, reconsideration of the requirement to elect is requested.

Respectfully submitted

Sanford Astor
Attorney for the Applicant

Dated: January 10, 1973

POL-85a
(REV. 5-73)

All communications regarding this
application should give the serial
number, date of filing, and name of
the applicant.

U.S. DEPARTMENT OF COMMERCE
Patent Office

Address Only: COMMISSIONER OF PATENTS
Washington, D.C. 20231

NOTICE OF ALLOWANCE
AND BASE ISSUE FEE DUE

The application identified below has been examined and found allowable for issuance of Letters Pater

	FILING DATE	SERIAL NO	NO OF CLAIMS ALLOWED	EXAMINER AND GROUP ART UNIT
	07/26/71	165937	4	Geoghegan 341
APPLICANT(S)	Maher, William A.; Sepulveda, Calif.			MAILED Jan. 24, 1974
TITLE OF INVENTION (X indicates as amended by examiner)	Steam propulsion system			

BASE FEE COMPUTATION					BASE FEE DUE	CLASS-SUB
$100.00	$6	(FOR DWG @$2 PER SHEET)	$10	(FOR FIRST PAGE PRINTED SPEC)	$116	060/105.000

The complete Issue Fee is one hundred dollars ($100) plus two dollars ($2) for each sheet of drawing, plus ten dollars ($10) for each printed page of specification (including claims) or portion thereof.

Inasmuch as the final number of printed pages cannot be determined in advance of printing, an initial BASE ISSUE FEE (con-; sisting of the fee for printing the first page of specification ($10) plus the fee of ($2) for each sheet of drawing, added to the fee of $100) *must be paid within three months from the date of this notice,* or the application shall be regarded as ABANDONED.

When remitting said Base Issue Fee, enclosed Form POL-85b should be used, and if use of a Deposit Account is being authorized, POL-85c should also be forwarded.

The Base Issue Fee will not be accepted from anyone other than the applicant, his assignee, attorney, or a party in interest, as shown by the records of the Patent Office.

If an assignment has not been previously filed and it is desired to have the patent issue to the assignee, the assignment must be received in this Office with the recording fee together with the Base Issue Fee. In any event, the appropriate space(s) under "Assignment Data" on POL-85b must be completed. Where there is an assignment, the assignee's address must be given to ensure its inclusion in the printed patent.

In connection with the address of the inventor(s), attention is directed to Form POL-231 enclosed.

A Notice of Balance of Issue Fee Due will be mailed together with the patentee's copy of the patent *if an additional fee is due.* Payment must be made within three months from the date shown on said Notice since FAILURE TO PAY THIS BALANCE WITHIN THE TIME SPECIFIED WILL RESULT IN LAPSE OF THE PATENT.

```
 Sanford Astor
 9036 Reseda Blvd.,
 Suite 203,
 Northridge, Calif. 91324        rlc 855
```

IMPORTANT

ATTENTION IS DIRECTED TO RULE 334
REVISED NOVEMBER 4, 1969.

THE PATENT WILL ISSUE TO APPLICANT
UNLESS AN ASSIGNEE IS SHOWN IN
ITEM 2 ON FORM POL-85b. ATTACHED

YOUR COPY—See reverse side for Base Issue Fee Record

United States Patent [19]

Maher

[11] **3,936,252**

[45] **Feb. 3, 1976**

[54] **STEAM PROPULSION SYSTEM**

[75] Inventor: **William A. Maher,** Sepulveda, Calif.

[73] Assignee: **Wilma Ryan,** Arlington Heights, Ill.

[22] Filed: **June 13, 1974**

[21] Appl. No.: **479,041**

Related U.S. Application Data

[62] Division of Ser. No. 165,987, July 26, 1971, Pat. No. 3,820,335.

[52] **U.S. Cl.** **418/173;** 418/177; 418/261
[51] **Int. Cl.²** **F04C 1/00**
[58] **Field of Search** 418/173, 172, 177, 261

[56] **References Cited**
UNITED STATES PATENTS

775,632	11/1904	Norden	418/261
2,907,307	10/1959	Striegl	418/177
2,969,743	1/1961	Menon	418/173
3,539,281	11/1970	Kramer	418/173

Primary Examiner—C. J. Husar
Attorney, Agent, or Firm—Sanford Astor

[57] **ABSTRACT**

The invention relates to a system for propulsion utilizing a vapor heat transfer generator to create high pressure steam directly from water vapor which is transferred to rotary cylinder motors of positive displacement design, which are run on ball and roller bearings to eliminate friction facilitating high speed operation.

3 Claims, 8 Drawing Figures

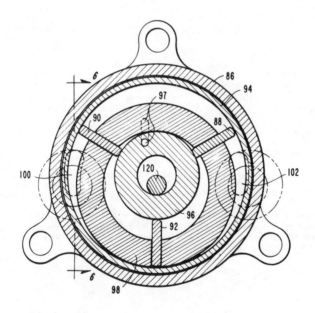

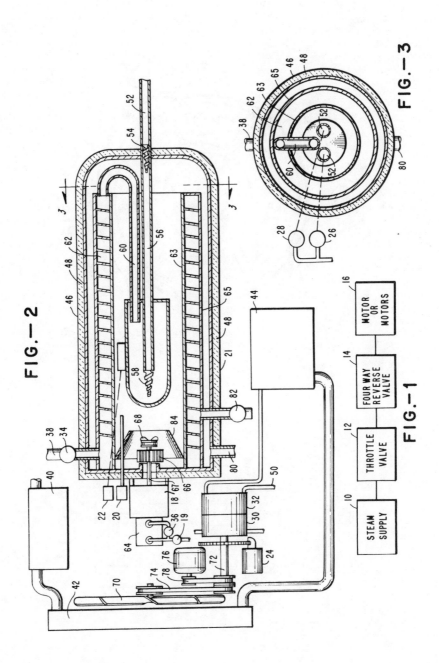

FIG.—1

FIG.—2

FIG.—3

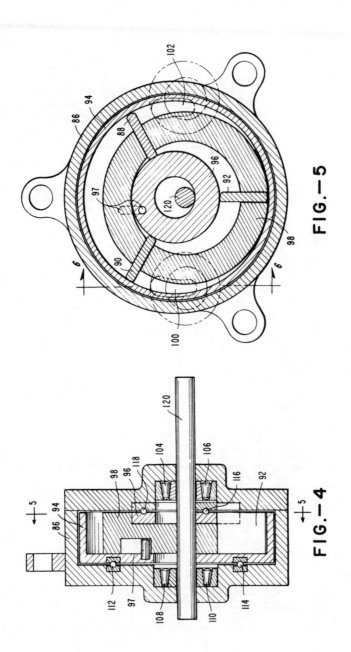

FIG.—5

FIG.—4

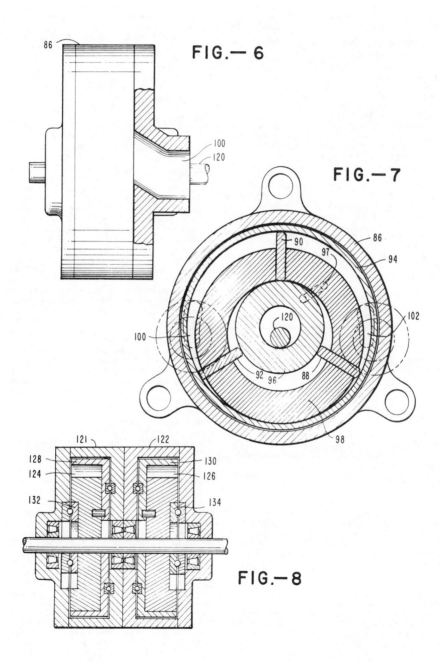

FIG.— 6

FIG.— 7

FIG.— 8

3,936,252

1

STEAM PROPULSION SYSTEM

This is a division of application Ser. No. 165,987, filed July 26, 1971 now U.S. Pat. No. 3,820,335.

BACKGROUND OF THE INVENTION

Present propulsion systems for automobiles as well as other means of movement are plagued with difficulties. The present internal combustion engine utilizes a carburetor which must be constantly cleaned and adjusted, an ignition system that must be constantly replaced, a transmission that needs adjustment and often replacement and brakes that must be relined often.

Furthermore, the high output of exhaust products including carbon monoxide and unburned hydrocarbons has caused an atmospheric pollution problem that has already reached the danger level.

It is an object of the present invention to develop a smog-free propulsion system, low in cost, free from service and replacement of parts, and light in weight.

It is a further object of this invention to provide a high pressure steam propulsion system that can be utilized for automobile travel and other means of propulsion.

The system of the present invention utilizes no carburetor, no spark plugs, points or distributor, no crank case, transmission or differential oil, no transmission, no drive shaft, no rear axle or differential and no separate brake system requiring adjustment or replacement.

The system of the present invention utilizes high pressure steam, is light in weight, low in cost and is smogfree.

The system further is far less noisy than the traditional internal combustion engine as power is from a continuous flow of steam rather than an explosion or pulsation and the fuel is non-explosive.

BRIEF DESCRIPTION OF THE DRAWINGS

FIG. 1 is a schematic diagram showing the flow of steam through the system.

FIG. 2 is a side elevation of the steam production system of the present invention.

FIG. 3 is a cross-section taken on lines 3—3 of FIG. 2.

FIG. 4 is a cross-sectional view of the motor of the system taken through its center line.

FIG. 5 is a cross-sectional view of the motor of the system taken on lines 5—5 of FIG. 4.

FIG. 6 is a side elevation partially broken away on lines 6—6 of FIG. 5.

FIG. 7 is a cross-sectional view along the same lines as FIG. 5 but showing the motor turned 60 degrees.

FIG. 8 is a cross-sectional view through the central axis showing a back-to-back arrangement of the water motor and pump assembly.

Referring now to FIG. 1, there is shown a schematic of the steam flow wherein the flow from the steam supply 10 passes through a throttle valve 12 to a four-way reverse valve 14 and then to the motor or motors 16.

Referring to FIG. 2 there is shown the steam generation system. Turning on the ignition switch (not shown) starts the burner motor 18, the igniter 20, and the fuel solenoid 19. This heats the generator 21. When the temperature reaches a predetermined level, for example 350° F., the thermal switch 22 turns on the starter motor 24, and also the water solenoid 26 shown in FIG. 3.

2

This pumps water vapor into the generator 21 building steam pressure. When the pressure reaches a predetermined level, for example 200 psi, a pressure switch (not shown) turns off the starter motor 24 and opens a second solenoid 28 and steam motor 30 takes over the operation of pump 32 during the further operation of the system.

When the pressure reaches a further predetermined level, for example 310 psi, pressure switch 34 closes solenoid 28 reducing pressure and temperature and regulates the pressure at operating conditions between 295 psi and 310 psi for example, by opening and closing solenoid 28.

When the maximum operating temperature, 500° F. for example, is reached temperature switch 22 opens fuel bypass solenoid 36 reducing the fuel volume and temperature and turns on and off solenoid 36 to maintain the operating temperature in operating limits such as 475° F. to 500° F. The operation is fully automatic.

When the system reaches full power, pressure and temperature, steam will flow from steam supply line 38 to the throttle valve 12 as shown in FIG. 1, through four-way reverse valve 14 to the motor or motors 16 and return to the surge tank 40. The steam will then travel to the condenser 42 and back to the hot well 44.

Referring also to FIG. 3, the generator 21 consists of an outer shell 46 with insulation 48. Water exits from the water supply pump 32 via supply line 50 and enters the generator 21 through dual entry lines 52. The water passes through fog nozzles 54 into a central feed line 56 into a second fog nozzle 58. By passing through the fog nozzles in this manner the water is in the form of water vapor more easily converted to steam. Dual entry lines and fog nozzles are provided, as shown in FIG. 3, to provide a greater volume of water vapor.

Water vapor usage rather than water liquid allows the radiating surfaces to be increased in temperature to 550° F. to allow for greater volume of heat transfer than prevails in a water tube boiler. Water is an insulating medium that prevents the temperature of the heat transfer surfaces from rising above 250° F. whereas this generator does not utilize water allowing the greater heat radiation. Having no water in the generator at the start, metal surfaces heat very rapidly and there is therefore a short heat-up period, after which steam is generated instantly.

The vapor then passes into an entry tube 60 which leads to outer jacket spiral 62. As the vapor passes through spiral 62 it is heated by an inner radiant tube 63 and an outer radiant tube 65 which are heated by flame from the burner system. The steam then passes, as stated, through pressure switch 34 to steam supply line 38.

A pump 64 run by burner motor 18 pumps fuel through the motor shaft 67 of pump 64 to aspirator 68 into the center of generator 21 to heat the water vapor in the generator. Blower 66 introduces air through louvers 84 into the combustion area.

Louvers 84 cause the air from blower 66 and the fuel from aspirator 68 to mix and flow into the combustion area.

The action of the apirator 68 draws hot gases from the combustion area into the louver 84 area causing the fuel droplets to turn to gas by the heat of the hot gases so that the fuel when burned is a gas. This allows more oxygen to mix with the gaseous fuel causing complete combustion not attainable with liquid fuel droplets.

3,936,252

3

Burner exhaust leaves the generator through exhaust 80. A pressure relief valve 82 is provided in the event the steam pressure gets abnormally high in the generator 21.

A fan 70 run by motor 32 through axle 72 and a belt 74 cools the condenser to condense the steam to water returning to hot well 44. An alternator 76 is operated by motor 32 through axle 72 and a belt 78 to provide electrical energy for the electrical system.

Referring now to FIGS. 4, 5, 6, and 7 there is shown the steam motor portion of the system. The motor is encased in an outer shell 86 cylinderical in shape. Multiple rotor blades or vanes 88, 90, 92, which may vary in number depending upon the particular design, rotate by steam pressure between rotating cylinder 94 and rotating disc 96. Said rotor blades 88, 90, 92 are slidingly engaged in a rotating carrier 98, said blades 88, 90, 92 being able to slide in a direction perpendicular to the outer circumference of carrier 98.

The disc 96 causes the rotor blades 88, 90, 92 to remain in contact with rotating cylinder 94 at all times.

A pin 97 in carrier 98 engages in a slot in the rotating cylinder 94 causing cylinder 94 to rotate together with carrier 98. As the carrier 98 rotates, pin 97 slides in and out of the slot in the rotary cylinder 94 because the relationship between the carrier 98 and cylinder 94 changes during rotation.

As the steam from the generator 21 via steam supply line 38 and after passing through throttle valve 12 and four-way reverse valve 14 enters the motor through an entrance port 100, the steam forces rotor 90, as shown, in a clockwise rotation until the steam reaches an outlet port 102 at which time the steam is returned to the surge tank 40.

Wheels (not shown) are mounted on motor shaft 120 which is fixedly attached to carrier 98, thus rotating as the steam rotates carrier 98 by forcing the rotor blades 88, 90, 92 in a clockwise direction. The wheels can be operated in the reverse direction by changing the position of four-way reverse valve 14 which causes the steam to enter the motor by port 102 and exit by port 100 causing the rotor blades 88, 90, 92 to rotate counter-clockwise.

Closing the throttle valve 12 will cause the motor to build up pressure and brake the rotation of the rotor blades, thus braking the wheels.

The motor assembly of the rotating cylinder 94, the rotor blades or vanes 88, 90, 92 and the disc 96 rotate as a unit around one center. The shaft 120 and carrier 98 rotate around another center. This causes the blades 88, 90, 92 to slide in and out of the carrier 98 exposing the blades to be forced in a circular pattern by steam pressure and retracting into the carrier 98 on the opposite side leaving no space for steam to leak which would cause steam pressure in the opposite direction.

The shaft 120 rotates with a minimum of friction within outer shell 86 due to roller bearings 104, 106, 108 and 110.

Carrier 98 and outer shell 86 are held in position by thrust bearings 112, 114, 116 and 118.

Referring now to FIG. 6 there is shown the outer shell 86, shaft 120 and the inlet port 100 for the steam.

FIG. 7 shows the motor with the rotor blades turned 60 degrees to show the release of the steam through exit port 102.

FIG. 8 shows the back-to-back arrangement of the motor and water pump assembly of this invention showing the outer shells 120 and 122. Rotor blades 124

4

and 126 rotate between rotary cylinders 128 and 130 and discs 132 and 134.

A back-to-back arrangement as described is utilized to provide the steam motor-pump arrangement 30, 32 used in the generator stage of this system. The steam motor must be larger than the water pump portion to provide greater pressure to force water vapor into the generator.

Many of the individual parts required to construct the system of the present invention are well known are are available commercially, for instance fog nozzles as described are availabe in a variety of types such as those manufactured by Bette and the burner motor and pump assembly is standard, manufactured by large pump manufacturers.

The system can be totally lubricated and anti-freeze protection provided by the addition of a silicone compound which travels through the system constantly with the steam. The rotary cylinder motor mounts in and drives each wheel, thus braking power is provided by action of the motor itself. The motor is practically friction-free with positive displacement and is so powerful it does not require gearing down to start the car, for instance.

The oil burner, furnishing the heat to make the steam, changes the fuel to gas and can burn jet fuel, light deisel oil, gasoline or any distillate without making smog.

In operation, one horsepower will require about 2545 BTU. One pound of fuel will generate about 19,000 BTU, one gallon (about eight pounds) about 152,000 BTU. Six gallons will generate about 912,000 BTU equalling 360 horsepower.

Having thus described the invention, I claim:

1. A rotary cylinder positive displacement motor comprising:
   a. an outer cylinderical shell
   b. an inner rotating cylinder
   c. a carrier adapted to receive
   d. rotor blades which slide in said carrier
   e. a rotating disc to position said rotor blades
   f. a motor shaft rotatably mounted on roller bearings attached to said carrier
   g. ports for the introduction and release of steam adapted to cause said rotors to rotate within said outer shell
   h. a thrust bearing assembly interconnecting said outer shell and said cylinder
   i. a second thrust bearing assembly interconnecting said disc and said outer shell

2. A rotary cylinder positive displacement motor comprising, an outer cylindrical shell having first and second ports and closed ends, each end having an aperture eccentric to the axis of the cylindrical shell, a cylinder having one closed end with a central aperture therein, said cylinder being concentrically mounted in said second outer cylindrical shell for rotation, the outer periphery of said cylinder being spaced from the inner periphery of said second outer shell, a thrust bearing assembly interconnecting the first of said closed ends of said second shell and the closed end of said cylinder, a shaft rotatably mounted on roller bearings in the eccentric apertures of said second outer shell and passing through the central aperture in said cylinder, a carrier fixedly mounted concentrically to said shaft, said carrier having a plurality of radial slots therein, an annular disc surrounding said shaft and having a second thrust bearing assembly interconnect-

3,936,252

5

ing said disc and the second closed end of said second outer shell, said disc being concentric to said cylinder, a plurality of vanes being slidably supported in each of said plurality of slots, each of said vanes having a first end in contacting relationship with the outer periphery

6

of said annular disc and a second end in contacting relationship with the inner periphery of said cylinder.

3. The motor of claim 2 including means for loosely connecting said cylinder and said carrier.

* * * * *

Part 3
Trademarks

THE TRADEMARK AND THE CORPORATE IDENTITY

The corporate identity is the image projected by the owner or management of a business, whether or not it's deliberate. At the heart of the corporate identity is the trademark. The importance of making an effective visual presentation with a trademark can't be understated. A well-groomed image can make a substantial impact on the bottom line—profits.

The corporate identity program comprises every aspect of the business that is open to public analysis, criticism, judgement, opinion, etc. It helps to shape other peoples' attitudes about your firm, your products, and your services. The following are parts of a corporate identity program:

- Printing
- Vehicles
- Packaging
- Decor
- Public relations
- Signs
- Buildings
- Advertising
- Colors
- Personnel
  - And, of course, the trademark!

Start by thinking big! Whether your business is a one-man enterprise or a leading corporation in your industry, project the image of success that you desire your business to attain. This is a very important step in the direction toward growth. A small business can appear substantial with the right look.

The subject of designing a trademark and creating a public image could fill volumes of books. A few recommended books are included in the "Resources" section which will provide a greater depth of understanding in this area. A visit to a public library will also provide new ideas.

Typically, advertising agencies or commercial artists are employed, but with careful thought, you can cultivate a good trademark or business image yourself and with equal success. The ad agency should be capable of handling every aspect of trademark and trade name creation. If an artist is consulted, determine his qualifications and experience with trademark design. His responsibility should be limited to typography, design, and color. The corporate or brand name should be created by persons with an understanding of the business and its products or services and/or someone who has experience with trade name invention.

First, start with the name, followed by the type style, design, and color. Experiment with your ideas until you're satisfied with one of your choices.

A name should be carefully selected. Besides visual appearance and meaning, it must sound good, too. If it doesn't sound right over the telephone, it probably won't sound good on radio, television, and in audio presentations. If that's the case, don't use it, even if the name qualifies in all other aspects. If the consumer or other customer can't pronounce the name correctly, or worse yet, if it sounds like the name of another product, then the name defeats its own purpose. If foreign markets are a possibility, consider the translation of the words. Will your brand name offend foreign customers when translated into their language? Does it retain its meaning? Will it have the same impact and effectiveness in another language?

The business owner or corporate executive should give the name adequate thought. If necessary, professional wordsmiths can be hired to do the job. These people know what's required to create an exceptional trade name. Their fees fluctuate with the size of the account and energy expended, fees of $20,000 to $100,000 are common. However, a local advertising agency or the do-it-yourself approach will be sufficient for most small businesses with limited budgets. If you contact ad agencies, ascertain their experience with trademarks and trade names. Samples will show their style.

The trademark should always convey the impression of consistency and quality. Trademarks that identify consumer products are frequently referred to as brand names. They should be:

1. Distinctive
2. Legible
3. Memorable
4. Simple
5. Unique

When examining your trademark ideas, ask yourself these questions:

- Does it reflect management's attitude?
- Does it enhance the present image of your business?
- Will it be acceptable in the marketplace?
- Does it project consistency and quality in your products and services?
- Is this the identity you want five years from now?
- Can it be adapted to all corporate identity requirements?

Boring and elementary designs aren't acceptable. Use your imagination, but don't forget that business is generally conservative. A type style that's too contemporary or timely might not be acceptable next year. There are many typefaces, too, but some are just not appropriate to your type of business or product. The typeface and design should have excellent reproductive capabilities. Lettering and lines that are too thin don't reproduce well and don't reflect strength and substance, and too bold is too much.

The name and design should be proportionately designed. Certain combinations will stand out immediately as inappropriate and others will appear more acceptable. Refine the best designs until you are completely satisfied.

It's best if you don't rush this process. Allow yourself the time to develop the trademark or trade name to its fullest potential. Trademark design books show good examples of trademarks in use today. These books can be found in your library or in art-supply stores. Graphic designers regularly use these books to get ideas.

The necessary tools to produce a trademark are available in a local art supply store. Refer to ''The Drawing'' section in Part 2 for recommendations of art supply firms that sell useful products for designing a trademark.

Your choice of trade names or brand names will determine the extent of protection you can expect to receive. There are four types (listed in order of desirability):

1. Fanciful
2. Arbitrary
3. Suggestive
4. Descriptive

Fanciful marks afford maximum legal protection for a trademark owner. These include such famous brand names as Xerox, Sanka, etc. Although these words may only apply to one product or certain types of products, because they are such well-known brand names, the owners receive maximum legal protection in any field which they choose to enter. Such trade names are manufactured words for the sole purpose of identifying a particular manufacturer's line of products. These words cannot be found in the dictionary because they have no meaning. Large companies have spent fortunes to make their products household knowledge through the use of clever trade names and massive advertising programs. Of the four categories, fanciful marks are the most difficult to develop, but are the most valuable to own. (So many of our English language words and combinations of these words have been used in commercial names that it's a real challenge to originate a new word.) This type of word mark can be protected through continued use and by registration for the specific categories that the product or service covers.

Arbitrary marks are the next best choice. Many American manufacturers became giants with arbitrary brand name products. These word marks consist of common words with which we are all familiar. These words have dictionary meanings, but don't indicate what the product is, what it does, or how it's manufactured.

Suggestive marks are words that imply something about the product. They may suggest strength, quality, durability, or other desirable features of the product. For instance, a brand of blue jeans with the trademark ''Bulldog'' suggests that the jeans are tough and durable.

Descriptive marks describe a characteristic of a product or service. These marks require a secondary meaning in order for them to be used as trademarks. The descriptive word alone holds no commercial value, and these are the weakest of word marks. However, the descriptive name may be very good for marketing the product, so that the importance of a strong trademark may not be a major concern. If the buyer is being sold the product at point of purchase, then this type of trademark may be sufficient to produce a desired number of sales.

TRADEMARK USE

Trademark ownership is the result of the continued and correct use of a mark. A trademark doesn't have to be registered to secure benefits for its user.

The proper use and display of the trademark is important, it sets an example for others to follow. Diligently guarding against improper use will ensure your legal claim to it. A trademark displayed incorrectly can confuse buyers, the public, and other people who may want to know the quality and source of the goods.

If the public misuses a brand name, it's possible that the trademark owner can lose his ownership right as a result of the word mark being reduced to a generic name through improper use. It's his responsibility to protect the proper use of the trademark or trade name.

Asking a waitress, "Please bring me the Tabasco," is incorrect use of a trade name. The same abuse can frequently be heard when someone asks for "a Kleenex," when actually he wants any brand of tissue. In both instances, the brand name is being used generically. Another similar example is when a person asks the clerk at the local copy shop for "a Xerox copy," rather than requesting a photocopy. Erosion of a brand name through improper use can eventually cause it to legally become a generic name. That's why major trademark owners go out of their way to protect their marks. Occasionally, you will see a large consumer-products company advertise on television or in magazines just to remind people of the proper way to refer to its product(s). This shows diligence on the part of the owner who is concerned about preserving the integrity of a mark.

There is a correct way to request a brand-name product that protects both the maker and the buyer, and only in this way can the customer be assured of consistent quality from a recognizable source. Next time, ask for a "Kleenex brand tissue," or, "Tabasco brand pepper sauce," etc. The word "mark" should always be followed by the word "brand" and the proper description of the item. This prevents any possible confusion as to the preferred brand. Trademark owners should always be alert as to how their trademarks and trade names are being used and to correct any abuses.

Additionally, when a trademark is printed on packaging, labels, in advertising, on signs, etc., it must always be a true fascimiles of the original design. Reproduction of the mark should be exercised with care. The colors must remain the same, the shape and design should be proportionally intact, the art and typography must not be altered, and nothing can be added or deleted from the trademark design.

The advantages of a good mark—quick identification, good will, the quality and source of your product—will be lost for a lack of strict adherence to the proper use of your trademark.

ADVANTAGES OF REGISTERING A TRADEMARK

1. The trademark owner can sue for infringement in Federal court.

2. The reparation of infringement damages can be claimed in Federal court, and the defendant can be forced to repay triple the damages and attorney's costs.

3. The trademark owner can display a notice of registration. The registered trademark symbol is constructive notice of a claim of ownership.

4. By recording the trademark with U.S. Customs, the trademark owner can prevent goods coming into the U.S. that bear an infringing mark.

5. A registered trademark is prima facie evidence that the mark is valid and entitles the owner exclusive right to use the mark in trade as stated in the certificate.

6. In the event a registered mark is challenged in court, the registration is indisputable evidence of the owner's exclusive right to use the trademark.

7. Once the registered mark is five years old, there is little chance that it can be successfully challenged.

8. Counterfeiting a registered trademark provides criminal penalties.

9. In many countries, previous U.S. registration is required for registration abroad.

10. The registered mark will appear on search reports obtained by others, which should discourage another party from using it.

MARKS AND NAMES

Trademarks, service marks, brand names, trade names, house marks, certification marks, and collective marks are created to distinguish a manufacturer or source's products and services from other similar items. They can be displayed on products, labels, in advertising, etc.

A *trademark* includes any word, number, name, symbol, or device, or any combination of these elements.

A *service mark* helps differentiate two or more services. It can be a design like a trademark or a combination of words similar to a trade name.

A *trade name* can be adopted by legal entities (including individuals) for the purpose of conducting business. It can identify a business, trade, vocation, or occupation.

A *certification mark* is used by persons, businesses, or associations other than the mark's owner to certify the origin, or some other aspect of the product or service.

A *collective mark* can be used by members of a cooperative, an association, a collective group, or an organization. It can be a trademark or service mark and may indicate membership in an organization.

TRADEMARK OWNERSHIP

Once the trademark design has been finalized and is ready to be incorporated in the promotion of the goods and services, immediate attention should be paid to legally protecting the mark.

In the United States, trademark ownership is determined by commercial use of the mark. Trademark use constitutes the regular trade of a branded product in interstate commerce or foreign trade. Interstate commerce is a shipment or sale of goods between two states. Foreign trade is a shipment or sale of goods between the U.S. and a foreign country. The normal sale of branded goods between the trademark owner and a customer in the same state doesn't satisfy the "use in commerce" requirement.

A mark used on products or services within a particular state doesn't necessarily need Federal registration. A state trademark is satisfactory for intrastate business; however, there are definite advantages to Federal registration. If Federal protection isn't possible, state registration may be an alternative solution. Dual Federal and state trademark registration affords the best national trademark protection. A Federal trademark can be barred from use within a state where previous registration has been established.

The first user of a trademark is the legal owner. It isn't necessary to register a trademark with the Patent and Trademark Office in order to use a mark. An unregistered trademark is protected by common law, but protection is limited to the states where the mark is used.

A mark must be used in interstate business to qualify for Federal registration. Upon applying for such registration, it's possible that a mark—although it has been in use—cannot be certified due to a previously registered Federal trademark. Additionally, a Federal trademark can be challenged for up to five years. Registration gives constructive notice of a trademark user's claim of ownership, but it's the date of first use that will determine the true owner of a mark.

In addition to Federal trademark registration, a mark owner might wish to register the trademark in certain states if registration in all 50 states is prohibitive. It's wise to register the mark in the states where branded products are frequently shipped. Most state applications request the first-use date within the state and elsewhere. It's the date the branded products were first in use anywhere that most states consider to be the first official date of use. Refer to "State Trademark Data" in this part for additional information on state trademark registration.

A mark can simultaneously be used as a trademark and service mark by simply registering it in the appropriate classifications of goods and services.

THE PRINCIPAL AND SUPPLEMENTAL REGISTERS

All registered trademarks fall into one of two categories: they are registered either on the Principal Register or the Supplemental Register. New trademarks are generally registered on the Principal Register (appropriate applications are included in this part). If for some reason the mark doesn't qualify for the Principal Register, the applicant should file an application to the Supplemental Register. Additional Federal trademark forms can be ordered from the PTO. See the "List of Trademark Forms" in this part for form numbers and titles.

Qualifications for both Principal and Supplemental Registers are explained in the Lanham-Trademark Act of 1946, the essence of which follows. The complete text can be found in the reference section of most large public libraries or in a law library.

Marks Registrable on the Principal Register

A mark will not be refused for registration on the Principal Register unless it falls into one of the following categories (registration is notice of the applicant's claim of ownership):

1. It comprises immoral, deceptive, or scandalous components.
2. It incorporates a flag or coat of arms or other insignia of the U.S. government, municipality, or state, or of a foreign nation.
3. It contains the name, portrait, or signature of a living individual, or of a deceased president of the United States during the lifetime of his widow, except if permission is granted.
4. It closely resembles a registered mark or trade name or one previously used but not abandoned.
5. It consists of a mark that is merely descriptive when applied to the goods or is deceptively misdescriptive; if it's primarily geographically descriptive or deceptively misdescriptive; or if it's primarily a surname.

Registrable Service Marks

Service marks are registered like trademarks. They have the same effect and are entitled to the same protection.

Registrable Collective and Certification Marks

Collective and certification marks are registered, treated, and entitled to the same protection as trademarks. They can indicate a regional origin used in commerce for the benefit of individuals, nations, states, municipalities, etc. It's not necessary that these types of marks be associated with industrial or commercial enterprises.

Use By Related Companies

A mark can be used by related companies in the conduct of legitimate business. It's at the discretion of the trademark owner to decide the use of the mark with related businesses provided it doesn't deceive the public.

Certificates

1. A certificate of registration of a mark on the Principal Register is issued to the trademark owner under the official PTO seal and signature of the Commissioner. The certificate contains.
   - Reproduction of the drawing of the mark
   - Statement of the applicant
   - Date of first use of the mark

- Date of first use of the mark in commerce
- Goods or services for which the mark is registered
- Number and date of registration
- Term
- Conditions and limitations

2. The certificate of registration is prima facie evidence of the validity of registration.

3. The mark can be assigned by the owner after the assignment has been recorded with the PTO. The new owner can obtain a certificate at the request of the original applicant if the proper fee is paid.

4. A registration may be surrendered, cancelled, or amended upon application by the owner and payment of the appropriate fee.

5. Documents related to marks and belonging to the PTO, or copies of certificates of registration bearing the official PTO seal and certified by the Commissioner, are evidence of authentication.

6. The PTO will correct any errors that it is responsible for in connection with registration and will issue a certificate stating the fact and nature of the mistake at its expense.

7. If an applicant makes an error and it occurred in good faith, the Commissioner will issue a certificate of correction or possibly a new certificate upon payment of the required fee.

Duration

Trademark registration is effective for 20 years. However, within 12 months prior to the sixth anniversary of registration, an affidavit must be filed showing that the mark is still in use in order for registration to continue in full force for the remaining 14 years.

Renewal

A trademark can be renewed at the end of its 20-year term. A new application, renewal fee, and affidavit must be filed within six months of the final expiration, stating that the mark is still in use in commerce.

Assignment

A registered mark is assignable with the good will of the business that owns it. An assignment is a written agreement that must be recorded with the Patent and Trademark Office and is prima facie evidence of execution. The assignment is required to be recorded prior to subsequent purchase or within three months after a transfer.

Publication

Once the application has been examined and it appears that the mark is registrable, the Commissioner will publish the mark in the official Trademark Gazette.

If the mark isn't registrable, the applicant will be notified of the reason and allowed six months to respond; otherwise, the application will be considered abandoned.

Opposition

Anyone who feels he would be adversely affected by the registration of a mark on the the Principal Register can file a verified notice of opposition within 30 days of publication and stating the grounds for such action.

Cancellation

Anyone who feels he would be damaged by the registration of a mark on the Principal Register can pay the required fee and apply to cancel registration under the following conditions:

1. Within five years of the registration date.
2. Anytime if the registration mark becomes the common descriptive name of the goods or has been abandoned, or if registration was fraudulent.
3. Anytime a registrant of a certification mark doesn't control its use, engages in the production or marketing or any goods or services to which the mark is applied, permits any use of the mark for purposes other than as a certification mark, or discriminately refuses to certify the goods or services of any person who maintains the standards that the mark certifies.

The Supplemental Register

All marks capable of distinguishing applicant's goods or services, but not registrable on the Principal Register, can be registered on the Supplemental Register.

A mark may be registered on the Supplemental Register if it consists of a trademark, symbol, label, package, configuration of goods, name, word, slogan, phrase, surname, geographical name, numeral, device or any combination of these, so long as the mark distinguishes the applicant's goods or services.

A separate trademark application is available from the PTO for filing on the Supplemental Register. A registration fee is required at filing time.

Registration on the Supplemental Register demands that the mark have been used for a full year prior to an application being made. This requirement can be waived at the discretion of the Commissioner if the mark has been used in foreign commerce and requires domestic registration as a basis for foreign protection.

Applications for registration not the Supplemental Register will not receive the advantages of sections 2(e), 2(f), 7(b), 12(a), 13 to 18, 22, 33, and 43 of the Act.

Registration on the Supplemental Register will not be filed in the Department of the Treasury nor can it be utilized to prevent importation by recording the mark with U.S. Customs.

Notice of Registration

One of the following notices of registration must be incorporated in the trademark:

1. "Registered in the U.S Patent and Trademark Office"
2. "Reg. U.S. Pat. & Tr. Off."
3. "®"

Failure to display the notice of registration will prevent the owner from recovering damages unless the defendant had actual notice of registration.

THE TRADEMARK SEARCH

A comprehensive trademark search is absolutely essential prior to using a mark or name. This also applies to corporate names, since a registered trademark or trade name has precedence. A trademark user who fails to take the appropriate cautionary measures is playing Russian roulette with the future good will of his business and product. The negligent act of infringing on another trademark might not surface for years, but if a competitor challenges the use of your trademark and wins (depending on many factors), the cost to correct the problem can range from a few hundred dollars to six figures.

An infringer might pay handsomely for poor judgment. The plaintiff receives damages, profits, and costs as a result of losses, expenses, and displaced good will. Under Federal law, the court can award the injured party up to three times the amount of actual damages, plus attorney's fees. In addition to the penalty setback, an infringer is then required to change his mark or name. Depending on how extensive promotional efforts were in connection with the old mark, this can entail changing all printing, including checks, signs, advertising, labels, packaging, stationery, brochures, catalogs, price sheets, etc.; the list is almost endless. Anything that bears the mark has to be changed.

The worst aspect of this scenario might be the public relations effort necessary to sustain consumer or buyer confidence, buyers become quickly attached to brand names. Remember, that's why a trademark was created for the product in the first place. A public relations campaign may be necessary and can require months or years to rectify the damage to the company's or product's good will or corporate image. So, a graceful trademark changeover would be desirable during this transitory period. Unfortunately, the problem is a reflection of the management of the business. A few eyebrows might be raised by creditors, suppliers, investors, and stockholders concerned with the bottom line of the business.

Advance planning and a thorough trademark search will minimize unnecessary difficulties and expense. However, before prematurely retaining an artist or designer to create a new trademark or logo, it's best to first check on the name. The name can be a proposed trademark or a name intended to be incorporated in the trademark design. If the same name or a similar name is discovered in use, the expense to change the artist's design of the trademark is spared. Otherwise, the designer of the mark has to change it when an acceptable name is found.

This preliminary step can be an informal name search that utilizes methods outlined in this chapter. The completed trademark should be followed up by a professional search prior to use and registration. The informal search might save design and search costs.

If the name is available for use, the trademark should then be designed by an artist or a trademark designer. If it's a trade name, then proceed to a professional search. A commercial artist might be less aware of the importance of a distinctive trademark design than one who specializes in this area. It's wise to ascertain in advance the qualifications of the party who will be responsible for creating the trademark. Remember, the mark will be a reflection of your product and business. It's important that the designer understand the product that the mark will promote, the company image desired, marketing channels and methods, the end buyer or consumer, the objectives of the trademark owner, management's philosophy, and so on.

An informal trademark search can be as expensive as you wish. After giving careful consideration to possible names, select at least several candidates, maybe even a couple dozen for the initial search. The object is to find a handful of names that will survive your investigation and are ready for further evaluation.

Once a list of names is chosen, check the following sources. The more leads you check, the better your chances of selecting a distinct name.

Begin looking at industry publications and directories for similar names. Contact associations and major suppliers in the same industry for companies that manufacture or market similar products under names that are spelled or sound close to the ones you have chosen. This is an important first step, since a similar name in the same or a related industry could easily confuse the buyer as to who is the source.

A large public library will have many of the following directories and other sources of information:

- Current and previous telephone directories
- *American Druggist Blue Book*
- *American Trademark Designs*
- *Annual Buyer's Guide*
- *Chemical Week Buyer's Guide Issue*
- *Commercial Names and Sources*
- *Consumer Sourcebook*
- *Drug Topics Red Book*
- *Dun & Bradstreet's Million Dollar Directory*
- *Handbook of Material Trade Names*
- *Jewelers Brand Name and Trademark Guide*
- *MacRae's Blue Book*
- *New Trade Names*

- *NPN Factbook*
- *Official Trademark Gazette* (published by PTO)
- *Polk's City Directory*
- *Trademark Register of the United States*
- *Thomas' Register of American Manufacturers*
- *Trademark Design Register*
- *Trademark Directory*
- *Trademark Stylesheet*
- *Trademark Symbols of the World*
- *Tradenames Directory*
- *Tradenames of the Man-Made Fibers*
- *U.K. Trade Names*

Many other directories are not mentioned in this list, so check the *Directory of Directories* for other sources. Additional library research can include a scan of the magazine article file, card catalog, microfiche, etc. for potential sources of trademark or brand name information.

Local, State, and Federal government offices are storehouses of information. Try a county clerk's office or the equivalent; the Secretary of State, Corporation Division & Trademark Division; the State Department of Taxation or the equivalent; or various state agencies (i.e., Department of Agriculture).

A search must have national scope. An informal search is only beneficial if it is economically feasible; otherwise, it is more efficient and cost-effective to use a professional search service. A thorough check of library information is very useful in eliminating the most obvious names in use.

Upon completion of your investigation, do a professional trade name search or, in the case of a trademark, begin the design phase, which should then be followed by a professional national or international search.

Before the design sequence is finished, contact one or all of the following firms and obtain information and rates on their professional trademark-search services. The services of these firms will be more comprehensive than a search by a lawyer. Additional firms can be found in your local Yellow Pages. A search can take a few days or a few weeks, depending on how thorough it is. The more comprehensive the investigation, the better your chances of landing a distinctive, nonconflicting mark.

Remember, the cost of a search is minimal in comparison to the problems that can arise from using a conflicting mark.

COMPUMARK U.S.
1333 F Street, N.W.
Washington, D.C. 20004
(202) 737-7900
1-800-421-7881

IFI/PLENUM DATA CORPORATION
302 Swann Ave.
Alexandria, VA 22301
(302) 998-0478
(800) 331-4955

RAPID PATENT SERVICE
P.O. Box 2527 Eads Station
Arlington, VA 22202
(703) 920-5050
1-800-336-5010

THOMSON & THOMSON, INC.
120 Fulton St.
Boston, MA 02109
1-(617) 479-1600
1-800-692-8833

TRADEMARK SERVICE COMPANY
A Division of the Company Corporation
725 N. Market St.
Wilmington, DE 19801
1-800-458-MARK

TRADEMARK SERVICES CORPORATION
747 Third Ave.
New York, NY 10017
(212) 421-5730
1-800-872-6275

The first user of a trademark is the legal owner whether or not the trademark is registered. Still, even though a thorough investigation is made, there's no assurance that the mark or name won't be challenged in the future. A trademark can have recently been used or used on a limited basis, thereby avoiding detection during the search. Since a trademark is owned through use rather than registration alone, the possibility always exists that a similar mark may appear someday.

An effective method in selecting a risk-free mark is to have an attorney or search firm begin with a Federal search of the name that survived the information search. This preliminary undertaking can be done in a day and will eliminate all but a few of the marks originally picked. This method is good when trying to determine a name to use for the trademark design, or if several trademarks are finished and are under consideration.

The remaining marks can then be investigated in all 50 states and in regard to common-law use. An international check is recommended in countries where foreign trade is anticipated. The trademark(s) that successfully survives the final journey will be a serious candidate for use and registration.

If it's essential that expense be kept to a minimum, it might be necessary to complete one trademark search at a time, but proceed according to the steps previously outlined. Attorneys and professional search firms base their fees per mark that is searched. A thorough, informal search will help reduce your overall expense in determining a distinguishable mark.

Up to 90 percent of all trademark applications are rejected for one reason or another. The mark might be too similar to another, or its generic or the application has been improperly submitted. Follow each step in the trademark process carefully to avoid unnecessary costs and delays.

After the trademark search has been completed, the attorney or search firm in charge of the investigation will return a report that will disclose similar marks or possible conflicting marks. At this point, you may wish to have an attorney review the trademark report and give an opinion on its findings even if you plan to register the mark yourself.

It's a good idea to contact the companies found in the attorney's report. Request information on the product to determine if the mark is still in use. If it is not being used, you might wish to have your attorney contact the trademark owners and see if they would be willing to sell the mark. However, this may not be cheaper or more advantageous than coming up with an alternative trademark.

"TOKEN" USE

Trademark ownership can be claimed in advance of marketing a new product. A "token" use sale and shipment can be arranged to satisfy the "date of first use in commerce" requirement that is necessary prior to apply for trademark registration.

Once prior use has been established, a Federal or state trademark application can be filed. The token-use method allows the trademark owner to register the mark quickly and with the least expense. When the Patent and Trademark Office issues the certificate, prima facie evidence is established. The trademark applicant can then be fairly sure that it's safe to begin promoting the branded product, including necessary printing, advertising, manufacturing, etc. Employing the token method of establishing first use for registration purposes will save the applicant unnecessary costs in marketing a branded product whose trademark or trade name may not be available.

The token-use practice must be a genuine, documented commercial transaction, and the owner must have the intent to begin distributing and marketing the new product. Prior to this stage, however (i.e., during product development), a trademark can be registered by exercising the token-use approach.

To document a branded product's first use, follow the steps outlined here:

1. Establish the date of first use by sale or shipment of the branded product to a legitimate customer (i.e., other than a relative or another branch of your company) in another state or foreign country. A sale can be arranged for this purpose.

2. Document the shipment of the first sale. Keep copies of the purchase order, invoice, bill of lading, etc.

3. Photograph the trademark as it's used on the goods. If the actual product label showing the trademark hasn't been printed yet, a specimen mark can be used for photographic purposes. A drawing of the label with the trademark is adequate for the photo.

4. Maintain a file for all documentation. Years from now, someone might challenge your trademark.

The first-use shipment can contain the actual goods for which the mark is used or a product that has the same description and purposes.

By employing the token-use approach, minimal expense is incurred to establish the date of first use in commerce and to meet trademark registration requirements. In most instances, this avenue provides the trademark owner the fastest way to trademark protection with the least risk.

A service mark can only be used with a genuine mark. It cannot be just a sundry element of a product.

INSTRUCTIONS FOR COMPLETION
OF THE FEDERAL TRADEMARK APPLICATION

At the time of filing, the trademark application, the trademark, service mark, trade name, etc. must already be in use with goods or services in interstate commerce.

The application must include the following four items or it will be rejected by the Trademark Office:

1. Application form
2. Drawing of the mark
3. Specimens
4. Filing fee

Application Form

Three Federal trademark application forms for registering on the Principal Register are included in this part. Only one application should be selected depending on whether the applicant is an individual, partnership, or corporation. The applicant will become the registered owner. In the case of a partnership or corporation, either a partner or corporate officer should sign the application as the representative of the trademark owner. Service mark applicants can also apply on the trademark application forms. A complete list of Federal trademark forms available from the Patent and Trademark Office is included in this part.

Before completing the application, carefully read the footnotes on the reverse side of the page. All spaces on the application must be correctly completed in English. The trademark application can be completed and filed by a lawyer on behalf of the applicant, or a power of attorney can be employed to authorize someone to execute the application. (A power of attorney form is included in this book.)

The Patent and Trademark Office will not recommend a lawyer. The name of an attorney specializing in patent and trademark law will be furnished by your local bar association on request. The association won't make recommendations, but will randomly select a qualified lawyer for consideration. A directory of patent attorneys and registered agents is available from the Superintendent of Documents listed in the Resource section. (Patent attorneys generally handle trademarks, too.)

In the top right-hand corner of the application is a box marked "Class No." The International Classification of Goods and Services list is incorporated in this chapter. Select the appropriate classification(s) that best describe the type of product or service for which the trademark is used. Write the respective classification number in the box marked "Class No."

The following numbers correspond to the numbering on the individual and partnership trademark applications. The explanations apply to the corporation form as well; here, however, the numbers do not correspond.

1. In addition to providing the name and address of the applicant, include a telephone number.

2./3. Give the first date that the trademark was used anywhere on the goods or in connection with services, and in what type of commerce. For instance, interstate commerce constitutes trade between two or more states or foreign trade, which would be commerce between the U.S. and one or more foreign countries. Indicate the appropriate trade activity by either writing "interstate commerce" or "commerce between the U.S. and (*a specific country or countries*) in the space provided on the form. This item also asks for the date when the trademark was first actually used in commerce. The dates can be the same, but the commerce date can't be earlier than the first date.

4. This blank space is for additional information necessary to describe distinctiveness, statements of disclaimer, or data pertaining to a foreign applicant. If not applicable, leave it blank.

5. Specify how the mark is used on goods or in connection with services. Is it printed on labels, directly on packaging, in conjunction with advertising, or otherwise?

6. Same as 4 above. Following the blank space provided for additional information, give the person's name who is making the application, whether an individual, partner, or corporate officer. At the bottom of the page, sign and date it.

Drawing of the Mark

An actual drawing of the trademark must accompany the application. Two types of drawings can illustrate the mark, only one of which will be appropriate:

1. Typed drawing
2. Special form drawing

Follow the parameters outlined below so that the drawing will meet all acceptable requirements:

- The drawing must be made on pure white paper not exceeding $8^1/_2 \times 11$ inches.
- The sheet should be vertical with the heading at the top.
- The Trademark Office prefers that the drawing measure $2^1/_4 \times 2^1/_4$ inches. The maximum acceptable size is 4×4 inches.
- A one-inch margin must encompass the drawing on both sides and at the bottom of the sheet. There must also be a one-inch space between the illustration and the heading.

The heading should run along the top of the vertical page, one inch above the drawing, but not more than one-quarter of the page. Type the heading to include the following information on separate lines:

1. Applicant's name
2. Post office address

3. Date of first use
4. Date first used in commerce
5. Goods or services

For a typed drawing, a trade name or word mark should be typed in capital letters in the center of the page. A typed drawing consists of words and/or numbers.

For a special-form drawing, an illustration of the mark must be prepared in accordance with PTO requirements. The drawing must adhere to these rules:

1. The drawing can only be in black and white.
2. Preferably, use India ink to draw the mark, or use a method that will permit outstanding reproduction of all its characteristics.
3. Everything but the white paper, which is the background, must be black (lines, letters, numbers, etc.).
4. All lines, letters, numbers, etc. must be clean, sharp, and solid.
5. If the mark can't be reduced clearly to less than $4'' \times 4''$ this can be explained in the application by writing a legible description of the details that distinguish the mark.
6. A photolithographic reproduction, printer's proof, or even a photocopy is acceptable if it is exceptionally clear with sharp black-and-white contrast.
7. Colors can be expressed by utilizing the conventional linings.

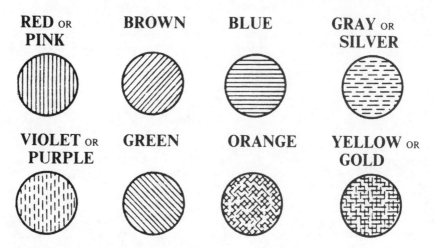

The drawing must not include half tones or photographs or corrections made with white-out fluid or other pigments.

Specimens

A specimen is an actual label, tag, container, display, or part that illustrates the trademark in use. Five specimens are required to be submitted with the application.

Containers, displays, or other cumbersome items can only be used as specimens if they are of a suitable material, can lie flat, and don't exceed $8^1/_2 \times 13$ inches. Otherwise, a good photograph or other sharp reproduction is acceptable, but again, not larger than $8^1/_2 \times 13$ inches. The trademark must appear clear and legible on the respective goods.

A service mark specimen can be a brochure or other form of advertising used in connection with the sale or promotion of the services. If the service mark is a sound recording, then three audio cassettes can be submitted in lieu of the five printed samples.

Filing Fee

The filing fee per classification is $175. Payment must be made to the Commissioner of Patents and Trademarks. Personal and business checks are accepted. Foreign remittances must be negotiable in the United States.

Send the required application, drawing, specimens, and fee to:

THE COMMISSIONER OF PATENTS AND TRADEMARKS
Washington, D.C. 20231

If the application isn't accepted upon examination, the applicant will be notified and allowed six months to respond before the application is considered void. Applications are examined in the order they are received.

Standard Industrial Classification (S.I.C.) Code List

After reading through the following list, select the four-digit number that most closely identifies your type of business. Write that four-digit number in the space provided on your form.

DIVISION A. AGRICULTURE, FORESTRY, & FISHING

0100	Agricultural Production-Crops
0200	Agricultural Production-Livestock
0700	Agricultural Services
0800	Forestry
0910	Commercial Fishing
0920	Fish Hatcheries & Preserves
0970	Hunting, Trapping & Game Propagation

DIVISION B. MINING

1000	Metal Mining
1100	Anthracite Mining
1200	Bituminous Coal & Lignite Mining
1300	Oil & Gas Extraction
1400	Nonmetallic Minerals Including Stone, Sand & Gravel

DIVISION C. CONSTRUCTION

1520	General Building Contractors — Residential Buildings
1530	Operative Builders Who Construct & Sell Buildings On Their Own Account Rather Than As Contractors
1540	General Building Contractors — Nonresidential Buildings
1610	Highway & Street Construction
1620	Heavy Construction
1710	Plumbing, Heating (except Electric) & Air Conditioning
1720	Painting, Paper Hanging & Decorating
1730	Electrical Work
1740	Masonry, Stonework, Tile Setting & Plastering
1750	Carpentering & Flooring
1760	Roofing & Sheet Metal Work
1770	Concrete Work
1780	Water Well Drilling
1790	Special Trade Contractors Not Otherwise Listed Above

DIVISION D. MANUFACTURING

2010	Meat Products
2020	Dairy Products
2030	Canned & Preserved Fruits & Vegetables
2040	Grain Mill Products
2050	Bakery Products
2060	Sugar & Confectionery Products
2070	Fats & Oils
2080	Beverages
2090	Food Preparations & Products
2100	Tobacco Manufacturers
2200	Textile Mill Products
2300	Apparel & Other Finished Products
2400	Lumber & Wood Products
2500	Furniture & Fixtures
2600	Paper & Allied Products
2700	Printing & Publishing
2810	Industrial Inorganic Chemicals
2820	Plastics Materials & Synthetics
2830	Drugs
2840	Soap, Detergents & Cleaning Preparations
2850	Paints, Varnishes & Allied Products
2860	Industrial Organic Chemicals
2870	Agricultural Chemicals
2890	Chemical Products Not Otherwise Listed Above
2910	Petroleum Refining
2950	Paving & Roofing Materials
2990	Products of Petroleum & Coal
3000	Rubber & Misc. Plastics Products
3100	Leather Tanning & Finishing & Leather Products
3200	Stone, Clay, Glass & Concrete Products
3300	Primary Metal Industries
3400	Fabricated Metal Products
3500	Machinery, Except Electrical
3600	Electrical & Electronic Machinery, Equipment & Supplies
3710	Motor Vehicles & Motor Vehicle Equipment
3720	Aircraft & Parts
3730	Ship & Boat Building & Repairing
3740	Railroad Equipment
3750	Motorcycles, Bicycles & Parts
3760	Guided Missiles, Space Vehicles & Parts
3790	Transportation Equipment Not Otherwise Listed Above
3800	Measuring, Analyzing & Controlling Instruments; Photographic, Medical & Optical Goods; Watches & Clocks
3910	Jewelry, Silverware & Plated Ware
3930	Musical Instruments
3940	Toys & Amusement, Sporting & Athletic Goods
3950	Pens, Pencils & Other Office & Artists' Materials
3960	Costume Jewelry, Novelties, Buttons & Notions
3990	Manufacturing Industries Not Otherwise Listed Above

DIVISION E. TRANSPORTATION, COMMUNICATIONS, ELECTRIC, GAS & SANITARY SERVICES

4000	Railroad Transportation
4110	Local & Suburban Passenger Transportation
4120	Taxicabs
4130	Intercity & Rural Highway Passenger Transportation
4140	Passenger Transportation Charter Service
4170	Terminal & Service Facilities for Motor Vehicle Passenger Transportation
4210	Trucking, Local & Long Distance
4220	Public Warehousing
4230	Terminal & Joint Terminal Maintenance Facilities for Motor Freight Transportation
4400	Water Transportation
4500	Transportation by Air
4600	Pipelines, Except Natural Gas
4700	Transportation Services Not Otherwise Listed Above
4810	Telephone Communication (Wire or Radio)
4820	Telegraph Communication (Wire or Radio)
4830	Radio & Television Broadcasting
4890	Communication Services Not Otherwise Listed Above
4910	Electric Services
4920	Gas Production & Distribution
4930	Combination Electric & Gas & Other Utility Services
4940	Water Supply
4950	Sanitary Services
4960	Steam Supply
4970	Irrigation Systems

DIVISION F. WHOLESALE TRADE

5010	Motor Vehicles, Automotive Parts & Supplies
5020	Furniture & Home Furnishings
5030	Lumber & Other Construction Materials
5040	Sporting, Recreational, Photographic & Hobby Goods & Toys & Supplies
5050	Metals & Minerals, Except Petroleum
5060	Electrical Goods
5070	Hardware, Plumbing & Heating Equipment & Supplies
5080	Machinery, Equipment & Supplies
5090	Durable Goods Not Otherwise Listed Above
5110	Paper & Paper Products
5120	Drugs, Proprietaries & Sundries
5130	Apparel, Piece Goods & Notions
5140	Groceries & Related Products
5150	Farm-Product Raw Materials
5160	Chemicals & Allied Products
5170	Petroleum & Petroleum Products
5180	Beer, Wine & Distilled Alcoholic Beverages
5190	Nondurable Goods Not Otherwise Listed Above

DIVISION G. RETAIL TRADE

5200	Building Materials Dealers (Including Lumber, Hardware & Mobile Home Dealers)
5300	General Merchandise Stores
5400	Food Stores Including Candy Stores
5510	Motor Vehicle Dealers (New & Used)
5520	Motor Vehicle Dealers (Used Only)
5530	Auto & Home Supply Stores
5540	Gasoline Service Stations
5550	Boat Dealers
5560	Recreation & Utility Trailer Dealers
5570	Motorcycle Dealers
5590	Automotive Dealers Not Otherwise Listed Above
5600	Apparel & Accessory Stores
5700	Furniture, Home Furnishings & Equipment Stores
5800	Eating & Drinking Places
5910	Drug Stores & Proprietary Stores
5920	Liquor Stores
5930	Used Merchandise Stores
5940	Retail Goods Stores Such As Sporting Goods, Bicycles, Books, Stationery, Jewelry & Hobby Stores
5960	Nonstore Retailers
5980	Fuel & Ice Dealers
5990	Retail Stores Not Otherwise Listed Above

DIVISION H. FINANCE, INSURANCE & REAL ESTATE

6000	Banking
6100	Credit Agencies Other Than Banks
6200	Security & Commodity Brokers, Dealers, Exchanges & Services
6300	Insurance Including Insurance Carriers Of All Types
6400	Insurance Agents, Brokers & Service
6500	Real Estate Including Cemeteries
6600	Any Combination of Real Estate, Insurance, Loans & Law Offices
6710	Holding Offices Which Hold Or Own Securities For The Purpose Of Exercising Some Degree Of Control Over Companies
6720	Investment Offices
6730	Trusts Consisting Of Establishments Primarily Engaged In The Management Of The Funds Of Individual Trusts & Foundations
6790	Investors Such As Oil Royalty Traders, Patent Owners & Investment Clubs

DIVISION I. SERVICES

7000	Hotels, Rooming Houses, Camps & Other Lodging Places
7210	Laundry, Cleaning & Garment Services
7220	Photographic Studios (Portrait)
7230	Beauty Shops & Barber Shops
7250	Shoe Repair, Shoe Shine & Hat Cleaning Shops
7260	Funeral Service & Crematories
7290	Personal Services
7310	Advertising
7320	Credit Reporting, Mercantile Reporting & Adjustment & Collection Agencies
7330	Mailing, Reproduction, Commercial Art & Photography & Stenographic Services
7340	Services to Dwellings & Other Buildings
7350	News Syndicates
7360	Personnel Supply Services
7370	Computer & Data Processing Services
7510	Automobile Rental & Leasing
7520	Automobile Parking
7530	Auto Repair Shops
7540	Automotive Services, except Repair
7620	Electrical Repair Shops
7630	Watch, Clock & Jewelry Repair
7640	Reupholstery & Furniture Repair
7690	Repair Shops Not Otherwise Listed Above
7810	Motion Picture Production & Distribution & Allied Services
7830	Motion Picture Theaters
7910	Dance Halls, Studios & Schools
7920	Theatrical Producers
7930	Bowling Alleys & Billiard & Pool Establishments
7940	Commercial Sports
7990	Amusement & Recreation Services Not Otherwise Listed Above
8010	Offices Of Licensed Physicians
8020	Offices Of Licensed Dentists
8030	Offices of Licensed Osteopathic Physicians
8040	Offices of Other Health Practitioners
8050	Nursing & Personal Care Facilities
8060	Hospitals
8070	Medical & Dental Laboratories
8080	Outpatient Care Facilities
8090	Health & Allied Services Not Otherwise Listed Above
8100	Legal Services
8200	Educational Services Such As Libraries, Schools, Including Nondegree Granting Schools, Except Dancing Schools
8320	Individual & Family Social Services
8330	Job Training & Related Social Services
8350	Child Day Care Services
8360	Residential Care
8380	Senior Citizens Associations
8390	Social Services Not Otherwise Listed Above
8400	Museums, Botanical & Zoological Gardens
8610	Business Associations
8620	Professional Associations
8630	Labor Organizations
8640	Civic & Social Associations
8650	Political Organizations
8660	Religious Organizations
8680	Farm Granges
8910	Engineering & Architectural Services
8920	Noncommercial Research Organizations
8930	Accounting, Auditing & Bookkeeping
8990	Services Not Otherwise Listed Such As Lecturers, Authors, & Artists
0000	Not Yet Organized Or Inactive

LIST OF TRADEMARK FORMS

Form Number	Title
4.1 (individual)	Trademark Application, Principal Register with, Oath
4.1a (individual)	Trademark Application, Principal Register, with Declaration
4.2	Power of Attorney at Law
4.4	Designation of Domestic Representative
4.5 (partnership)	Trademark Application, Principal Register, with Oath
4.5a (partnership)	Trademark Application, Principal Register, with Declaration
4.6 (corporation)	Trademark Application, Principal Register, with Oath
4.6a (corporation)	Trademark Application, Principal Register, with Declaration
4.7 (individual)	Service Mark Application, Principal Register, with Oath
4.7a (individual)	Service Mark Application, Principal Register with Declaration
4.7 (partnership)	Service Mark Application, Principal Register, with Oath
4.7a (partnership)	Service Mark Application, Principal Register, with Declaration
4.7 (corporation)	Service Mark Application, Principal Register, with Oath
4.7a (corporation)	Service Mark Application, Principal Register, with Declaration
4.8 (corporation)	Collective Trademark or Collective Service Mark Application, Principal Register, with Oath
4.8a (corporation)	Collective Trademark or Collective Service Mark Application, Principal Register, with Declaration
4.8(A) (corporation)	Collective Membership Mark Application, Principal Register, with Oath
4.8(A)a (corporation)	Collective Membership Mark Application, Principal Register, with Declaration
4.9 (individual)	Certification Mark Application, Principal Register, with Oath
4.9a (individual)	Certification Mark Application, Principal Register, with Declaration
4.9 (partnership)	Certification Mark Application, Principal Register, with Oath
4.9a (partnership)	Certification Mark Application, Principal Register, with Declaration
4.9 (corporation)	Certification Mark Application, Principal Register, with Oath

Form Number	Title
4.9a (corporation)	Certification Mark Application, Principal Register, with Declaration
4.10 (individual)	Trademark or Service Mark Application Based on Concurrent Use, Principal Register, with Oath
4.10a (individual)	Trademark or Service Mark Application Based on Concurrent Use, Principal Register with Declaration
4.10 (partnership)	Trademark or Service Mark Application Based on Concurrent Use, Principal Register, with Oath
4.10a (partnership)	Trademark or Service Mark Application Based on Concurrent Use, Principal Register, with Declaration
4.10 (corporation)	Trademark or Service Mark Application Based on Concurrent Use, Principal Register, with Oath
4.10a (corporation)	Trademark or Service Mark Application Based on Concurrent Use, Principal Register, with Declaration
4.11 (individual)	Trademark Application, Supplemental Register, with Oath
4.11a (individual)	Trademark Application, Supplemental Register, with Declaration
4.11 (partnership)	Trademark Application, Supplemental Register, with Oath
4.11a (partnership)	Trademark Application, Supplemental Register, with Declaration
4.11 (corporation)	Trademark Application, Supplemental Register, with Oath
4.11a (corporation)	Trademark Application, Supplemental Register, with Declaration
4.11 (individual)	Service Mark Application, Supplemental Register, with Oath
4.11a (individual)	Service Mark Application, Supplemental Register, with Declaration
4.11 (partnership)	Service Mark Application, Supplemental Register, with Oath
4.11a (partnership)	Service Mark Application, Supplemental Register, with Declaration
4.11 (corporation)	Service Mark Application, Supplemental Register, with Oath
4.11a (corporation)	Service Mark Application, Supplemental Register, with Declaration
4.11 (corporation)	Collective Trademark or Collective Service Mark Application, Supplemental Register, with Oath
4.11a (corporation)	Collective Trademark of Collective Service Mark Application, Supplemental Register, with Declaration

Form Number	Title
4.11 (corporation)	Collective Membership Mark Application, Supplemental Register, with Oath
4.11a (corporation)	Collective Membership Mark Application, Supplemental Register, with Declaration
4.11 (individual)	Certification Mark Application, Supplemental Register, with Oath
4.11a (individual)	Certification Mark Application, Supplemental Register, with Declaration
4.11 (partnership)	Certification Mark Application, Supplemental Register, with Oath
4.11a (partnership)	Certification Mark Application, Supplemental Register, with Declaration
4.11 (corporation)	Certification Mark Application, Supplemental Register, with Oath
4.11a (corporation)	Certification Mark Application, Supplemental Register, with Declaration
4.13	Application for Renewal of Registration of a Mark, with Oath
4.13a	Application for Renewal of Registration of a Mark, with Declaration
4.14	Affidavit for Publication of a Mark under Section 12(c), with Oath
4.14a	"Affidavit" for Publication of a Mark under Section 12(c), with Declaration
4.15	Affidavit of Use of a Mark Required by Section 8, with Oath
4.15a	"Affidavit" of Use of a Mark Required by Section 8, with Declaration
4.16	Affidavit of Incontestability of a Mark under Section 15, with Oath
4.16a	"Affidavit" of Incontestability of a Mark under Section 15, with Declaration
4.16(A)	Combined Affidavit of Use and Incontestability of a Mark under Sections 8 and 15, with Oath
4.16(A)a	Combined "Affidavit" of Use and Incontestability of a Mark under Sections 8 and 15, with Declaration
4.17	Opposition to the Registration of a Mark, with Oath
4.17a	Opposition to the Registration of a Mark, with Declaration
4.18	Petition to Cancel a Registration of a Mark, with Oath

Form Number	Title
4.18a	Petition to Cancel a Registration of a Mark, with Declaration
4.19	Ex Parte Appeal from Examiner of Trademarks to Trademark Trial and Appeal Board
4.21	Assignment of Application for Registration of a Mark
4.22	Assignment of Registration of a Mark
4.23	Certificate of Mailing under Rule 1.8(a)

PREVENTION OF UNFAIR FOREIGN COMPETITION IN THE U.S.

Trademarks registered in the U.S. Patent and Trademark Office can be protected by the U.S. Customs Service against the importation of articles bearing marks that are deceptively similar or that are counterfeits.

If the trademark owner is a U.S. citizen or corporation, the owner can file a copy of the certificate of registration with the Treasury Department to prevent unfair competition. Thereafter, merchandise with confusingly similar or counterfeit marks will be denied entry into the United States. The only way the importer can then bring the goods into the country is if the mark is removed from all merchandise or a written consent is obtained from the legal trademark owner.

Importing goods with the intent to infringe on a registered U.S. trademark is common practice and big business. Certain countries in particular are known for this sort of activity. The U.S. Customs Service will prohibit the importation of foreign-made goods of this nature if the mark has been recorded with that department. To secure this valuable protection under Section 526 of the Tariff Act of 1930 (Section 1526, Title 19, U.S. Code), send the following items to the Commissioner of Customs, Washington, D.C.:

1. A letter requesting the service.
2. A $190 fee for each class of goods to be covered or for each mark.
3. A certified copy of the certificate of registration from the Patent and Trademark Office, or the Copyright Office in the case of copyrighted goods.
4. One thousand copies of the trademark or of pertinent information concerning the copyrighted work (such as the title page).

UNITED STATES TRADEMARK ASSOCIATION

The United States Trademark Association is a national nonprofit association with over 1,700 members worldwide. The organization boasts a membership roster that includes trademark and service mark owners, trade name owners, marketing and law firms, advertising and public relation concerns, graphic designers, professional associations, and trademark agencies.

The United States Trademark Association was founded in 1878 in New York City and has been a prominent influence in the development of trademark legislation ever since, including the Federal Trademark Act of 1946. It promotes the trademark system, influences public policy, and educates business people, the public, and the media on the importance and proper use of trademarks. Large and small companies unite under the umbrella of the USTA to express their concerns and interests to trademark owners everywhere.

Members are kept abreast of trademark news through several USTA publications and a series of books intended to educate readers. Periodicals include *The Trademark Reporter*, a bimonthly law journal; the *Bulletin Service* provides over 50 updates per year; *The Executive Letter* is published with business and marketing professionals in mind; and the *Annual Membership Roster* is the USTA membership directory.

Books include *Trademark Management, The Trademark Law Handbook, Protection of Corporate Names, The Paralegal Handbook,* and *Handbook for the Executive as a Witness.* Informational pamphlets available in quantity are *Guide to the Care of Trademarks* and *When ® Should and Should Not Be Used.*

For more information, contact:

DIRECTOR OF MEMBERSHIP SERVICES
The United States Trademark Association
6 East 45th St.
New York, NY 10017
(212) 986-5880
Fax: 212-986-5880
Telex: 192818002 USTA

TRADEMARK DEFINITIONS

The following terms have been defined by the Lanham-Trademark Act.

applicant and registrant   The legal representatives, successors, and assigns of such persons.

certification mark   A mark used upon or in connection with the products or services of one or more persons—other than the owner of the mark—to certify a regional or other origin, material, mode of manufacture, quality, accuracy, or other characteristic(s) of such goods or services, or that the work or labor on the goods or services was performed by members of a union or other organization.

collective mark   A trademark or service mark used by the members of a cooperative, an association, or some other collective group or organization; includes marks used to indicate membership in a union, an association, or some other organization.

commerce   All commerce that can lawfully be regulated by Congress.

Commissioner   The Commissioner of Patents.

juristic person   A firm, corporation, union, association, or other organization capable of suing and of being sued in a court of law.

mark   Any trademark, service mark, collective mark, or certification mark entitled to registration under the Act, whether registered or not.

person   This includes any other word or term used to designate the applicant or other entitled to benefits or privileges, or who is rendered liable under the provisions of this Act; includes a juristic person as a natural person.

Principal Register   The register provided for by sections 1 through 22 of the Act.

related company   Any person who legitimately controls or is controlled by the registrant or applicant for registration in respect to the nature and quality of the goods or services in connection with which the mark is used.

service mark   A mark used in the sale or advertising of services to identify the services of one person and to distinguish them from the services of others; includes, without limitation, the marks, names, symbols, titles, designations, slogans, character names, and distinctive features of radio or other advertising used in commerce.

Supplemental Register   Refers to the register provided for by sections 23 through 28 of the Act.

trademark   Any word, name, symbol, or device, or any combination thereof, that is adopted and used by manufacturer or merchant to identify his goods and to distinguish them from those manufactured or sold by others.

trade name and commercial name   Individual names and surnames, firm names, and trade names used by manufacturers, industrialists, merchants, agriculturists, and others to identify their businesses, vocations, or occupations; the names or titles lawfully adopted and used by persons, firms, associations, corporations, companies, unions, and any manufacturing, industrial, commercial agricultural, or other organizations in trade or commerce and capable of suing and of being sued in a court of law.

STATE TRADEMARK APPLICATIONS

To secure trademark protection, an application to register the mark or name must be satisfactorily completed and filed with the Secretary of State, along with specimens, possibly a drawing, and the appropriate filing or registration fee.

Each application contains a set of questions requiring the applicant to furnish appropriate answers. Complete all spaces provided on the form(s) and type in black ink. Properly completing the application will prevent unnecessary delays.

Remember, the mark or name must be in use prior to the time of registration. Let's take a "dry run" through this application.

1. *Applicant.* The full legal name of the person filing the application for registration of a trademark, service mark, or trade name, or the legal representative.

2. *Applicant's address.* The applicant's mailing address. It doesn't have to be within the state of registration; however, some states might require a process agent in the state of registration.

3. *If incorporated, state of incorporation.* Explanatory enough, except that if an incorporated business of one state wished to file a trademark, service mark, or trade name in another state, it may be required to "qualify" in that state prior to registration. If the state considers the corporation to be "doing business" there as a result of registering a trademark, the corporation is then required to "qualify." It is beneficial for the corporation to qualify, anyway, if it plans to conduct business in that state. A complete discussion of incorporating and doing business in all 50 states can be found in another book by the author entitled *HOW TO INCORPORATE YOUR BUSINESS IN ANY STATE*, from Liberty House Books.

4. *Type of business.* An easy way to describe a business is to utilize the Standard Industrial Classification Code. Just choose the SIC Code that best describes your business. The complete code is included in this section.

5. *Name, title or designation to be registered.* The words incorporated in the trademark, service mark, or trade name.

6. *Description of the goods or services in connection with the mark.* A brief description in the applicant's own words that best describes the goods or services to be registered.

7. *Classification—number and title.* Refer to the International Classification List in this part and choose the most appropriate category that best describes your goods or services. Limit your selection to one classification, unless you wish the mark to be protected in other categories as well. Most states require additional fees to be paid for each new classification, and some require each category to be filed on a separate application. Refer to the "State Trademark Data" section or the state application form for clarification.

8. *Description of mark.* Be specific and brief. Include colors, shape, type styles, designs, etc. Cover all elements that characterize the mark's uniqueness.

9. *Specimens or facsimiless of mark.* Each state requires a different number of specimens to be submitted with the application. Some states are very specific about the size of the specimens. Other states won't accept certain types of specimens. Don't glue or tape specimens to the application; use only staples or paperclips. Drawings are generally preferred in black ink on crisp white paper. India ink or white bristol board is recommended.

10. *How will the mark be used?* Will the mark be used on labels, packaging, containers, etc? Specify all intended uses.

11. *Date of first use.* All states request the date the mark was first used in the state where registration is sought, and most want to know when it was first used elsewhere.

12. *How is the trademark affixed to products, containers, etc.?* Is it printed on the package, is it a label that is affixed to the package, or is some other method used?

13. *Is the trademark also registered with the U.S. Patent and Trademark Office?* If so, give the date.

14. *Has the trademark been previously registered?* Give the complete name and address of the previous registered owner, if any.

15. *Name(s) of partners.* If the business is a partnership, furnish the names and addresses of each partner.

16. *Filing/Registration fee.* Be sure to include the correct filing fee along with specimens, drawings, and the application. Refer to the "State Trademark Data" section for appropriate filing fees.

17. *Notarization.* Most states require the application to be notarized. The applicant must sign the form on his behalf, as a legal representative or as an officer of a corporation. Specify your corporate title. An attorney can represent the applicant, but the latter should have a power of attorney form to avoid unnecessary delays.

STATE TRADEMARK ACTS

Each state has its own trademark laws that govern the application, registration, and use of various types of marks and names. Although there are variations between states, most have similar acts and registration procedures.

Trade names aren't necessarily covered by trademark acts. Many states don't have specific legislation regarding them and therefore don't accept trade name registration at the state level. In general, however, if a trade name is used as a trademark, it can be registered as a trademark. Otherwise, the only alternative is to file a fictitious or assumed name in the county where the business or individual is located.

States that do accept trade name registration don't allow the use of certain words in the name, such as "company," "incorporated," "corporation," or abbreviations of these words, since a trade name isn't a business or legal entity, but rather a brand name for use in trade.

Upon request, a Secretary of State will furnish a copy of the state's trademark act; it can also be located in a law library or universary library. The Secretary can also furnish appropriate registration applications and other pertinent information.

STATE TRADEMARK DATA

All information in this section applies to trademarks, service marks, and trade names unless otherwise indicated. The following abbreviations will be used throughout this section:

TM = Trademark
SM = Service mark
TN = Trade name

ALABAMA

1. Number of copies of application to be filed with Secretary of State:
   One

2. Filing fee and form of payment:
   TM/SM/TN—$30

3. Duration of trademark/service mark/trade name:
   TM/SM/TN—10 years

4. Trademark/service mark/trade name that must be filed with county instead of state, if any:

5. Number of specimens or fascimiles of mark required to be submitted with application (trademarks/service marks only):
   Three

6. Secretary of State's address for filing application:

   SECRETARY OF STATE
   Lands and Trademark Division
   Room 528
   State Office Building
   Montgomery, AL 36130-7701
   (205) 261-7200

7. Additional information:
   Trade name is only registrable when used as a trademark or service mark.
   One classification only.

ALASKA

1. Number of copies of application to be filed with Secretary of State:
   One application for TM/SM
   Two applications for TN

2. Filing fee and form of payment:
   TM/SM—$10
   TN—$25

3. Duration of trademark/service mark/trade name:
   TM/SM—10 years
   TN—5 years

4. Trademark/service mark/trade name that must be filed with county instead of state, if any:

5. Number of specimens of fascimiles of mark required to be submitted with application (trademarks/service marks only):
   Three; not to exceed 5″ × 8″

6. Secretary of State's address for filing application:
   DEPARTMENT OF COMMERCE AND ECONOMIC DEVELOPMENT
   Corporation Section
   P.O. Box D
   Juneau, AK 99811
   (907) 465-2530

7. Additional information:
   One classification only.

ARIZONA

1. Number of copies of application to be filed with Secretary of State:
   One

2. Filing fee and form of payment:
   TM/SM—$15
   TN—$10

3. Duration of trademark/service mark/trade name:
   TM/SM—10 years
   TN—5 years

4. Trademark/service mark/trade name that must be filed with county instead of state, if any:

5. Number of specimens or fascimiles of mark required to be submitted with application (trademarks/service marks only):
   Three

6. Secretary of State's address for filing application:
   SECRETARY OF STATE
   Capitol West Wing
   Phoenix, AZ 85007
   (602) 255-4285

7. Additional information:
   One classification only.

ARKANSAS

1. Number of copies of application to be filed with Secretary of State:
   Two

2. Filing fee and form of payment:
   TM/SM—$20 per classification

3. Duration of trademark/service mark/trade name:
   TM/SM—10 years

4. Trademark/service mark/trade name that must be filed with county instead of state, if any:
   Trade name

5. Number of specimens or fascimiles of mark required to be submitted with application (trademarks/service marks only):
   Three

6. Secretary of State's address for filing application:

   SECRETARY OF STATE
   State Capitol
   Little Rock, AR 72201-1094

7. Additional information:
   A single application may include any and all goods and/or services for which the mark is actually used.

CALIFORNIA

1. Number of copies of application to be filed with Secretary of State:
   One

2. Filing fee and form of payment:
   TM/SM—$10

3. Duration of trademark/service mark/trade name:
   NA

4. Trademark/service mark/trade name that must be filed with county instead of state, if any:

5. Number of specimens or fascimiles of mark required to be submitted with application (trademarks/service marks only):
   Five

6. Secretary of State's address for filing application:

   SECRETARY OF STATE
   1230 "J" St.
   Suite 100
   Sacramento, CA 95814
   (916) 445-9872

7. Additional information:
   Do not write the classification number on the application; leave it blank. The Secretary of State's office will complete the "Office Use Only" box.

COLORADO

1. Number of copies of application to be filed with Secretary of State:
   One

2. Filing fee and form of payment:
   TM/SM—$11

3. Duration of trademark/service mark/trade name:
   10 years

4. Trademark/service mark/trade name that must be filed with county instead of state, if any:

5. Number of specimens or fascimiles of mark required to be submitted with application (trademarks/service marks only):
   Three

6. Secretary of State's address for filing application:

   SECRETARY OF STATE
   Corporation Office
   1575 Sherman Street, 2nd Floor
   Denver, CO 80203

7. Additional information:
   The trade name is filed as a trademark.

CONNECTICUT

1. Number of copies of application to be filed with Secretary of State:
   Two

2. Filing fee and form of payment:
   TM/SM—$25 per application

3. Duration of trademark/service mark/trade name:
   TM/SM—10 years

4. Trademark/service mark/trade name that must be filed with county instead of state, if any:

5. Number of specimens or fascimiles of mark required to be submitted with application (trademarks/service marks only):
   Four; not to exceed 3″ × 5″.

6. Secretary of State's address for filing application:

    SECRETARY OF STATE
    30 Trinity St.
    Hartford, CT 06106
    Attn.: Trademarks

7. Additional information:
    One classification only.

DELAWARE

1. Number of copies of application to be filed with Secretary of State:
    One

2. Filing fee and form of payment:
    TM/SM/TN—$25 per application

3. Duration of trademark/service mark/trade name:
    TM/SM/TN—10 years

4. Trademark/service mark/trade name that must be filed with county instead of state, if any:

5. Number of specimens or facsimiles of mark required to be submitted with application (trademarks/service marks only):
    Two

6. Secretary of State's address for filing application:

    DEPARTMENT OF STATE
    Division of Corporations
    Townsend Building
    P.O. Box 898
    Dover, DE 19903

7. Additional information:
    N/A

FLORIDA

1. Number of copies of application to be filed with Secretary of State:
    Two

2. Filing fee and form of payment:
    TM/SM—$15

3. Duration of trademark/service mark/trade name:
    TM/SM—10 years

4. Trademark/service mark/trade name that must be filed with county instead of state, if any:
    Trade name must be filed as a fictitious name in the circuit court in the county where the business or individual is located.

5. Number of specimens or fascimiles of mark required to be submitted with application (trademarks/service marks only):
   Three

6. Secretary of State's address for filing application:
   DIVISION OF CORPORATIONS, TRADEMARK SECTION
   P.O. Box 6327
   Tallahassee, FL 32314

7. Additional information:
   More than one classification can be listed on the application; if applicable, however, the filing fee is required for each classification.

GEORGIA

1. Number of copies of application to be filed with Secretary of State:
   One

2. Filing fee and form of payment:
   TM/SM—$5

3. Duration of trademark/service mark/trade name:
   TM/SM—10 years

4. Trademark/service mark/trade name that must be filed with county instead of state, if any:

5. Number of specimens or fascimiles of mark required to be submitted with application (trademarks/service marks only):
   Three

6. Secretary of State's address for filing application:
   SECRETARY OF STATE
   306 West Tower
   #2 Martin Luther King, Jr. Drive
   Atlanta, GA 30334
   (404) 656-2861

7. Additional information:
   One classification only.

HAWAII

1. Number of copies of application to be filed with Secretary of State:
   Two

2. Filing fee and form of payment:
   TM/SM/TN—$25

3. Duration of trademark/service mark/trade name:
   One year, when renewed, it becomes valid for 10 years

4. Trademark/service mark/trade name that must be filed with county instead of state, if any:

5. Number of specimens or fascimiles of mark required to be submitted with application (trademarks/service marks only):
    Three

6. Secretary of State's address for filing application:
    DEPARTMENT OF COMMERCE AND CONSUMER AFFAIRS
    Business Registration Division
    1010 Richards St.
    P.O. Box 40
    Honolulu, HI 96810

7. Additional information:
    N/A

IDAHO

1. Number of copies of application to be filed with Secretary of State:
    One

2. Filing fee and form of payment:
    TM/SM—$20

3. Duration of trademark/service mark/trade name:
    TM/SM—10 years

4. Trademark/service mark/trade name that must be filed with county instead of state, if any:
    Trade name

5. Number of specimens or fascimiles of mark required to be submitted with application (trademarks/service marks only):
    Three; not to exceed $8^1/2'' \times 11''$ or smaller than $1'' \times 2''$

6. Secretary of State's address for filing application:
    SECRETARY OF STATE
    Room 203, State House
    Boise, ID 83720

7. Additional information:
    One classification only.

ILLINOIS

1. Number of copies of application to be filed with Secretary of State:
    One

2. Filing fee and form of payment:
    TM/SM/TN—$10

3. Duration of trademark/service mark/trade name:
   TM/SM/TN—10 years

4. Trademark/service mark/trade name that must be filed with county instead of state, if any:

5. Number of specimens or fascimiles of mark required to be submitted with application (trademarks/service marks only):
   Three; not to exceed 3″ × 3″

6. Secretary of State's address for filing application:
   SECRETARY OF STATE
   Index Dept.
   Springfield, IL 62756
   (217) 782-7017

7. Additional information:
   Each classification requires a separate application, a set of specimens, and a fee.

INDIANA

1. Number of copies of application to be filed with Secretary of State:
   One

2. Filing fee and form of payment:
   TM/SM—$10

3. Duration of trademark/service mark/trade name:
   TM/SM—10 years

4. Trademark/service mark/trade name that must be filed with county instead of state, if any:
   Trade names are filed in the County Recorder's office in the county where the business or individual is located.

5. Number of specimens or fascimiles of mark required to be submitted with application (trademarks/service marks only):
   Three

6. Secretary of State's address for filing application:
   SECRETARY OF STATE
   Trademark Clerk
   Room 155, State House
   Indianapolis, IN 46204
   (317) 232-6540

7. Additional information:
   One classification only.

IOWA

1. Number of copies of application to be filed with Secretary of State:
   Two originals

2. Filing fee and form of payment:
   TM/SM—$10

3. Duration of trademark/service mark/trade name:
   TM/SM—10 years

4. Trademark/service mark/trade name that must be filed with county instead of state, if any:

5. Number of specimens or facsimiles of mark required to be submitted with application (trademarks/service marks only):
   One

6. Secretary of State's address for filing application:

   SECRETARY OF STATE
   Hoover Building
   Des Moines, IA 50319
   (515) 281-8367

7. Additional information:
   Trade names are not filed with the Secretary of State. Only one classification per application.

KANSAS

1. Number of copies of application to be filed with Secretary of State:
   One

2. Filing fee and form of payment:
   TM/SM—$25
   No provisions for trade names; however, a business name can qualify for registration as a service mark

3. Duration of trademark/service mark/trade name:
   TM/SM—10 years

4. Trademark/service mark/trade name that must be filed with county instead of state, if any:

5. Number of specimens or facsimiles of mark required to be submitted with application (trademarks/service marks only):
   Three

6. Secretary of State's address for filing application:
   SECRETARY OF STATE
   2nd Floor,State Capitol
   Topeka, KS 66612-1594

7. Additional information:
   One classification only.

KENTUCKY

1. Number of copies of application to be filed with Secretary of State:
   One copy for the Secretary of State and one copy for each county where the business conducts business.

2. Filing fee and form of payment:
   TM/SM—$10
   TN—$20

3. Duration of trademark/service mark/trade name:
   TM/SM/TN—10 years

4. Trademark/service mark/trade name that must be filed with county instead of state, if any:

5. Number of specimens or facsimiles of mark required to be submitted with application (trademarks/service marks only):
   Three

6. Secretary of State's address for filing application:
   SECRETARY OF STATE
   Frankfort, KY 40601-3493

7. Additional information:
   The trade name is filed as an "assumed name." Make your check payable to the "Kentucky State Treasurer."

LOUISIANA

1. Number of copies of application to be filed with Secretary of State:
   One original

2. Filing fee and form of payment:
   TM/SM/TN—$50

3. Duration of trademark/service mark/trade name:
   N/A

4. Trademark/service mark/trade name that must be filed with county instead of state, if any:

5. Number of specimens or fascimiles of mark required to be submitted with application (trademarks/service marks only):
   Three

6. Secretary of State's address for filing application:
   SECRETARY OF STATE
   Corporation Division
   P.O. Box 94125
   Baton Rouge, LA 70804-9125
   (504) 925-4698

7. Additional information:
   Each classification requires an additional $50 registration fee. TM/SM/TN reservations are accepted for 60 days for a $20 fee.

MAINE

1. Number of copies of application to be filed with Secretary of State:
   One

2. Filing fee and form of payment:
   TM/SM—$25

3. Duration of trademark/service mark/trade name:
   TM/SM—10 years

4. Trademark/service mark/trade name that must be filed with county instead of state, if any:

5. Number of specimens or fascimiles of mark required to be submitted with application (trademarks/service marks only):
   Three; not to exceed $8^1/2''$ × 11″ or smaller than 2″square

6. Secretary of State's address for filing application:
   SECRETARY OF STATE
   State House Station 101
   Augusta, ME 04333

7. Additional information:
   Each classification requires an additional $25 registration fee.

MARYLAND

1. Number of copies of application to be filed with Secretary of State:
   One

2. Filing fee and form of payment:
   TM/SM—$10

3. Duration of trademark/service mark/trade name:
   TM/SM—10 years

4. Trademark/service mark/trade name that must be filed with county instead of state, if any:

    Trade name—$10 plus $1 per name

5. Number of specimens or fascimiles of mark required to be submitted with application (trademarks/service marks only):

    Three

6. Secretary of State's address for filing application:

    SECRETARY OF STATE
    Trademark Division Executive Dept.
    State House
    Annapolis, MD 21404
    (301) 269-2844

7. Additional information:

    One classification only. Request *Filing a Trade Name in Maryland* for additional information. It's available from:

    STATE DEPT. OF ASSESSMENTS AND TAXATION
    Corporate Charter Division
    301 W. Preston St.
    Baltimore, MD 21201
    (301) 225-1340

MASSACHUSETTS

1. Number of copies of application to be filed with Secretary of State:

    Two

2. Filing fee and form of payment:

    TM/SM—$35

3. Duration of trademark/service mark/trade name:

    TM/SM—10 years

4. Trademark/service mark/trade name that must be filed with county instead of state, if any:

    Trade names are filed with the town or city hall where the business is located.

5. Number of specimens or fascimiles of mark required to be submitted with application (trademarks/service marks only):

    Three; no larger than 3" × 3"

6. Secretary of State's address for filing application:
   OFFICE OF THE SECRETARY OF STATE
   Trademark Division
   Room 1711
   One Ashburton Place
   Boston, MA 02108
   (617) 727-8329

7. Additional information:
   One classification only.

MICHIGAN

1. Number of copies of application to be filed with Secretary of State:
   One

2. Filing fee and form of payment:
   TM/SM—$50

3. Duration of trademark/service mark/trade name:
   TM/SM—10 years

4. Trademark/service mark/trade name that must be filed with county instead of state, if any:

5. Number of specimens or facsimiles of mark required to be submitted with application (trademarks/service marks only):
   Two

6. Secretary of State's address for filing application:
   DEPARTMENT OF COMMERCE
   Corporation and Securities Bureau, Corporation Division
   P.O. Box 30054
   Lansing, MI 48909
   (517) 334-6302

7. Additional information:
   One classification only.

MINNESOTA

1. Number of copies of application to be filed with Secretary of State:
   One

2. Filing fee and form of payment:
   TM/SM—$25
   TN—$15

3. Duration of trademark/service mark/trade name:
   TM/SM/TN—10 years

4. Trademark/service mark/trade name that must be filed with county instead of state, if any:

5. Number of specimens or fascimiles of mark required to be submitted with application (trademarks/service marks only):
   Three

6. Secretary of State's address for filing application:
   SECRETARY OF STATE
   180 State Office Building
   St. Paul, MN 55155
   Attn.: Trademarks
   (612) 296-2803

7. Additional information:
   One classification only per application.

MISSISSIPPI

1. Number of copies of application to be filed with Secretary of State:
   One

2. Filing fee and form of payment:
   TM/SM—$25 (Mississippi residents only)
   TM/SM—$35 (non-Mississippi residents)

3. Duration of trademark/service mark/trade name:
   10 years

4. Trademark/service mark/trade name that must be filed with county instead of state, if any:

5. Number of specimens or fascimiles of mark required to be submitted with application (trademarks/service marks only):
   Three

6. Secretary of State's address for filing application:
   SECRETARY OF STATE
   401 Mississippi St.
   P.O. Box 136
   Jackson, MS 39205

7. Additional information:
   One classification only.

MISSOURI

1. Number of copies of application to be filed with Secretary of State:
   Two

2. Filing fee and form of payment:
   TM/SM—$15

3. Duration of trademark/service mark/trade name:
   TM/SM/TN—10 years

4. Trademark/service mark/trade name that must be filed with county instead of state, if any:

5. Number of specimens or fascimiles of mark required to be submitted with application (trademarks/service marks only):
   Three

6. Secretary of State's address for filing application:
   SECRETARY OF STATE
   Jefferson City, MO 65102

7. Additional information:
   One classification only.

MONTANA

1. Number of copies of application to be filed with Secretary of State:
   Two

2. Filing fee and form of payment:
   TM/SM—$20
   TN—$15

3. Duration of trademark/service mark/trade name:
   10 years

4. Trademark/service mark/trade name that must be filed with county instead of state, if any:

5. Number of specimens or fascimiles of mark required to be submitted with application (trademarks/service marks only):
   One

6. Secretary of State's address for filing application:
   SECRETARY OF STATE
   Montana State Capitol
   Helena, MT 59620
   (406) 444-3665

7. Additional information:
   One classification only.

NEBRASKA

1. Number of copies of application to be filed with Secretary of State:
   Two

2. Filing fee and form of payment:
   TM/SM/TN—$100

3. Duration of trademark/service mark/trade name:
   TM/SM/TN—10 years

4. Trademark/service mark/trade name that must be filed with county instead of state, if any:

5. Number of specimens or facsimiles of mark required to be submitted with application (trademarks/service marks only):
   Two

6. Secretary of State's address for filing application:

   SECRETARY OF STATE
   State Capitol Building
   Suite 2305
   Lincoln, NE 68509

7. Additional information:
   One classification only. Trademarks and service marks are registered on separate applications

NEVADA

1. Number of copies of application to be filed with Secretary of State:
   Two

2. Filing fee and form of payment:
   TM/SM/TN—$25

3. Duration of trademark/service mark/trade name:
   TM/SM/TN—10 years

4. Trademark/service mark/trade name that must be filed with county instead of state, if any:

5. Number of specimens or facsimiles of mark required to be submitted with application (trademarks/service marks only):
   Three

6. Secretary of State's address for filing application:

   SECRETARY OF STATE
   State Capitol Complex
   Carson City, NV 89710

7. Additional information:
   Each classification requires a separate application and fee.

NEW HAMPSHIRE

1. Number of copies of application to be filed with Secretary of State:
     One

2. Filing fee and form of payment:
     TM/SM—$20
     TN—$40

3. Duration of trademark/service mark/trade name:
     TM/SM/TN—10 years

4. Trademark/service mark/trade name that must be filed with county instead of state, if any:

5. Number of specimens or fascimiles of mark required to be submitted with application (trademarks/service marks only):
     Three

6. Secretary of State's address for filing application:

     DEPARTMENT OF STATE
     State House
     Concord, NH 03301

7. Additional information:
     One classification only.

NEW JERSEY

1. Number of copies of application to be filed with Secretary of State:
     Two

2. Filing fee and form of payment:
     TM/SM—$25

3. Duration of trademark/service mark/trade name:
     TM/SM—10 years

4. Trademark/service mark/trade name that must be filed with county instead of state, if any:
     Trade names are filed at the county level where the business is located.

5. Number of specimens or fascimiles of mark required to be submitted with application (trademarks/service marks only):
     Three

6. Secretary of State's address for filing application:

     SECRETARY OF STATE
     Trademark Section
     CN300
     State House
     Trenton, NJ 08625

7. Additional information:
   Include self-addressed stamped envelope with application, one classification only.

NEW MEXICO

1. Number of copies of application to be filed with Secretary of State:

2. Filing fee and form of payment:
   TN—$10 (State Corporation Commission)
   TM/SM/TN (Secretary of State)

3. Duration of trademark/service mark/trade name:
   N/A

4. Trademark/service mark/trade name that must be filed with county instead of state, if any:

5. Number of specimens or fascimiles of mark required to be submitted with application (trademarks/service marks only):

6. Secretary of State's address for filing application:

   SECRETARY OF STATE
   Legislative-Executive Building
   Room 400
   Sante Fe, NM 87503

7. Additional information:
   An Application for Trade Name Clearance must first be completed and returned to:

   STATE CORPORATION COMMISSION
   P.O. Drawer 1269
   Santa Fe, NM 87504-1269
   along with the $10 fee. Allow 10 days for the application to be processed. If the name is cleared and is available, a certificate will be returned that must then be forwarded to the Secretary of State along with their application and a $25 fee.

NEW YORK

1. Number of copies of application to be filed with Secretary of State:
   One

2. Filing fee and form of payment:
   TM/SM—$20

3. Duration of trademark/service mark/trade name:
   TM/SM—10 years

4. Trademark/service mark/trade name that must be filed with county instead of state, if any:

   Trade names are filed in the Office of the County Clerk where the business is located.

5. Number of specimens or fascimiles of mark required to be submitted with application (trademarks/service marks only):
   Four; not to exceed 5" × 8"

6. Secretary of State's address for filing application:

   DEPARTMENT OF STATE
   Misc. Records
   162 Washington Ave.
   Albany, NY 12231

7. Additional information:
   A separate application and fee must be submitted for each classification.

NORTH CAROLINA

1. Number of copies of application to be filed with Secretary of State:
   One

2. Filing fee and form of payment:
   TM/SM—$25

3. Duration of trademark/service mark/trade name:
   TM/SM—10 years

4. Trademark/service mark/trade name that must be filed with county instead of state, if any:

   Trade name

5. Number of specimens or fascimiles of mark required to be submitted with application (trademarks/service marks only):
   Three

6. Secretary of State's address for filing application:

   Trademark Specialist
   SECRETARY OF STATE
   300 N. Salisbury St.
   Room 302
   Raleigh, NC 27611
   (919) 733-4161

7. Additional information:
   One classification only per application.

NORTH DAKOTA

1. Number of copies of application to be filed with Secretary of State:
   One

2. Filing fee and form of payment:
   TM/SM—$20
   TN—$25

3. Duration of trademark/service mark/trade name:
   TM/SM—10 years
   TN—5 years

4. Trademark/service mark/trade name that must be filed with county instead of state, if any:

5. Number of specimens or fascimiles of mark required to be submitted with application (trademarks/service marks only):
   Three

6. Secretary of State's address for filing application:

   SECRETARY OF STATE
   Capitol Building
   Bismarck, ND 58505

7. Additional information:
   One classification only.

OHIO

1. Number of copies of application to be filed with Secretary of State:
   One

2. Filing fee and form of payment:
   TM/SM/TN—$20

3. Duration of trademark/service mark/trade name:
   TM/SM—10 years
   TN—5 years

4. Trademark/service mark/trade name that must be filed with county instead of state, if any:

5. Number of specimens or fascimiles of mark required to be submitted with application (trademarks/service marks only):
   One

6. Secretary of State's address for filing application:

> SECRETARY OF STATE
> 30 E. Broad St.
> 14th Floor
> Columbus, OH 43266-0418

7. Additional information:
   One classification only.

OKLAHOMA

1. Number of copies of application to be filed with Secretary of State:
   Two

2. Filing fee and form of payment:
   TM/SM—$25
   TN—$10

3. Duration of trademark/service mark/trade name:
   TM/SM/TN—10 years

4. Trademark/service mark/trade name that must be filed with county instead of state, if any:

5. Number of specimens or fascimiles of mark required to be submitted with application (trademarks/service marks only):
   One

6. Secretary of State's address for filing application:

> SECRETARY OF STATE
> 101 State Capitol
> Oklahoma City, OK 73105

7. Additional information:
   One classification only.

OREGON

1. Number of copies of application to be filed with Secretary of State:
   One

2. Filing fee and form of payment:
   TM/SM/TN—$10

3. Duration of trademark/service mark/trade name:
   TM/SM/TN—5 years

4. Trademark/service mark/trade name that must be filed with county instead of state, if any:

5. Number of specimens or fascimiles of mark required to be submitted with application (trademarks/service marks only):
   One

6.   Secretary of State's address for filing application:

   SECRETARY OF STATE
   Corporation Division
   Commerce Building
   158 12th St. NE
   Salem, OR 97310
   (503) 378-3478

7. Additional information:
   A TM or SM can be registered in all appropriate classes.

PENNSYLVANIA

1. Number of copies of application to be filed with Secretary of State:
   One

2. Filing fee and form of payment:
   TM/SM—$25;
   TN—corp./individual, $65; corporation, $40; individual, $25

3. Duration of trademark/service mark/trade name:
   TM/SM—10 years
   TN—N/A

4. Trademark/service mark/trade name that must be filed with county instead of state, if any:

5. Number of specimens or fascimiles of mark required to be submitted with application (trademarks/service marks only):
   One

6. Secretary of State's address for filing application:

   SECRETARY OF COMMONWEALTH
   Room 308
   North Office Building
   Harrisburg, PA 17120

7. Additional information:

   Trade name must be published in a local newspaper in the country where the business is located. One classification only.

RHODE ISLAND

1. Number of copies of application to be filed with Secretary of State:
   Two

2. Filing fee and form of payment:
   TM/SM—$25
   TN—$10

3. Duration of trademark/service mark/trade name:
   TM/SM—10 years

4. Trademark/service mark/trade name that must be filed with county instead of state, if any:

5. Number of specimens or fascimiles of mark required to be submitted with application (trademarks/service marks only):
   Three; not to exceed 3″ × 3″

6. Secretary of State's address for filing application:

   SECRETARY OF STATE
   State House
   Providence, RI 02903
   Attn.: Trademark Division

7. Additional information:
   One classification only.

SOUTH CAROLINA

1. Number of copies of application to be filed with Secretary of State:
   One

2. Filing fee and form of payment:
   TM/SM—$15

3. Duration of trademark/service mark/trade name:
   TM/SM—10 years

4. Trademark/service mark/trade name that must be filed with county instead of state, if any:
   Trade name

5. Number of specimens or fascimiles of mark required to be submitted with application (trademarks/service marks only):
   Three

6. Secretary of State's address for filing application:

   SECRETARY OF STATE
   P.O. Box 11350
   Columbia, SC 29211

7. Additional information:
   One classification only per application.

SOUTH DAKOTA

1. Number of copies of application to be filed with Secretary of State:
   One

2. Filing fee and form of payment:
   TM/SM/TN—$10

3. Duration of trademark/service mark/trade name:
   TM/SM/TN—10 years

4. Trademark/service mark/trade name that must be filed with county instead of state, if any:

5. Number of specimens or fascimiles of mark required to be submitted with application (trademarks/service marks only):
   Three

6. Secretary of State's address for filing application:

   SECRETARY OF STATE
   State Capitol Building
   Pierre, SD 57501
   (605) 773-4845

7. Additional information:
   One classification only.

TENNESSEE

1. Number of copies of application to be filed with Secretary of State:
   One

2. Filing fee and form of payment:
   TM/SM/TN—$5

3. Duration of trademark/service mark/trade name:
   TM/SM/TN—10 years

4. Trademark/service mark/trade name that must be filed with county instead of state, if any:

5. Number of specimens or fascimiles of mark required to be submitted with application (trademarks/service marks only):
   Three

6. Secretary of State's address for filing application:

   DEPARTMENT OF STATE
   James K. Polk Building
   Nashville, TN 37219-5040

7. Additional information:
   One classification only.

TEXAS

1. Number of copies of application to be filed with Secretary of State:
   Two

2. Filing fee and form of payment:
   TM/SM—$25

3. Duration of trademark/service mark/trade name:
   TM/SM—10 years

4. Trademark/service mark/trade name that must be filed with county instead of state, if any:

5. Number of specimens or fascimiles of mark required to be submitted with application (trademarks/service marks only):
   Two

6. Secretary of State's address for filing application:

   SECRETARY OF STATE
   Statutory Filing Division, Corporation Section
   Attn.: Trademark Examiner
   P.O. Box 13697
   Austin, TX 78711

7. Additional information:
   Use state-furnished "drawing sheet" to illustrate trademark. One classification only.

UTAH

1. Number of copies of application to be filed with Secretary of State:
   One

2. Filing fee and form of payment:
   TM/SM—$20

3. Duration of trademark/service mark/trade name:
   TM/SM—10 years

4. Trademark/service mark/trade name that must be filed with county instead of state, if any:
   Trade name

5. Number of specimens or fascimiles of mark required to be submitted with application (trademarks/service marks only):
   Three; not to exceed $8^1/_2'' \times 11''$ or smaller than the size of a business card.

6. Secretary of State's address for filing application:

SECRETARY OF STATE
Division of Corporations and Commercial Code
160 E. 300 S.
Box 45801
Salt Lake City, UT 84145-0801
(801) 530-6006

7. Additional information:
Limit the description of the mark on line #3 of the application to 54 spaces as their computer cannot accommodate more. One classification only.

VERMONT

1. Number of copies of application to be filed with Secretary of State:
One original

2. Filing fee and form of payment:
TM/SM—$10
TN—$20

3. Duration of trademark/service mark/trade name:
TM/SM—10 years

4. Trademark/service mark/trade name that must be filed with county instead of state, if any:

5. Number of specimens or fascimiles of mark required to be submitted with application (trademarks/service marks only):
A facsimile, copy, or counterpart of the trademark in each class must accompany the application.

6. Secretary of State's address for filing application:

SECRETARY OF STATE
Pavilion Building
Montpelier, VT 05602
(802) 828-2386

7. Additional information:
Nonresidents must appoint a process agent. Trade name reservations are accepted for 120 days for a $10 fee.

VIRGINIA

1. Number of copies of application to be filed with Secretary of State:
One

2. Filing fee and form of payment:
TM/SM—$30

3. Duration of trademark/service mark/trade name:
   TM/SM—10 years

4. Trademark/service mark/trade name that must be filed with county instead of state, if any:

5. Number of specimens or facsimiles of mark required to be submitted with application (trademarks/service marks only):
   Three

6. Secretary of State's address for filing application:

   STATE CORPORATION COMMISSION
   Division of Securities and Retail Franchising
   P.O. Box 1197
   Richmond, VA 23209

7. Additional information:
   One classification only.

WASHINGTON

1. Number of copies of application to be filed with Secretary of State:
   Two

2. Filing fee and form of payment:
   TM/SM—$50; TN—$5

3. Duration of trademark/service mark/trade name:
   TM/SM—10 years

4. Trademark/service mark/trade name that must be filed with county instead of state, if any:

5. Number of specimens or facsimiles of mark required to be submitted with application (trademarks/service marks only):
   Three

6. Secretary of State's address for filing application:

   SECRETARY OF STATE
   Corporation Division
   2nd Floor
   Republic Building
   505 E. Union, MS: PM-21
   Olympia, WA 98504
   (Check payable to "Secretary of State")

7. Additional information:
   Send trade name application to: BUSINESS LICENSE SERVICES, Department of Licensing, Olympia, WA 98504 (Check payable to "State Treasurer").

WEST VIRGINIA

1. Number of copies of application to be filed with Secretary of State:
   Two

2. Filing fee and form of payment:
   TM/SM/TN—$5

3. Duration of trademark/service mark/trade name:
   Perpetual

4. Trademark/service mark/trade name that must be filed with county instead of state, if any:

5. Number of specimens or fascimiles of mark required to be submitted with application (trademarks/service marks only):
   Three

6. Secretary of State's address for filing application:

   SECRETARY OF STATE
   State Capitol
   Charleston, WV 25305

7. Additional information:
   N/A

WISCONSIN

1. Number of copies of application to be filed with Secretary of State:
   One

2. Filing fee and form of payment:
   TM/SM/TN—$15

3. Duration of trademark/service mark/trade name:
   TM/SM/TN—20 years

4. Trademark/service mark/trade name that must be filed with county instead of state, if any:

5. Number of specimens or fascimiles of mark required to be submitted with application (trademarks/service marks only):
   Two

6. Secretary of State's address for filing application:

   Secretary of State
   Trademark Records
   P.O. Box 7848
   Madison WI 53707
   (608) 266-5653

7. Additional information:
   One name or mark only per application.

WYOMING

1. Number of copies of application to be filed with Secretary of State:
   Two

2. Filing fee and form of payment:
   TM/SM/TN—$10

3. Duration of trademark/service mark/trade name:
   TM/SM—10 years

4. Trademark/service mark/trade name that must be filed with county instead of state, if any:

5. Number of specimens or facsimiles of mark required to be submitted with application (trademarks/service marks only):
   Three

6. Secretary of State's address for filing application:

   SECRETARY OF STATE
   Capitol Building
   Cheyenne, WY 82002
   (307) 777-7311

7. Additional information:
   Trade name reservations are accepted for 120 days for a $5 fee. One classification only.

International schedule of classes of goods and services

Goods

1   Chemicals products used in industry, science, photography, agriculture, horticulture, forestry; artificial and synthetic resins; plastics in the form of powders, liquids or pastes, for industrial use; manures (natural and artificial); fire extinguishing compositions; tempering substances and chemical preparations for soldering; chemical substances for preserving foodstuffs; tanning substances; adhesive substances used in industry.

2   Paints, varnishes, lacquers; preservatives against rust and against deterioration of wood; colouring matters, dyestuffs; mordants; natural resins; metals in foil and powder form for painters and decorators.

3   Bleaching preparations and other substances for laundry use; cleaning, polishing, scouring and abrasive preparations; soaps; perfumery, essential oils, cosmetics, hair lotions; dentifrices.

4   Industrial oils and greases (other than oils and fats and essential oils); lubricants; dust laying and absorbing compositions; fuels (including motor spirit) and illuminants; candles, tapers, night lights and wicks.

5   Pharmaceutical, veterinary, and sanitary substances; infants' and invalids' foods; plasters, material for bandaging; material for stopping teeth, dental wax, disinfectants; preparations for killing weeds and destroying vermin.

6   Unwrought and partly wrought common metals and their alloys; anchors, anvils, bells, rolled and cast building materials; rails and other metallic materials for railway tracks; chains (except driving chains for vehicles); cables and wires (nonelectric); locksmiths' work; metallic pipes and tubes; safes and cash boxes; steel balls; horseshoes; nails and screws; other goods in nonprecious metal not included in other classes; ores.

7   Machines and machine tools; motors (except for land vehicles); machine couplings and belting (except for land vehicles); large size agricultural implements; incubators.

8   Hand tools and instruments; cutlery, forks, and spoons; side arms.

9   Scientific, nautical, surveying and electrical apparatus and instruments (including wireless), photographic, cinematographic, optical, weighing, measuring, signalling, checking (supervision), life-saving and teaching apparatus and instruments; coin or counterfreed apparatus; talking machines; cash registers; calculating machines; fire extinguishing apparatus.

10   Surgical, medical, dental, and veterinary instruments and apparatus (including artificial limbs, eyes and teeth).

11   Installations for lighting, heating, steam generating, cooking, refrigerating, drying, ventilating, water supply, and sanitary purposes.

12   Vehicles; apparatus for locomotion by land, air or water.

13   Firearms; ammunition and projectiles; explosive substances; fireworks.

14   Precious metals and their alloys and goods in precious metals or coated therewith (except cutlery, forks and spoons); jewelry, precious stones, horological and other chronometric instruments.

15   Musical instruments (other than talking machines and wireless apparatus).

16   Paper and paper articles, cardboard and cardboard articles; printed matter, newspaper and periodicals, books; bookbinding material; photographs; stationery, adhesive materials (stationery); artists' materials; paint brushes; typewriters and office requisites (other than furniture); instructional and teaching material (other than apparatus); playing cards; printers' type and cliches (stereotype).

17   Gutta percha, india rubber, balata and substitutes, articles made from these substances and not included in other classes; plastics in the form of sheets, blocks and rods, being for use in manufacture; materials for packing, stopping or insulating; asbestos, mica and their products; hose pipes (nonmetallic).

18   Leather and imitations of leather, and articles made from these materials and not included in other classes; skins, hides; trunks and travelling bags; umbrellas, parasols and walking sticks; whips, harness and saddlery.

19   Building materials, natural and artificial stone, cement, lime, mortar, plaster and gravel; pipes of earthenware or cement; roadmaking materials; asphalt, pitch and bitumen; portable buildings; stone monuments; chimney pots.

20   Furniture, mirrors, picture frames; articles (not included in other classes) of wood, cork, reeds, cane, wicker, horn, bone, ivory, whalebone, shell, amber, mother-of-pearl, meerschaum, celluloid, substitutes for all these materials, or of plastics.

21   Small domestic utensils and containers (not of precious metals, or coated therewith); combs and sponges; brushes (other than paint brushes); brushmaking materials; instruments and material for cleaning purposes, steel wool; unworked or semi-worked glass (excluding glass used in building); glassware, porcelain and earthenware, not included in other classes.

22   Ropes, string, nets, tents, awnings, tarpaulins, sails, sacks; padding and stuffing materials (hair, kapok, feathers, seaweed, etc.); raw fibrous textile materials.

23   Yarns, threads.

24   Tissues (piece goods); bed and table covers; textile articles not included in other classes.

25   Clothing, including boots, shoes and slippers.

26   Lace and embroidery, ribands and braid; buttons, press buttons, hooks and eyes, pins and needles; artificial flowers.

27   Carpets, rugs, mats and matting; linoleums and other materials for covering existing floors; wall hangings (nontextile).

28   Games and playthings; gymnastic and sporting articles (except clothing); ornaments and decorations for Christmas trees.

29   Meats, fish, poultry and game; meat extracts; preserved, dried and cooked fruits and vegetables; jellies, jams; eggs, milk and other dairy products; edible oils and fats; preserves, pickles.

30   Coffee, tea, cocoa, sugar, rice, tapioca, sago, coffee substitutes; flour, and preparations made from cereals; bread, biscuits, cakes, pastry and confectionery, ices; honey, treacle; yeast, baking powder; salt, mustard, pepper, vinegar, sauces, spices; ice.

31   Agricultural, horticultural and forestry products and grains not included in other classes; living animals; fresh fruits and vegetables; seeds; live plants and flowers; foodstuffs for animals, malt.

32   Beer, ale and porter; mineral and aerated waters and other nonalcoholic drinks; syrups and other preparations for making beverages.

33   Wines, spirits and liqueurs.

34   Tobacco, raw or manufactured; smokers' articles; matches.

Services

35   Advertising and business.

36   Insurance and financial.

37   Construction and repair.

38   Communication.

39   Transportation and storage.

40   Material treatment.

41   Education and entertainment.

42   Miscellaneous.

TRADEMARK APPLICATION, PRINCIPAL REGISTER, WITH DECLARATION (Individual)	MARK *(identify the mark)*
	CLASS NO. *(if known)*

TO THE COMMISSIONER OF PATENTS AND TRADEMARKS:

NAME OF APPLICANT, AND BUSINESS TRADE NAME, IF ANY

BUSINESS ADDRESS

RESIDENCE ADDRESS

CITIZENSHIP OF APPLICANT

The above identified applicant has adopted and is using the trademark shown in the accompanying drawing for the following

goods: _____

_____

and requests that said mark be registered in the United States Patent and Trademark Office on the Principal Register established by the Act of July 5, 1946.

The trademark was first used on the goods on _____ ; was first used on the goods in
                                              (date)

_____ commerce on _____ ; and is now in use in such
        (type of commerce)   *(date)*

commerce.

The mark is used by applying it to _____

_____

and five specimens showing the mark as actually used are presented herewith.

_____
(name of applicant)

being hereby warned that willful false statements and the like so made are punishable by fine or imprisonment, or both, under Section 1001 of Title 18 of the United States Code and that such willful false statements may jeopardize the validity of the application or any registration resulting therefrom, declares that he/she believes himself/herself to be the owner of the trademark sought to be registered; to the best of his/her knowledge and belief no other person, firm, corporation, or association has the right to use said mark in commerce, either in the identical form or in such near resemblance thereto as may be likely, when applied to the goods of such other person, to cause confusion, or to cause mistake, or to deceive; the facts set forth in this application are true; and all statements made of his/her own knowledge are true and all statements made on information and belief are believed to be true.

_____
(signature of applicant)

_____
(date)

FORM PTO-1476FB (REV. 4-87)   U.S. DEPARTMENT OF COMMERCE/Patent and Trademark Office

TRADEMARK APPLICATION, PRINCIPAL REGISTER, WITH DECLARATION (Partnership)	MARK *(identify the mark)*
	CLASS NO. *(if known)*

TO THE COMMISSIONER OF PATENTS AND TRADEMARKS:

NAME OF PARTNERSHIP

NAMES OF PARTNERS

BUSINESS ADDRESS OF PARTNERSHIP

CITIZENSHIP OF PARTNERS

The above identified applicant has adopted and is using the trademark shown in the accompanying drawing for the following

goods: _____

_____

and requests that said mark be registered in the United States Patent and Trademark Office on the Principal Register established by the Act of July 5, 1946.

The trademark was first used on the goods on _____ ; was first used on the goods in
                                                            (date)

_____ commerce on _____ ; and is now in use in such
     (type of commerce)   *(date)*

commerce.

The mark is used by applying it to _____

_____

and five specimens showing the mark as actually used are presented herewith.

_____
(name of partner)

being hereby warned that willful false statements and the like so made are punishable by fine or imprisonment, or both, under Section 1001 of Title 18 of the United States Code and that such willful false statements may jeopardize the validity of the application or any registration resulting therefrom, declares that he/she believes himself/herself to be the owner of the trademark sought to be registered; to the best of his/her knowledge and belief no other person, firm, corporation, or association has the right to use said mark in commerce, either in the identical form or in such near resemblance thereto as may be likely, when applied to the goods of such other person, to cause confusion, or to cause mistake, or to deceive; the facts set forth in this application are true; and all statements made of his/her own knowledge are true and all statements made on information and belief are believed to be true.

_____
(signature of applicant)

_____
(date)

TRADEMARK APPLICATION, PRINCIPAL REGISTER, WITH DECLARATION (Corporation)	MARK *(identify the mark)*
	CLASS NO. *(if known)*

TO THE COMMISSIONER OF PATENTS AND TRADEMARKS:

NAME OF CORPORATION

STATE OR COUNTRY OF INCORPORATION

BUSINESS ADDRESS OF CORPORATION

The above identified applicant has adopted and is using the trademark shown in the accompanying drawing for the following

goods: _____

_____

and requests that said mark be registered in the United States Patent and Trademark Office on the Principal Register established by the Act of July 5, 1946.

The trademark was first used on the goods on _____ ; was first used on the goods in
(date)

_____ commerce on _____ ; and is now in use in such
(type of commerce) *(date)*

commerce.

The mark is used by applying it to _____

_____

and five specimens showing the mark as actually used are presented herewith.

_____
(name of officer of corporation)

being hereby warned that willful false statements and the like so made are punishable by fine or imprisonment, or both, under Section 1001 of Title 18 of the United States Code and that such willful false statements may jeopardize the validity of the application or any registration resulting therefrom, declares that he/she is

_____
(official title)

of applicant corporation and is authorized to execute this instrument on behalf of said corporation; he/she believes said corporation to be the owner of the trademark sought to be registered; to the best of his/her knowledge and belief no other person, firm, corporation, or association has the right to use said mark in commerce, either in the identical form or in such near resemblance thereto as may be likely, when applied to the goods of such other person, to cause confusion, or to cause mistake, or to deceive; the facts set forth in this application are true; and all statements made of his/her own knowledge are true and all statements made on information and belief are believed to be true.

_____
(name of corporation)

By _____
(signature of officer of corporation, and official title of officer)

_____
(date)

Part 4
Intellectual
Property Protection
In Foreign Countries

INTRODUCTION

This part provides important international information for anyone seeking a foreign copyright, patent, or trademark.

Determine your objectives (if you haven't already done so), prior to filing an application with the Copyright Office or the Patent and Trademark Office in Washington D.C. What are the chances that your new book, song, computer program, invention, or merchandise will find its way abroad? If there's a real possibility, now is the time to begin planning how you intend to secure appropriate protection.

An individual profile of more than 60 countries is included in this part, highlighting their copyright, patent, and trademark laws. Contacts have been provided for most countries if you need additional information. Remember, property protection abroad is accomplished by meeting the requirements of the individual countries.

Unlike U.S. trademarks, foreign trademarks are generally registered prior to use. The registered owner of a trademark is the legal owner, but continued use of the mark may be necessary to ensure continued ownership. Many foreign countries require that trademark registration be effective in the United States (or the owner's country) prior to a foreign filing. Copyright protection—as in the U.S.—is covered by national laws, and registration isn't usually necessary.

Patents and Foreign Countries

The following is a general rule-of-thumb concerning foreign patents:

- A patent made public or disclosed in a publication or an application open for examination by another country is not patentable.
- Patent laws vary from country to country.
- Annual maintenance fees are often required.
- The invention must be manufactured in the country of registration within a specific number of years (typically three years).
- An individual patent application must be filed in each country where protection is desired, or must conform to one or more international agreements or treaties.
- A foreign patent agent or attorney is required to handle the filing.

Attorneys and Registered Agents

Many countries require a native legal agent or representative to execute the application and filing on behalf of the foreign applicant. The third party may also be necessary as a resident agent of record who will transmit the annual maintenance fees and other requirements to the foreign patent or trademark office.

It's worth the expense to have a competent registered agent or attorney handle the myriad details when you are confronted with a multitude of foreign country laws. To this end, the Government Printing Office publishes a comprehensive directory,

Patent Attorneys and Agents Registered to Practice Before the U.S. Patent and Trademark Office. A copy can be purchased for $21 and ordered through the Superintendent of Documents, Government Printing Office, Washington, D.C. 20402. Also, a competent lawyer who specializes in copyright, patent, and trademark laws can be found in your local Yellow Pages under "Patent Attorney," or contact your local bar association for a referral.

Before consulting a legal representative or agent, know what you wish to accomplish. If possible, find several competent lawyers who specialize in the area where you seek protection and compare fees quoted for the same services(s). Legal fees vary considerably and don't necessarily indicate the type of service a client can expect or the level of competence.

After selecting two or three candidates, you might wish to personally visit the least expensive one first. If you feel comfortable with your choice, then proceed; otherwise, visit another attorney before making a final decision.

If you prefer to go direct, a list of foreign patent agents is contained in this part along with a list of foreign consulates in the United States. The consulate offices can provide the names and addresses of patent agents in their respective countries. The biggest problem in dealing with foreign agents is the question of their competence. This is particularly true if an agent wasn't referred by your attorney or someone whose opinion you value. If a U.S. patent attorney doesn't specialize in foreign filings, the counselor might deal with an affiliate law firm that does and that can satisfactorily execute the foreign filings. You can also locate patent agents in foreign telephone directories found in most large public libraries. Communicate with several agents in each country before selecting one.

Agreements and Treaties

International agreements and treaties exist between countries for their benefit and protect nationals and foreign owners of copyrights, patents, and trademarks. Intellectual property laws in the United States don't afford legal protection in foreign countries. Major international treaties that affect Americans include the Paris Union International Convention, The Patent Cooperation Treaty, The European Patent Convention, and The Universal Copyright Convention.

WORLDWIDE COPYRIGHT PROTECTION

U.S. citizens are entitled to receive international copyright protection in member countries under the Universal Copyright Convention (UCC) if the copyright notice is properly displayed. All copies of the work (from the date of first publication) must display the copyright symbol, the copyright owner's name, and the year of publication. Follow the example shown here:

© Hoyt L. Barber 1990

The countries listed on the following pages are members of the Universal Copyright

Convention. Correct use of the copyright notice will provide copyright protection in each of these countries. Refer to Part 1 for additional copyright information.

The profiles here cover intellectual property protection in over 60 countries. In addition to patent and trademark information, specific information is provided on copyrights by country.

The text of the Geneva and Paris Universal Copyright Convention treaties can be found in most reference sections of large public libraries, or you may want to try a university or law library.

UNIVERSAL COPYRIGHT CONVENTION COUNTRIES

Effective Sept. 30, 1986

Country	Geneva, 1952	Paris, 1971
Algeria	Aug. 28, 1973	July 10, 1974
Andorra	Feb. 16, 1955	
Argentina	Feb. 13, 1958	
Australia	May 1, 1969	Feb. 28, 1978
Austria	July 2, 1957	Aug. 14, 1982
Bahamas	Dec. 27, 1976	Dec. 27, 1976
Bangladesh	Aug. 5, 1975	Aug. 5, 1975
Barbados	June 18, 1983	June 18, 1983
Belgium	Aug. 31, 1960	
Belize	Sept. 21, 1981	
Brazil	Jan. 13, 1960	Dec. 11, 1975
Bulgaria	June 7, 1975	June 7, 1975
Cameroon	May 1, 1973	July 10, 1974
Canada	Aug. 10, 1962	
Chile	Sept. 16, 1955	
Colombia	June 18, 1976	June 18, 1976
Costa Rica	Sept. 16, 1955	March 7, 1980
Cuba	June 18, 1957	
Czechoslovakia	Jan. 6, 1960	April 17, 1980
Denmark	Feb. 9, 1962	July 11, 1979
Dominican Republic	May 8, 1983	May 8, 1983
Ecuador	June 5, 1957	
El Salvador	March 29, 1979	March 29, 1979
Fiji	Oct. 10, 1970	
Finland	Apr. 16, 1963	
France	Jan. 14, 1956	July 10, 1974
German Democratic Republic	Oct. 5, 1973	Dec. 10, 1980
German Federal Republic	Sept. 16, 1955	July 10, 1974
Ghana	Aug. 22, 1962	

Country	Geneva, 1952	Paris, 1971
Greece	Aug. 24, 1963	
Guatemala	Oct. 28, 1964	
Guinea	Nov. 13, 1981	Nov. 13, 1981
Haiti	Sept. 16, 1955	
Hungary	Jan. 23, 1971	July 10, 1974
Iceland	Dec. 18, 1956	
India	Jan. 21, 1958	
Ireland	Jan. 20, 1959	
Israel	Sept. 16, 1955	Jan. 25, 1980
Italy	Jan. 24, 1957	Jan. 25, 1980
Japan	April 28, 1956	Oct. 21, 1977
Kampuchea	Sept. 16, 1955	
Kenya	Sept. 7, 1966	July 10, 1974
Khmer Republic	Sept. 16, 1955	
Laos	Sept. 16, 1955	
Lebanon	Oct. 17, 1959	
Liberia	July 27, 1956	
Liechtenstein	Jan. 22, 1959	
Luxembourg	Oct. 15, 1955	
Malawi	Oct. 26, 1965	
Malta	Nov. 19, 1968	
Mauritius	March 12, 1968	
Mexico	May 12, 1957	Oct. 31, 1975
Monaco	Sept. 16, 1955	Dec. 13, 1974
Morocco	May 8, 1972	June 28, 1976
Netherlands	June 22, 1967	Nov. 30, 1985
New Zealand	Sept. 11, 1964	
Nicaragua	Aug. 16, 1961	
Nigeria	Feb. 14, 1962	
Norway	Jan. 23, 1963	Aug. 7, 1974
Pakistan	Sept. 16, 1955	
Panama	Oct. 17, 1962	
Paraguay	March 11, 1962	
Peru	Oct. 16, 1963	
Poland	March 9, 1977	March 9, 1977
Portugal	Dec. 25, 1956	July 30, 1981
Saint Vincent and the Grenadines	April 22, 1985	April 22, 1985
Senegal	July 9, 1974	July 10, 1974
Soviet Union	May 27, 1973	
Spain	Sept. 16, 1955	July 10, 1974
Sri Lanka	Jan. 25, 1984	Jan. 25, 1984
Sweden	July 1, 1961	July 10, 1974
Switzerland	March 30, 1956	

Country	Geneva, 1952	Paris, 1971
Tunisia	June 19, 1969	June 10, 1975
United Kingdom	Sept. 27, 1957	July 10, 1974
United States	Sept. 16, 1955	July 10, 1974
Vatican City	Oct. 5, 1955	May 6, 1980
Venezuela	Sept. 30, 1966	
Yugoslavia	May 11, 1966	July 10, 1974
Zambia	June 1, 1965	

PARIS CONVENTION

Members of the Paris Convention for the Protection of Industrial Property have agreed that foreigners will be afforded the same treatment as nationals in regard to patent and trademark protection. This is known as the "Right of National Treatment." Intellectual property protection varies by country, but Paris Convention countries don't discriminate against foreign applicants.

In many countries, once an invention is revealed to the public or is published, it's no longer patentable (this also applies to inventions where the application is under inspection). An inventor might lose the rght to register in another country for one of these reasons. Fortunately, another advantage of the Paris Convention is known as the "Right of Priority." After a patent or trademark application has been filed in a Paris Convention country, all applications filed in subsequent member countries become effective with the filing date of the first appliation.

The "one-year foreign filing rule" permits you a full year—after the first filing in a member country—to make application in other member countries and still preserve the benefits of the original filing date. This negates the necessity of your having to simultaneously file in each country where protection is desired. Preferably, file subsequent registrations as soon after the first one as possible. If the one-year deadline is missed, you can still file if the invention hasn't become public, the late filing(s) will become a non-Convention application. In the case of a design patent or trademark, the period is six months. Although some countries aren't members of the Paris Convention, similar benefits can be extended, possibly under another agreement or treaty.

PARIS CONVENTION COUNTRIES

Algeria	Lebanon
Argentina	Libyan Arab Jamahiriya
Australia	Liechtenstein
Austria	Luxembourg
Bahamas	Madagascar
Belgium	Malawi
Benin	Malta
Brazil	Mauritania

Bulgaria
Burundi
Cameroon
Canada
Central African Republic
Chad
Congo
Cuba
Cyprus
Czechoslovakia
Denmark
Dominican Republic
Eygpt
Finland
France
Gabon
German Democratic Republic
    (East Germany)
Germany, Federal Republic of
    (West Germany)
Ghana
Greece
Haiti
Holy See
Hungary
Iceland
Indonesia
Iran
Iraq
Ireland
Israel
Italy
Ivory Coast
Japan
Jordan
Kenya
Korea

Mauritius
Mexico
Monaco
Morocco
Netherlands
New Zealand
Niger
Nigeria
Norway
Philippines
Poland
Portugal
Romania
San Marino
Senegal
South Africa
Southern Rhodesia
Soviet Union
Spain
Sri Lanka
Suriname
Sweden
Switzerland
Syria
Tanzania
Togo
Trinidad and Tobago
Tunisia
Turkey
Uganda
United Kingdom
United States of America
Upper Volta
Uruguay
Viet Nam
Yugoslavia
Zaire
Zambia

EUROPEAN PATENT CONVENTION
AND THE PATENT COOPERATION TREATY

The European Patent Convention and the Patent Cooperation Treaty help simplify the procedure for U.S. business people to obtain foreign patent protection in member countries.

European Patent Convention (EPC)

U.S. citizens can file a patent application with the European Patent Office (EPO) to secure patent protection in selected contracting states. These countries are Austria, Belgium, Federal Republic of Germany, France, Italy, Liechtenstein, Luxembourg, Netherlands, Sweden, Switzerland, and the United Kingdom. As with the PCT, the EPC is easier, cheaper, and more reliable than individual country filings by offering a more uniform procedure for granting patents. The term of the European patent is 20 years.

The EPC will handle the application as follows:

1. Examine it for formalities and accept or reject it.
2. Upon acceptance, a search will be conducted.
3. The application is then published 18 months after the official filing date.
4. When the search report is completed, it will accompany the application.
5. Within six months of publication of the search report, the applicant must file a "request for examination"; otherwise, the application will be considered withdrawn.
6. When a request is made, the EPO examines the application for novelty and inventive merit, and it will either be refused or a patent will be granted.
7. The grant of a patent is published in the *European Patent Bulletin,* and for nine months thereafter, anyone can file an opposition.

Two informative publications are available from the European Patent Office; *How To Get a European Patent: Guide for Applicants* and *National Law Relating to the EPC.*

Applications are filed with either of the following offices (the latter is the branch office):

EUROPEAN PATENT OFFICE
Erhardtstr. 27
D-8000 Munich 2
Telephone (089) 2399-0
Telex 523656 epmu d

EUROPEAN PATENT OFFICE
Branch at the Hague
Patentlaan 2
Rijswijk

Mailing address:

POSTBUS 5818
2280 HV Rijswijk 2H
Netherlands

Patent Cooperation Treaty (PCT)

With the PCT, the applicant files a standardized international patent application with the U.S. Patent and Trademark Office and indicates in which PCT member countries patent protection is desired. This eliminates the need to file separate applications in each country for the same invention.

The application is subject to a search for prior art by the U.S. Patent and Trademark Office, which is one of the designated international searching authorities. The applicant receives a copy of the International Search Report. Prior art is cited in the report that might disclose patents and other published technology on the invention. This provides additional information to help determine whether it's advantageous to proceed in one or more countries.

This process saves time and money and allows the appliant up to 20 months instead of the usual 12 months to file translations and pay national fees to each foreign country.

The Patent Cooperation Treaty does not issue international patents; rather, it simplifies patent filing procedures. The World Intellectual Property Organization (WIPO) administers the PCT, and publishes the *PCT Applicants Guide* that provides detailed information on filing international applications, governing regulations, instructions, and more. The guide is available through:

RAPID PATENT SERVICE
1921 Jefferson Davis Hwy.
Suite 1821D
Arlington, VA 22202
(703) 920-5050

The headquarters for WIPO is:

WORLD INTELLECTUAL PROPERTY ORGANIZATION
34 Chemin des Colombettes
1211 Geneva 20, Switzerland

The PCT International Services Division handles international applications and can provide you with a copy of its *PCT Helpful Hints* bulletin which is regularly updated. PCT International applications and transmittal letter forms are available upon request. A sample of a completed applicatin, specification (description, claims, abstract, and drawing), and fee schedule is included also available. (Refer to Part 2, for drawing dimensions (A-4 size) for international filings.) The address is:

CRYSTAL PLAZA 6-12
Washington, D.C.
(703) 557-2003

The mailing address is:

COMMISSIONER OF PATENTS AND TRADEMARKS
Box PCT
Washington, D.C. 20231

Basic PCT procedures can be found in Chapter 1800 of the PTO *Manual of Patent Examining Procedure* (MPEP). The Patent Cooperation Treaty can be located in Appendix T of the *MPEP*, and the Patent Rules are in Appendix L.

PATENT COOPERATION TREATY COUNTRIES

(Effective January 1, 1988)

Country	Date of Entry	Country	Date of Entry
Australia	March 31, 1980	Liechtenstein	March 19, 1980
Austria	April 23, 1979	Luxembourg	April 30, 1978
Barbados	March 12, 1985	Madagascar	January 24, 1978
Belgium	December 14, 1981	Malawi	January 24, 1978
Benin	February 26, 1987	Mali	October 19, 1984
Brazil	April 9, 1978	Mauritania	April 13, 1983
Bulgaria	May 21, 1984	Monaco	June 22, 1979
Cameroon	January 24, 1978	Netherlands	July 10, 1979
Central Africa Republic	January 21, 1978	Norway	January 1, 1980
		Republic of Korea	August 10, 1984
Chad	January 24, 1978		
Congo	January 24, 1978	Romania	July 23, 1979
Democratic People's		Senegal	January 24, 1978
Republic of Korea		Soviet Union	March 29, 1978
Denmark	July 8, 1980		
Finland	December 1, 1978	Sri Lanka	February 26, 1982
France	October 1, 1980	Sudan	April 16, 1984
Gabon	February 25, 1978	Sweden	May 17, 1978
Federal Republic of Germany	January 24, 1978	Switzerland	January 24, 1978
Hungary	January 24, 1978	United Kingdom	January 24, 1978
	June 27, 1980	United States of America	Janaury 24, 1978
Italy			
Japan	March 28, 1985		
	October 1, 1978		

INTERNATIONAL TRADEMARK AGREEMENTS

The International Convention for the Protection of Industrial Property, also known as the "Paris Convention" or "Paris Union," is the most significant multilateral agreement for incorporating trademark rights. The United States and 89 other countries are members. Rights in this pact include a "right or priority" that allows an applicant six months to file corresponding trademark applications in convention countries following the initial application with the U.S. Patent and Trademark Office (USPTO) or another member country. It also eliminates the former requirement of a prior "home country" registration of the mark in the U.S. It covers patents, trademarks, industrial designs, utility models, trade names, and inventor's certificates.

The United States is also a party to the General Inter-American Convention for Trademark and Commercial Protection of 1929 agreement which has 11 Western Hemisphere member countries. Both the Paris Convention and Inter-American Convention agreements have similar advantages and rights.

Twenty-two countries, including the United States, adhere to the Madrid Agreement Concerning the International Registration of Trademarks. A trademark registered in the country of origin (home country) can automatically gain protection in one or more other member countries by a single international application filed with WIPO in Geneva, Switzerland. This is achieved through the applicant's own country. In the case of U.S. citizens, it is handled by the USPTO. When the Central Bureau in Geneva receives the application, it's registered and published in an international journal, and copies are sent to other countries where the applicant seeks registration. Each country has the right to refuse to register a mark, and has up to one year from the date of publication to inform the WIPO. This agreement is effected by the "home country" provision.

The United States employs the Arangement of Nice Concerning the International Classification of Goods and Services to Which Trademarks Apply to uniformly classify goods and services. Sixty other countries use the same system, often referred to as the International Classification of Goods and Services. Refer to Part 3 for a review of the complete list.

Other treaties and agreements are subscribed to by foreign countries for the protection of trademark rights that don't pertain to U.S. citizens (unless they establish a company or subsidiary in one of the foreign countries). Two such agreements are the African Intellectual Property Organization (OAPI) and the Central American Agreement (CAA). Members of OAPI include Benin, Cameroon, Central African Republic, Chad, Congo, Gabon, Ivory Coast, Mauritania, Niger, Senegal, Togo, and Upper Volta. Members of CAA include Costa Rica, Guatemala, and Nicaragua.

COUNTRY PROFILES

The information contained in this section is divided into copyrights, patents, and trademarks, each consisting primarily of these elements: duration, law, international treaty membership, administering agency, plus other pertinent information. If the administering agency is the same for patents and trademarks, which is often the case, the address appears in the trademarks category. If the agencies are different, the address is listed under its respective heading, unless an address isn't provided at all. The same applies to copyrights, as some government agencies handle all three; frequently, though, it is an entirely separate agency.

The Paris Convention governs both patents and trademarks. If a country is a member, rather than listing its membership twice, it is included under the patent heading.

ALGERIA

Copyrights

Duration: Author's life plus 25 years
Law: The Algerian Copyright Ordinance No. 73-14
Member: Universal Copyright Convention
Administered by the Ministry of Information and Culture

Patents

Duration: 20 years
Law: The Algerian Patent Law, Ordinance No. 66-54
Member: Paris Union International Convention

Trademarks

Duration: 10 years
Law: The Algerian Trademark Law, Ordinance No. 66-57
Patent and trademark applications are filed with:

> DIRECTOR GENERAL Country Profiles
> Institut Algerien de Normalisation et
>   de Propriete Industrielle
> 5, Rue Abau Hamou Moussa
> Algiers, Algeria

Additional information concerning copyright, patent, and tradmark laws can be obtained by writing:

> FOREIGN BUSINESS PRACTICES DIVISION
> Office of International Service
> Bureau of International Economic Policy

ARGENTINA

Copyrights

Administered by The Office of Intellectual Property (judicial branch of the government)
Member: Universal Copyright Convention

Patents

Duration: 5, 10, or 15 years

Trademarks

Duration: 10 years
Patents and Trademarks are administered by:

> SECRETARIA DE ESTADO DE INDUSTRIA Y COMERCIO COMERCIO INTERIOR
> Direccion Nacional de la Propriedad Industrial
> Av. Julio A. Roca 651
> Buenos Aires, Argentina

AUSTRALIA

Copyrights

Duration: Author's life plus 50 years
Member: Universal Copyright Convention

Patents

Duration: 16 years
Law: Patent Act 1952
Member: Paris Union International Convention and Patent Cooperation Treaty

Trademarks

Duration: 7 years
Law: Trademark Act of 1955

Copyright, patent, and trademark inquiries and filings are handled by:

> PATENTS, TRADEMARKS AND DESIGN OFFICE
> Scarsborough House, Phillip
> P.O. Box 200
> Woden, A.C.T. 2606
> Canberra, Australia

AUSTRIA

Copyrights

Duration: Author's life plus 70 years
Law: Copyright Statute, April 9, 1936, including amendments through 1972
Member: Universal Copyright Convention and Berne International Union

Copyright inquires and filings are handled by:

> FEDERAL MINISTRY OF EDUCATION
> Bundesministeriumfuer Unterricht and Kunst
> Minoritenplatz 5
> 1014 Wien I, Austria

Patents

Duration: 18 years

Law: Current patent law effective October, 1969

Member: Patent Cooperation Treaty, the European Patent Convention, and the Paris Convention.

Trademarks

Duration: 10 years

Law: Trademark Protection Law effective November 30, 1970

Uses the Nice International Classification System

Patent and trademark inquiries and filings should be directed to:

> FEDERAL PATENT OFFICE
> Oesterreichisches Patentamt
> Kohlmarkt 8-10
> Wein I, Vienna

BELGIUM

Copyrights

Duration: Author's life plus 50 years

Member: Universal Copyright Convention

Patents

Duration: 20 years

Member: Paris Union International Convention, Patent Cooperation Treaty, and the European Patent Convention

Trademarks

Duration: 10 years

Law: The Benelux Uniform Law

Administered by:

>   Benelux Trademark Bureau
>   The Hague

Copyright and patent inquiries and filings should be addressed to:

>   SERVICE DE LA PROPRIETE INDUSTRIELLE ET COMMERCIALE
>   Ministere des Affaires Ecenomiques
>   Rue de Mot 24
>   1040 Brussels, Belgium

Or write:

>   OFFICE OF INDUSTRIAL PROPERTY
>   19 Avenue de la Porte Neuve
>   Luxembourg

BULGARIA

Copyrights

Duration: Author's life plus 50 years
Law: Copyright Statute, amended April, 1972
Member: Universal Copyright Convention and the Berne Union International Convention
Copyright inquiries and applications should be submitted to:

>   JUSAUTOR
>   11 Slaveikov Square
>   Sofia, Bulgaria

Patents

Duration: 15 years
Law: Inventions and Innovations, effective January 1, 1969
Member: Paris Union International Convention and Patent Cooperation Treaty
Bulgaria also issues Inventors' Certificates.

Trademarks

Duration: 10 years
Law: Trademarks and Industrial Design Law, effective January 1, 1968

Patents, Inventors' Certificates, industrial designs, and trademarks are administered by:

THE INSTITUTE OF INVENTIONS AND RATIONALIZATIONS
5 Zhdandov St.
Sofia, Bulgaria

Foreigners should inquire with:

PATENT AND TRADEMARK BUREAU OF THE BULGARIAN CHAMBER OF COMMERCE AND INDUSTRY
42 Parchevitch St.
Sofia, Bulgaria

CANADA

Copyrights

Duration: Author's life plus 50 years
Member: Universal Copyright Convention

Patents

Duration: 17 years
Member: Paris Union International Convention
Canada also issues Investors' Certificates pursuant to the 1967 Stockholm Provision.

Trademarks

Duration: 18 years
Law: Trademark and Design Act of July 1, 1954
Inquiries should be directed to:

BUREAU OF CORPORATE AFFAIRS
Patents, Trademarks, Copyrights and Industrial Design Office
Consumer and Corporate Affair Canada
Ottawa, Ontario, Canada KIA OC9

CHINA

Copyrights

China has no copyright laws. Copyright infringement in China should be addressed to:

U.S. COMMERCE DEPARTMENT
Office of China Affairs

Alternately, write the U.S. Copyright Office in Washington, DC.

Patents

China has no patent laws, nor are trade secrets protected.

Trademarks

Duration: 10 years
Law: The new trademark law became effectve March 1, 1983
Administered by the Bureau of the State Administration for Industry and Commerce
Contact:

NATIONAL BUREAU OF STANDARDS
Ministry of Economic Affairs
No. 1, 1st St.
Pei Men Road
Tainan, Taiwan

COLOMBIA

Copyrights

Member: Universal Copyright Convention

Patents

Duration: 5 years
Law: Andean Pact, Decision 85

Trademarks

Duration: 5 years
Law: Andean Pact, Decision 85

Contact:

MINISTERIO DE DESARROLLO ECONOMICO
Division de Propiedad Industrial
Edificio Bochico
Bogota, Colombia

COSTA RICA

Copyrights

Duration: Author's life plus 50 years
Member: Universal Copyright Convention
Law: Act No. 6683 and compliances with international treaties

Patents

Duration: 12 years
Law: Assembly Act No. 6867, June, 1983
Administered by the Patent Registry

Trademarks

Duration: 15 years
Law: Central American Treaty; civil codes and Legislative Assembly
Administered by the Ministry of Economy, Industry and Commerce

DENMARK

Copyrights

Duration: Author's life plus 50 years
Law: Law No. 158, Copyright in Literary and Artistic Works, 1961
Member: Universal Copyright Convention, Berne Union International Convention, and the International Convention for the Protection of Producers and Phonograms (sound recordings)

Patents

Duration: 17 years
Law: Patent Act No. 479, 1967
Member: Paris Union International Convention and Patent Cooperation Treaty

Trademarks

Duration: 10 years
Law: Trade Marks Act No. 211, June 11, 1959
Uses the Nice International Classification System
Copyright, patent, and trademark inquiries and applications are handled by:

> DIRECTORATET FOR PATENT
> Varmaei kevaesenet
> 45 Nyropsgade
> DK, Copenhagen V, Denmark

DOMINICAN REPUBLIC

Copyrights

Member: Universal Copyright Convention
Law: Inter-American Convention on the Rights of Authors, 1946

Patents

Duration: 15 years
Member: Paris Union International Convention
Copyrights and patents are administered by:

> THE SECRETARIA DE EDUCACION
> Santo Domingo, Dominican Republic

Trademarks

Duration: 5, 10, 15 or 20 years
Administered by the Secretaria de Industria y Comercio

EGYPT

Copyrights

N/A

Patents

Duration: 15 years

Administerd by:

> PATENTS DIRECTORATE
> Academy of Scientific Research
> 101 Sharia Kast
> El Aini, Cairo, Egypt

Trademarks

Duration: 10 years

FINLAND

Copyrights

Duration: Author's life plus 50 years
Member: Universal Copyright Convention
Law: Law No. 404, July 8, 1961, amended August 23, 1971; literary and artistic works

Patents

Duration: 17 years
Law: Patent Act, January 1, 1968
Member: Paris Union International Convention and Patent Cooperation Treaty

Industrial Designs

Duration: 5 years
Law: Registered Design Act, March 12, 1971

Trademarks

Duration: 10 years
Law: Trade Marks Act, effective June 1, 1964
Uses the Nice International Classification System
Patent, industrial designs, and trademark inquiries and filings are handled by:

> PATENTTI-JA REHISTERIHALLITUS
> Bulevardi 21
> 00180 Helsinki 18, Finland

FRANCE

Copyrights

Duration: Author's life plus 50 years
Member: Universal Copyright Convention
Law: Copyright Law of 1957

Patents

Duration: 20 years (Standard Patent); six years (Certificate of Utility)
Member: Paris Union International Convention, Patent Cooperation Treaty, and European Patent Convention

Trademarks

Duration: 10 years
Patents and trademarks are administerd by:

> NATIONAL INSTITUTE OF INDUSTRIAL PROPERTY
> Ministry of Industry and Research
> 26 bis, rue de Leningrad
> 75008 Paris,France

GABON

Copyrights

Member: Berne Industrial Union

Patents

Duration: 20 years
Member: Office Africain et Malagache de la Propriete Industrielle and Patent Cooperation Treaty

Trademarks

Duration: 20 years
Administered by: Same as patents

GERMAN DEMOCRATIC REPUBLIC

Copyrights

Duration: Author's life plus 50 years
Member: Universal Copyright Convention and Berne Industrial Union

Patents

Duration: 18 years
Law: Patent Law, September 6, 1950, amended 1963
Member: Paris Union International Convention

Trademarks

Duration: 10 years
Member: The Madrid Agreement (Stockholm version) and Paris Union International Convention.
Patents and trademarks are filed with:

> OFFICE OF INVENTIONS AND PATENTS
> 1080 Berlin
> Mohrenstrasse 37-B

GERMANY, FEDERAL REPUBLIC OF

Copyrights

Duration: Author's life plus 70 years
Member: Universal Copyright Convention and the Berne Industrial Convention.

Patents

Duration: 20 years (Basic Patent); Three years (Gebrauchsmuster, utility model, or petty patent)
Member: Paris Union International Convention, Patent Cooperation Treaty, and European Patent Convention
Contact:

> DEUTSCHES PATENTAMT
> Zweibruckenstrasse 12
> 8 Munchen 2, Germany

Trademarks

Duration: 10 years
Uses the Nice International Classification System

GHANA

Copyrights

Member: Universal Copyright Convention

Patents

Law: Patent Registration Ordinances

Trademarks

Duration: 14 years

GREECE

Copyrights

Law: Legal protection provided through signed agreements with the United States
and Greek Legislation
Member: Berne Industrial Convention, Universal Copyright Convention

Patents

Duration: 15 years
Member: Paris Union International Convention
Law: Legal protection provided through a signed agreement with the U.S.
Contact:

> MINISTERE DU COMMERCE SERVICE DE LA PROPRIETE INDUSTRIELLE
> Platia Caningoos
> Athenes, Greece

Trademarks

Duration: 10 years
Law: Greek Trademark Law

GUATEMALA

Copyrights

N/A

Patents and Trademarks

Trademark duration: 10 years
Patent duration: 15 years (maximum)
Patents, trademarks, and trade names are administered by the Office of Trademarks and Patents in Commerce, Industry and Controls Administration.

HONG KONG

Copyrights

Law: United Kingdom Copyright Act of 1956, amended by the Design Copyright Act of 1968

Patents

Hong Kong has no patent laws; however, a patent holder may register the patent under the Registration of United Kingdom Patents Ordinance.
Inquires and applications are handled by:

REGISTRAR GENERAL'S DEPARTMENT
Central Government Offices (West Wing)
11th Floor
Hong Kong

Trademarks

Law: Hong Kong Trade Marks Ordinance
Additional trademark information, forms, fees, etc. are available by writing:

GOVERNMENT PUBLICATION CENTER
Stan Ferry Concourse
Hong Kong
Be sure to include HK $9 with your request.

ICELAND

Copyrights

Duration: Author's life plus 50 years
Law: Copyright Statute of May 29, 1972
Member: Universal Copyright Convention and the Berne Industrial Union.
Administered by:

> MINISTER OF EDUCATION
> Hverfisgotu 4-6
> 101 Reykjavik

Patents

Duration: 15 years
Member: Paris Union International Convention
Administered by:

> SECRETARY GENERAL
> Ministry of Industries
> Arnarhvoli, Reykjavik

Trademarks

Duration: 10 years
Law: Trademark Act No. 47, May 2, 1968
Administered by:

> OFFICE OF THE CHIEF MAGISTRATE
> Trademark Secretary
> Skolavordustig 11
> Reykjavik

INDIA

Copyrights

Duration: Author's life plus 50 years
Law: Copyright Statute, Act No. 14, 1957
Member: Universal Copyright Convention
Administered by:

Administered by:

> REGISTRAR OF COPYRIGHTS
> Copyright Office
> New Delhi, India

Patents

Duration: 14 years
Law: Patents Act of 1970
Member: Berne Industrial Union

Designs

Duration: 5 years
Patents and designs are filed with:

> CONTROLLER GENERAL OF PATENTS, DESIGNS AND TRADEMARKS
> 214 Lower Circular Rd.
> Calcutta, India

Trademarks

Duration: 7 years
Law: The Trade and Merchandise Marks Act of 1958
Uses the Nice International Classification System
Trademark applications should be submitted to:

> CONTROLLER GENERAL OF PATENTS
> Central Building
> Maharshi Karve Rd.
> Bombay, India

INDONESIA

Copyrights

Duration: Author's life plus 50 years
Law: Netherlands Copyright Act of 1912
Member: Universal Copyright Convention, and the Berne Industrial Convention

Patents

Law: Presently, there's no Indonesian patent law; however, an inventor can file for the record, so when a patent law is adopted, it will become effective.
Member: Paris Union International Convention

Trademarks

Duration: 10 years
Law: Trade Name and Trade Marks Act No. 21, 1961

ISRAEL

Copyrights

Duration: Author's life plus 70 years
Law: United Kingdom Copyright Act of 1911, effective 1924
Member: Universal Copyright Convention

Patents

Duration: 20 years
Law: Patent Law 5727-1967, effective April 1, 1968
Member: Paris Union International Convention

Trademarks

Law: Trademarks Ordinance of 1938
Uses the Nice International Classification System
Patent and trademark information and filings should be addressed to:

THE COMMISSIONER OF PATENTS, DESIGNS AND TRADEMARKS
Ministry of Justice
Jaffa Road 19
P.O. Box 767
Jerusalem, Israel

Copyright inquiries should be mailed to the same address, to the attention of:

Administrative Director in Charge of Copyrights
Ministry of Justice

ITALY

Copyrights

Duration: Author's life plus 50 years
Law: Law No. 633, April 22, 1941, amended as Law No. 82, August 23, 1946
Member: Universal Copyright Convention and the Berne Industrial Union
Send copyright inquiries and filing to:

> PRESIDENZA DEL CONSIGLIO DEI MINISTRI
> Ufficio del Proprieta Letteraria
> Artistics e Scientificia
> Via Boncompagni, 15
> 00187 Rome, Italy

Patents

Duration: 15 years
Law: Italian Legislation
Member: Paris Union International Convention, Patent Cooperation Treaty, and European Patent Convention

Trademarks

Duration: 20 years
Law: Trademark Registration Laws
Address patent and trademark inquiries and applications to:

> MINISTERO DEL'INDUSTRIA E COMMERCIO
> Ufficio Centrale Bervetti per Invenzioni
> Modelli e Marchi
> Via Molise, 19
> 00187 Rome, Italy

IVORY COAST

Copyrights

Member: Berne Industrial Convention

Patents and Trademarks

Duration: 20 years (both)

Member: Paris Union International Convention and the Office Africain et Malgache de la Propriete Industrielle (OAMPI)

Patent and Trademark inquiries and filings should be addressed to:

OAMPI
B.P. 887
Yaounde, Cameroon

JAPAN

Copyrights

Duration: 3 to 50 years
Member: Universal Copyright Convention
Administered by the Cultural Affairs Agency, Ministry of Education

Patents

Duration: 20 years (maximum)
Member: Paris Union International Convention and Patent Cooperation Treaty
Administered by the World Intellectual Organization
Applications should be submitted to:

JAPANESE PATENT OFFICE
1-3-1 Kasumigseki
Chiyoda-ku
Tokyo, Japan

Trademarks

Duration: 10 years

KENYA

Copyrights

Member: Universal Copyright Convention

Patents

Kenya doesn't have a patent law; however, U.K. patent holders can obtain patent protection upon registration.
Member: Paris Union International Convention

Trademarks

Duration: 7 years
Trademark applications are accepted by:

> DEPARTMENT OF REGISTRAR GENERAL
> P.O. Box 30031
> Wairobi, Kenya

KUWAIT

Copyrights

N/A

Patents

Duration: 15 years
Law: Patent Law No. 4/1962
Administered by the Patent Office

Trademarks

Duration: 10 years
Law: Trademark Statute Law No. 2/1961
Uses a classification similar to the Nice International Classification System
Administered by the Registrar of Trademarks

LIBERIA

Copyrights

Duration: 20 years
Member: Universal Copyright Convention

Patents

Duration: 20 years

Trademarks

Duration: 15 years

Copyrights, patents, and trademarks are administered by:

BUREAU OF ARCHIVES, PATENTS, COPYRIGHTS AND TRADEMARKS
Ministry of Foreign Affairs

MALAYSIA

Copyrights

Law: Copyright Act of 1969, amended 1975 and 1979

Patents

Duration: 15 years
Law: Patent Act of 1983

Trademarks

Duration: 7 years
Law: Trademark Ordinance of 1950
Uses the Nice International Classification System

MEXICO

Copyrights

Duration: Author's life plus 30 years
Law: Federal Copyright Law of December 28, 1956, amended November 4, 1963
Member: Universal Copyright Convention
Administered by the Copyright Directorate of the Secretariat of Education

Patents

Duration: 14 years
Law: Inventions and Trademarks Law of 1976, amended September, 1986
Member: Paris Union International Convention
Mexico also issues Certificates of Invention.

Trademarks

Duration: 5 years

Patents and trademarks are filed with:

DIRECTOR GENERAL OF INDUSTRIAL PROPERTY
Secretariat of Commerce
Hermosillo 26
Mexico D.F., Mexico

MOROCCO

Copyrights

Duration: Author's life plus 50 years
Member: Universal Copyright Convention and the Berne Industrial Union

Patents

Duration: 20 years
Laws: Specific laws exist for former French Morocco and former Tangier. There's confusion, however, over requirements and protection concerning the former Spanish Zone and Western Sahara.
Member: Paris Union International Convention
Uses the Nice International Classification System
Patent and trademark applications must be filed in several regions of Morocco. Patent applications should be sent to the appropriate address:

Former French Morocco:
Office Marocain de la Propriete Industrielle,Casablanca
Former Tangier Zone:
Bureau de la Propriete Industrielle, Tangier

Trademarks

N/A

NETHERLANDS

Copyrights

Duration: Author's life plus 50 years
Member: Universal Copyright Convention and the Berne Industrial Union

Patents

Duration: 20 years

Member: Paris Union International Convention, Patent Cooperation Treaty, and European Patent Convention
Administered by:

> OCTROOITSSF
> Patentlaan 2
> Rijswijk (Z.H.)
> The Netherlands

Trademarks

Duration: 10 years
Law: The Uniform Benelux Law on Trademarks
Administerd by:

> Benelux Law on Trademarks
> The Hague

NEW ZEALAND

Copyrights

Member: Universal Copyright Convention and the Berne Industrial Convention

Patents

Duration: 16 years
Law: Patents Act of 1953 and the Design Act of 1953
Member: Paris Union International Convention

Designs

Duration: 5 years

Trademarks

Law: Trade Marks Act of 1953
Administered by the Commissioner of Trade Marks
Contact:

> PATENT OFFICE (PATENTS & TRADEMARKS)
> Departmental Building
> Stout St.
> Wellington C.1., New Zealand

NORWAY

Copyrights

Duration: Author's life plus 50 years
Member: Universal Copyright Convention and the Berne Industrial Union

Patents

Duration: 17 years
Law: The Patents Act of 1967, effective January 1, 1968
Member: Paris Union International Convention and Patent Cooperation Treaty

Trademarks

Duration: 10 years
Law: Trade Marks Act of March 3, 1961, effective October 1, 1961
Uses the Nice International Classification System
Send patent and trademark inquiries and applications to:

> NORWEGIAN PATENT OFFICE
> Styret for det Industrielle Rettsvern
> Middlthunsgate 156, Oslo. 3

PAKISTAN

Copyrights

Duration: Author's life plus 50 years
Member: Universal Copyright Convention

Patents

Duration: 16 years
Member: World Intellectual Property Organization (WIPO)
Administered by:

> THE PATENT OFFICE
> 30-A Maqbool Chambers
> Shaheed-e-Millat
> Karachi, Pakistan

Trademarks

Duration: 15 years
Administered by:

TRADEMARKS REGISTRY
Karachi, Pakistan

PARAGUAY

Copyrights

Member: Universal Copyright Convention

Patents

Duration: 15 years
Law: Law 773, September, 1925
Administered by the Office of Patents and Invention

Trademarks

Duration: 10 years
Law: Law 751, July, 1979

PHILIPPINES

Copyrights

Duration: Author's life plus 50 years
Administered by the Philippines National Library

Patents

Duration: 17 years
Member: Berne Industrial Union and Paris Union International Convention

Trademarks

Duration: 20 years

Send patent and trademark inquiries and filings to:

> ATTORNEY CESAR C. SAN DIEGO, ACTING DIRECTOR
> Philippine Patent Office
> P.O. Box 296
> Manila, Philippines

POLAND

Copyrights

Duration: Author's life plus 20 years
Law: Copyright Statute Law No. 234, July 10, 1952
Member: Universal Copyright Convention and the Berne Industrial Union

Patents

Duration: 15 years
Law: Inventive Activity No. 272, October 29, 1972
Member: Paris Union International Convention
Administered by:

> PATENT OFFICE OF POLISH PEOPLE'S REPUBLIC
> 188/192 Aleja
> Niepodleglosci, Warsaw 68, Poland

Trademarks

Duration: 10 years
Law: Act of March 28, 1963
Send patent and trademark inquiries and filings to:

> PATENT ATTORNEY OFFICE (PATPOL)
> Polish Chamber of Foreign Trade
> P.O. Box 168
> 2 Stawki St.
> Warsaw 00950, Poland

PORTUGAL

Copyrights

Duration: Author's life plus 50 years

Member: Berne Industrial Union, Geneva Convention (1952), Stockholm Convention (1967), and Universal Copyright Convention

Administered by the Bureau of Literary, Scientific and Artistic Property

Patents

Duration: 15 years

Member: International Convention for the Protection of Industrial (Paris Union) Property and the Madrid Agreements

Trademarks

Duration: 10 years

Administered by Industrial Property Bureau.

Contact:

> MINISTERIO DE ECONOMIA
> Secretaria de Estado do Comercio
> Reparticao da Propriedad Industrial
> Campo das Cebolas
> Liboa, Portugal

This address can be used for patent and trademark inquiries and applications.

QATAR

Copyrights

N/A

Patents

There's no patent law.

Trademarks

N/A

ROMANIA

Copyrights

Member: Universal Copyright Convention and the Berne Industrial Union

Patents

Duration: 15 years
Law: Law No. 62, October 30, 1974, Inventions and Innovations
Member: Paris Union International Convention and Patent Cooperation Treaty
Administered by the State Office for Inventions and Trademarks (OSIM)

Trademarks

Duration: 10 years
Law: Law No. 28, December 29, 1976, Trade and Service Marks and Branch.
Member: Madrid Agreement
Patent and trademark applications are filed through ROMINVENT, the Bureau of Foreign Patents and Inventions of the Chamber of Commerce and Industry.
Contact:

> DIRECTIA GENERALA PENTRU METROLOGIE STANDARDE SI INVENTII
> Officiul de Stut Pentru Inventii si Marci
> Strada Popow 24-B.P. 52
> Bucuresti, Romania

This address can be used for patent and trademark inquiries and applications.

SAUDI ARABIA

Copyrights

There are no copyright laws.

Patents

There are no patent laws.

Trademarks

Duration: 10 years
Law: Royal Degree 33/1/4 of 1939, amended Decree No. 8 of 1973 and No. M/24 of 1974.
Administered by the Ministry of Commerce in Riyadh

SENEGA

Copyrights

Member: Berne Industrial Union and Universal Copyright Convention

Patents

Duration: 20 years
Member: Africain Intellectual Property Organization, Paris Union International Convention, and Patent Cooperation Treaty

Trademarks

Duration: 20 years
Patents and trademarks are administered by:

> OFFICE AFRICAIN ET MALAGACHE DE LA PROPRIETE INDUSTRIELLE
> Yaounde
> Cameroon, Senega

SINGAPORE

Copyrights

Law: United Kingdom Act of 1911

Patents

Law: Only patents registered under U.K. law can be patented.

Trademarks

Duration: 7 years
Law: Trademark Act, effective February 1, 1939, and the Trademark Act, effective May 1, 1968
Patents and trademarks are administered by:

> REGISTRAR OF TRADE MARKS AND PATENTS, 305
> Tanglin Rd., Singapore 1024

SOUTH AFRICA

Copyrights

Duration: Author's life plus 50 years
Law: Copyright Act of 1978

Patents

Duration: 20 years
Law: Patents Act of 1978
Member: Paris Union International Convention

Trademarks

Duration: 10 years
Uses the Nice International Classification System
All intellectual property protection inquiries and applications should be submitted to:

> REGISTRAR OF PATENTS, DESIGN, TRADE MARKS AND COPYRIGHT
> Zania Building
> 116 Proes St
> Pretoria, South Africa

SOUTH KOREA

Copyrights

Law: Korean Copyright Law

Patents

Duration: 12 years
Member: Paris Union International Convention

Trademarks

Duration: 10 years
Contact: T'ukhoguk, Seoul, Republic of Korea

SPAIN

Copyrights

Member: Universal Copyright Convention

Patents

Duration: 20 years
Law: Decree Law, July 26, 1929
Member: Paris Union International Convention

Trademarks

Duration: 20 years
All intellectual property protection inquiries and applications should be addressed to:

> REGISTRO DE LA PROPRIEDAD INDUSTRIAL
> Ministry of Industry and Energy
> Avenue Generalisimo 59
> Madrid, Spain

SRI LANKA

Copyrights

Member: Berne Industrial Union and Universal Copyright Convention

Patents and Trademarks

Member: Paris Union International Convention, World Intellectual Property Organization, and Patent Cooperation Treaty

SUDAN

Copyrights

N/A

Patents

Member: Universal Copyright Convention

Trademarks

Sudan's trademark law is similar to British law.

SWEDEN

Copyrights

Duration: Author's life plus 50 years
Law: Number 729, 1960
Member: Universal Copyright Convention and Berne Industrial Union

Patents

Duration: 20 years
Law: Patents Act of 1978, effective June 1, 1978
Member: Paris Union International Convention, Patent Cooperation Treaty, and European Patent Convention

Trademarks

Duration: 10 years
Law: Trademark Act of 1960, effective January 1, 1961
Uses the Nice International Classification System
Patents and trademark inquiries and applications should be directed to:

> DIRECTOR GENERAL
> Patent and Registeringsverket
> Box 5055
> S-102 42 Stockholm, Sweden

SWITZERLAND

Copyrights

Member: Universal Copyright Convention

Patents

Member: European Patent Convention (effective 1977), Paris Union International Convention, and Patent Cooperation Treaty

Trademarks

Duration: 20 years
Law: Federal Trademark Law of 1980
Member: Madrid Arrangement of 1891
Copyright, patent, and trademark applications can be filed with:

> THE FEDERAL OFFICE FOR THE PROTECTION OF
> INTELLECTUAL PROPERTY (Eidgenossiche Amt fur
> Geistiges Eigentum/Bureau de la propriete intellectuelle)
> Eschmannstrasse 2
> 3000 Bern,Switzerland

TAIWAN

Copyrights

Member: Ministry of Interiors Copyright Committee

Patents

Duration: 15 years

Trademarks

Duration: 10 years
Patent and trademarks are administered by the National Bureau of Standards.

THAILAND

Copyrights

Law: Copyright Act of B.E. 2521 (1978)
Member: Bern Industrial Convention

Patents

Duration: 15 years
Law: Patent Act of B.E. 2522 (1979)

Trademarks

Law: Trademarks Act of B.E. 2474 (1931) and B.E. 2504 (1961)

TUNISIA

Copyrights

Duration: Author's life plus 50 years
Member: Universal Copyright Convention and Berne Industrial Convention

Patents

Duration: 5, 10 and 20 years
Member: Paris Union International Convention

Trademarks

Duration: 15 years
Patent and trademark inquiries and applications should be sent to:

> DIRECTOR OF COMMERCE
> Bureau of Industrial Property Protection
> Ministry of National Economy
> 19 rue al-Djazira, Tunisia

TURKEY

Copyrights

Member: Bern Industrial Convention
Law: Number 5846, December 5, 1951, Artistic and Intellectual Works

Patents

Duration: 5, 10 or 15 years
Law: March 23, 1879 as amended
Member: World Intellectual Property Organization, European Patent Convention, and Paris Union International Convention

Trademarks

Duration: 10 years
Law: Trademark Law 511, March 3, 1965

Information concerning patents and trademarks should be addressed to:

SINAI MULKIYET MUDURLUGU
Sanayi Bahanligi
Konur Sokak
Yenirsehir, Anakara, Turkey

UNITED ARAB EMIRATES

Copyrights

N/A

Patents

There are no patent laws.

Trademarks

Duration: 10 years

UNITED KINGDOM

Copyrights

Duration: Author's life plus 50 years
Member: Universal Copyright Convention

Patents

Duration: Basic patents—16 years; secret patents—16 years
Member: Paris Union International Convention, Patent Cooperation Treaty, and European Patent Convention

Industrial Designs

Duration: 5 years

Trademarks

Duration: 7 years
Administered by the Trade Marks Registry located at the same adddress as the Patent Office

Patent and industrial design inquiries and applications should be directed to:

COMPTROLLER
The Patent Office
25 Southhampton Buildings
Chancery Lane
London, W.C.

U.S.S.R.

Copyrights

Duration: Author's life plus 25 years
Recognizes the Universal Copyright Convention, effective May 27, 1973
Administered by the Copyright Agency of the U.S.S.R. (VAAP)
Arrangements for collaboration with Soviet authors must be made through:

VAAP
613 Bronnaya
Moscow 103104, U.S.S.R.

Patents

Duration: 15 years
Member: Patent Cooperation Treaty
Law: Statute on Discoveries, Inventions and Innovation Proposals, effective January 1, 1974
Investors' Certificates are commonly issued.

Industrial Designs

Law: Industrial Designs, effective July 9, 1965

Trademarks

Duration: 10 years
Law: Statute on Trademarks, effective January 23, 1972
Patents and trademarks are administered by:

PATENT BUREAU OF THE U.S.S.R.
Chamber of Commerce
6 Kuibyshev, Moscow

ZAMBIA

Copyrights

Duration: Author's life plus 25 years
Member: Universal Copyright Convention
Law: Zambia Copyright Law

Patents

Duration: 16 years
Law: Zambian Patents Act of 1957
Member: Paris Union International Convention

Trademarks

Duration: 7 years
Copyrights, patents, and trademarks are handled by:

> REGISTRAR OF PATENTS, TRADEMARKS AND DESIGNS
> Ministry of Commerce
> Box 1968
> Lusaka, Zambia

FOREIGN-PATENT ATTORNEYS

ARGENTINA
ALLENDE & BREA
Juncal 691, 6th Floor
Buenos Aires, Argentina

ESTUDIO BECCAR VARELA
Cerrito 740
Buenos Aires, Argentina

HAUSHEER BELGRANO & FERNANDEZ
Florida 142, 1337
Buenos Aires, Argentina

AUSTRALIA

BLAKE & RIGGALL
140 William Street
Melbourne, Victoria, Australia

ARTHUR ROBINSON & HEDDERWICKS
G.P.O. Box 1776Q
Melbourne, 3001, Victoria
Australia

AUSTRIA

DR. ERICH ZEINER
Dr. Hans-Georg Zeiner
Dr. Norbert Pirker
Schellinggasse 6
Vienna, Austria

BAHAMAS

HARRY B. SANDS
330 Bay Street
Nassau, Bahamas

WALLACE WHITFIELD & CO.
Queen Street
Nassau, Bahamas

BELGIUM

BUREAU GEVERS, S.A.
7, rue de Livourne, B-1050
Brussels, Belgium

LEBRUN, DE SMEDT & DASSESSE
Franklin D. Roosevelt Avenue 96A
Brussels, Belgium

BOLIVIA

BUFETE HINOJOSA ANTEZANA
Avenida Arce No. 2071
3er Piso, Ofincina 7
La Paz, Bolivia

C.R. & F. ROJAS
Loayza 250 (5° Piso) (Edificio Castilla)
La Paz, Bolivia

BRAZIL

DANIEL & CIA
Rua da Alfandega 108, 7° andar
Rio de Janeiro, 20070, Brazil

MOMSEN, LEONARDOS & CIA
Rua Teofilo Otoni, 63°–8°/9°/10°
Rio de Janeiro, Brazil

CAYMAN ISLANDS (BRITISH WEST INDIES)

HUNTER & HUNTER
Huntlaw Building
Grand Cayman, Cayman Islands

MAPLES & CALDER
Cayman International Trust Building
Grand Cayman, Cayman Islands

CHILE

ESTUDI ARTURO ALESSANDRI
Huerfanos 1376, 3rd Floor
Santiago, Chile

ESTUDIO JURIDICO OTERO
Paseo Ahumunda 179, 5th Floor
Santiago, Chile

COLUMBIA

BRIGARD & CASTRO
Carrera 7a No. 16-56, 9th Floor
P.O. Box Airmail 36-92
Bogota, Columbia

CAVELIER ABOGADOS
Edificio Siski, Carrera 4a. No. 72-35, 8
Bogota, Columbia

POMBO URIBE & CIA
Calle 13 No. 8-39, Apartado 11351
Bogota, Columbia

COSTA RICA

BUFETE DAREMBLUM
Apartado Postal 1756
San Jose, Costa Rica

FOURNIRE GUTIERREZ & ASOCIADOS
Apartado 348, Centro Colon
San Jose, Costa Rica

ZURCHER, MONTOYA & ZURCHER
P.O. Box 4066
San Jose, Costa Rica

CYPRUS

DR. ANDREAS P. POETIS & CO.
19, Makarios, 3rd Avenue
Larnaca, Cyprus

DENMARK

LAW FIRM HOLM-NIELSEN & PLESNER
37 Amaliegade
Copenhagen, Denmark

ECUADOR

BARRAGAN ROMERO & BARRAGAN
MEDINA
Calles 10 de Agosto y Riofrio
Esquina Edificio Benalcazar 1000
P.O. Box 515
Quito, Ecuador

BUSTAMANTE & CRESPO
Avenues Patria & Amazonas
Cofiec Building, 10th Floor
P.O. Box 2455
Quito, Ecuador

QUEVEDO & PONCE Y CARBO
Avenida 747
P.O. Box 600
Quito, Ecuador

EGYPT

HASHEM, IBRAHIM & TAWFIK
23, Kasr El-Nil Street
Cairo, Egypt

ENGLAND

HASELTINE LAKE & CO.
Haslitt House
28 Southampton Buildings
London, WC2A 1AT, England

LADAS & PARRY (AMERICAN ATTOR-
NEYS)
High Holborn House
52-54 High Holborn
London, WCIV 6RR, England

MORGAN Y MORGAN
(PANAMANIAN ATTORNEYS)
Suite 6, 52 Haymarket
London SW1, England

FINLAND

DITTMAR & IDRENIUS
Pohjoisesplanadi 25 B
Helsinki, Finland

PROCOPE & HORNBORG
Mannerheimintie 20B
Helsinki, Finland

FRANCE

CHARTIER, HOURCADE, JOBARD, CON-
NOR,
    ASSOCIATION d'AVOCATS
83 Avenue Foch
Paris, France

COURTPIS BOULOY LEBEL & ASSOCIES
5 Rue de Chaillot
Paris, France

WEINSTEIN LAW OFFICES
20, Avenue de Friedland
Paris, France

LAW OFFICES OF WILLIAM J. REZAC
    (AMERICAN aTTORNEY)
49 Avenue Franklin D. Roosevelt
Paris, France

GOODRICH, RIQUELME Y ASOCIADOS
    (MEXICAN ATTORNEYS)
15 Rue Greuze
Paris 75116 France

GERMANY

AXSTER & PARTNER
Kaiser-Wilhelm-Ring 43
Dusseldorf, Germany

HEUKING, KUHN, HEROLD,
    KUNZ & PARTNER
Wasserstrasse 13
Dusseldorf, Germany

PETER VON ROSPATT
Dr. Horst von der Osten
Dr. Ulrich Pross
Postfach 110935
Dusseldorf, Germany

BOESEBECK, BARZ & PARTNER
Burnitzstrasse 42-44
P.O. Box 700126
Frankfurt, 6000 Germany

KLAKA & PARTNER
Delpstrasse 4
Munich, Germany

LADAS & PARRY (AMERICAN ATTOR-
NEYS)
Isartorplatz 5, D-8000
Munich, Germany

GHANA

VIDAL L. BUCKLE & CO.
Wuowoti Chambers
10 Cantonments Road Accra
P.O. Box 362 Accra
Accra, Ghana

GREECE

C.B.E. & D. LAMBADARIOS
7, Voulis Street
Athens, Greece

ZEPOS & ZEPOS
120 Vas. Sophias Avenue
Athens, Greece

GUATEMALA

SARAVIA Y MUNOZ
14 Calle 4-32, Zona 10, Cuarto Nivel
Guatemala City, Guatemala

JORGE SKINNER-KLEE
9a Calle 3-72, Zona 1
Guatemala City, Guatemala

HAITI

CABINET LAMARRE
Rue Americaine, 27
Port-au-Prince, Haiti

TALLEYRAND & TALLEYRAND
159, Rue Des Miracles
Georges Talleyrand's Building
P.O. Box 1263
Port-au-Prince, Haiti

HONDURAS

BUFETE ORTEZ COLINDRES Y ASO-
CIADOS
Edificio El Centro
Tegucigalpa, Honduras

HONG KONG

DEACONS
Chater Road
Hong Kong

JOHNSON, STOKES & MASTER
11th Floor, Alexandra House
16-20 Chater Road
Hong Kong

INDIA

LITTLE & COMPANY
Mahatma Gandhi Road
Bombay, India

MULLA & MULLA & CRAIGIE BLUNT &
CAROE
51 Mahatma Gandhi Road
Bombay, India

ISRAEL

YAACOV SALOMON, LIPSCHUTZ & CO.
Yoel House, 64 Hameginim Avenue
P.O. Box 303
Haifa, Israel

SANFORD T. COLB & CO.
Bet Eliahu, 2 Ibn Gvirol Street
Tel Aviv, Israel

ITALY

JACOBACCI-CASETTA & PERANI
Via Visconti di Modrone
Milan, Italy

UGHI & NUNZIANTE
Via Venti Settembre 1
Rome, Italy

JAMAICA

PERKINS, TOMLINSON, GRANT,
    STEWART & CO.
11A Swallowfield Road
P.O. Box 358, 5
Kingston, Jamaica

JAPAN

NAKAMURA & PARTNERS
New Tokyo Building, 3-1
Marunouchi 3-Chome,
    Chiyoda-Ku, 100
Tokyo, Japan

ADACHI, HENDERSON, MIYATAKA &
FUJITA
    (AMERICAN ATTORNEYS)
10th Floor, Time & Life Building
3-6, Otemachi 2-Chome, Chiyoda-Ku
Central
Tokyo, Japan

KENYA

HAMILTON HARRISON & MATHEWS
Kenyatta Avenue
Nairobi, Kenya

KOREA

KIM MYUNG SHIN PATENT & LAW
OFFICE
Room No. 1503, Sam Jung Building
69-5, 2-Ka, Taepyong-Ro, Choong-Ku
Seoul, Korea

LEBANON

LAW OFFICES OF DR. MUHAMED
MUGRABY
202 Lions Building, Sorati Street,
    Hamra
P.O. Box 11-4780
Beirut, Lebanon

LIECHTENSTEIN

RITTER, WOHLWEND, WOLFF
Pflugstrasse 10 (Kastanienhof)
Vaduz, Liechtenstein

LUXEMBOURG

OFFICE DANNEMEYER
    (AMERICAN ATTORNEYS)
21-25 Alle Scheffer
P.O. Box 41
Luxembourg

MEXICO

ANGULO, CALVO, ENRIQUEZ Y GONZA-
LEZ,
    S.C.
Paseo Triunfo de la Republica 3980-201
Ciudad Juarez, Chihuahua, Mexico

GOODRICH, RIQUELME Y ASOCIADOS
Paseo de la Reforma 355, 06500
Mexico, D.F., Mexico

BUFETE SONI
Avenida Presidente Masaryk 101,
    11570
Mexico, D.F., Mexico

NETHERLANDS ANTILLES

SPEETJENS, STEEMAN & LOPEZ
7 Frontstreet
Phililsburg, St. Maarten
Netherlands Antilles

CIVIL LAW NOTARY OFFICE PALM &
SENIOR
50 de Ruyterkade
Willemstad, Curacao
Netherlands Antilles

NEW ZEALAND

NICHOLSON GRIBBIN
Corner Customs & Albert Streets
Auckland, New Zealand

A.J. PARK & SON
140-150 Lambton Quay
Wellington, New Zealand

NICARAGUA

CARRION, HUECK & MANZANARES
Edificio Juris, Apartado 2422
Managua, Nicaragua

NIGERIA

BENTLEY, EDU & COMPANY
24/26 Campbell Street, 7th Floor
Lagos, Nigeria

NORWAY

ADVOKATFIRMAET SCHJODT
Grensen 12
Oslo, Norway

PAKISTAN

ABRAHAM & SARWANA
410 Press Center, Shahrah Kamal
   Ataturk
Karachi, Pakistan

SURRIDGE & BEECHENO
Ghulam Rasool Building
60, Shahrah-e-Quaid-e-Azam
Lahore, Pakistan

REPUBLIC OF PANAMA

ALFARO, FERRER, RAMIREZ & ALEMAN
Avenida Federico Boyd No. 33
Panama

MORGAN Y MORGAN
Torre Bancosur Building, 16th Floor
Calle 53 E., Urbanizacion Nuevo
   Obarrio
Panama

PARAGUAY

ESTUDIO MERSAN ABOGADOS
F.R. Moreno 509
Asuncion, Paraguay

VOUGA & OLMEDO
3rd Floor, Banco Sudameris
Asuncion, Paraguay

PERU

BARRIOS, FUENTES, URQUIAGA Y
DANINO
Arias Araguez 250, San Antonio
Lima, Peru

OSTERLING, ARIAS-SSHREIBER, VEGA,
   ROSSELLO & ASOCIADOS
Avenida Pardo y Aliaga 640
Piso 8 San Isidro
Lima, Peru

REPUBLIC OF THE PHILIPPINES

CASTILLO, LAMAN, TAN & PANTALEON
Singapore Airlines Building
138 H.V. de la Costa Street,
Salcedo Village
Manila, Philippines

SYCIP, SALAZAR, HERNANDEZ & GAT-
MAITAN
PAIC Building, 105 Paseo de Raxas
Makati, Metro Manila, Philippines

PORTUGAL

JOSE VERA JARDIM, JULIO CASTRO
CALDAS,
   JORGE SAMPAIO
Av. Duque de Avila, 66-5th Floor
Lisbon, Portugal

Goncalves Pereira
Praca Marques de Pombal, No 1, 8°
   andar
Lisbon, Portugal

SOUTH AFRICA

ADAMS & ADAMS
2817 Trust Bank Centre
Heerengracht, 8001
P.O. Box 1513
Cape Town, South Africa

D.M. KISH INCORPORATED
11th Floor, Glen Cairn,
   73 Market Street
P.O. Box 668, 2000
Johannesburg, South Africa

SPAIN

BUFETE ARBOLEYA
General Oraa, 68
Madrid, Spain

Despacho, Luis Lamana, Abogados
Calle de Montalban No. 5
Madrid, Spain

SWEDEN

ADVOKATFIRMAN FRITZ ENGSTROM AB
Drottninggatan 25, P.O. Box 16 282,
S-103 25
Stockholm, Sweden

SWITZERLAND

EGLI PATENT ATTORNEYS
Horneggstrasse 4,
P.O. Box 473, CH-8034
Zurich, Switzerland

TAIWAN (REPUBLIC OF CHINA)

BAKER & MCKENZIE
685 Min Sheng East Road
Taipei, Taiwan

SAINT ISLAND INTERNATIONAL PATENT
& TRADEMARK OFFICE
3rd Floor, 52, Chang-An East Road
Section 2, 104
Taipei, Taiwan

TAIWAN INTERNATIONAL PATENT & LAW
   OFFICE
7th Floor, We Shang First Building,
   No. 125
Nanking East Road, Section 2
P.O. Box 39-243
Taipei, Taiwan

THAILAND

DOMNERN SOMGAIT & BOONMA
719 Siphya Road G.P.O. Box 203,
10500
Bangkok, Thailand

Dr. Mana Law & Tax Office
16/7 North Sathorn Road
   (near Wireless Square)
Bangkok, Thailand

TUNISIA

SAMIR EL ANNABI & ASSOCIATES
Immeuble Errouki (Bloc A),
Voie X-X4 El-Manar 2
Tunis, Tunisia

TURKEY

MORDO DINAR
Set Ustu, Derya Han
Istanbul, Turkey

URUGUAY

GUYER & REGULES
Plaza Independencia 811, P.B.
Montevideo, Uruguay

VENEZUELA

BENTATA, HOET & ASOCIADOS
Torre Europa, Pent House Avenida
    Generalisimo Francisco de Miranda
    (con Campo Alegre)
Caracas, Venezuela

YUGOSLAVIA

DJURDJE M. NINKOVIC
Milovana Milovanovica 1
Belgrade, Yugoslavia

FOREIGN CONSULAR OFFICES IN THE U.S. (1987)

(Area Code 202)

AFGHANISTAN, DEMOCRATIC REPUBLIC OF,	
2341 Wyoming Avenue, NW., 20008	234-3770
ALGERIA, DEMOCRATIC & POPULAR REPUBLIC OF, 2118 Kalorama Road, NW.,	
20008	328-5300
IRANIAN INTERESTS SECTION, 2139 Wisconsin Ave. NW., 20007	965-4990
ANTIGUA AND BARBUDA, 3400 International Dr. NW., #2H, 20008	362-5122
ARGENTINE REPUBLIC, 1600 New Hampshire Ave. NW., 20009	939-6400
AUSTRALIA, 1601 Massachusetts Ave. NW., 20036	797-3000
AUSTRIA, 2343 Massachusetts Ave. NW., 20008	483-4474
BAHAMAS, COMMONWEALTH OF THE,	
600 New Hampshire Ave. NW., Suite 865, 20037	944-3390
BAHRAIN, STATE OF, 3502 International Dr. NW., 20008	342-0741
BANGLADESH, PEOPLE'S REPUBLIC OF, 2201 Wisconsin Ave. NW., 20007	342-8372
BARBADOS, 2144 Wyoming Ave. NW., 20008	939-9200
BELGIUM, 3330 Garfield St. NW., 20008	333-6900
BELIZE, 3400 International Dr. NW., 20008, Suite 2J	363-4505
BENIN, PEOPLE'S REPUBLIC OF, 2737 Cathedral Ave. NW., 20008	232-6656
BOLIVIA, 3014 Massachusetts Ave. NW., 20008	483-4410
BOTSWANA, REPUBLIC OF, 4301 Connecticut Ave. NW., Suite 404, 20008	244-4990
BRAZIL, 3006 Massachusetts Ave. NW., 20008	745-2700
BRUNEI, 2600 Virginia Ave. NW., Suite 300, 20037	342-0159
BULGARIA, PEOPLE'S REPUBLIC OF, 1621 22nd St. NW., 20008	387-7969
BURKINA-FASO, 2340 Massachusetts Ave. NW., 20008	332-5577
BURMA, SOCIALIST REP. OF THE UNION OF, 2300 S ST. NW., 20008	332-9044
BURUNDI, REPUBLIC OF, 2233 Wisconsin Ave., NW., Suite 212, 20007	342-2574
CAMEROON, UNITED REPUBLIC OF, 2349 Massachusetts Ave. NW., 20008	265-8790
CANADA, 1746 Massachusetts Ave. NW., 20036	785-1400
CAPE VERDE, REPUBLIC OF, 3415 Massachusetts Ave. NW., 20007	965-6820
CENTRAL AFRICAN REPUBLIC, 1618 22nd St. NW., 20008	483-7800
CHAD, REPUBLIC OF, 2002 R St. NW., 20009	462-4009

CHILE, 1732 Massachusetts Ave. NW., 20036	785-1746
CHINA, PEOPLE'S REPUBLIC OF, 2300 Connecticut Ave. NW., 20008	328-2500
COLOMBIA, 2118 Leroy Pl. NW., 20008	387-8338
CONGO, PEOPLE'S REPUBLIC OF THE, 4891 Colorado Ave. NW., 20011	726-5500
COMOROS, FEDERAL AND ISLAMIC REPUBLIC, 336 E. 45th, 2d Fl., NY 10017	(212) 972-8010
COSTA RICA, 1825 Connecticut Ave., Suite 213, NW., 20009	234-2945
COTE D'IVOIRE, 2424 Massachusetts Avenue NW., 20008	483-2400
CYPRUS, REPUBLIC OF, 2211 R St. NW., 20008	462-5772
CZECHOSLOVAK SOCIALIST REPUBLIC, 3900 Linnean Ave. NW., 20008	363-6315
CUBAN INTERESTS SECTION, 2630 and 2639 16th St. NW., 20009	797-8518
DENMARK, 3200 Whitehaven St. NW., 20008	234-4300
DJIBOUTI, REPUBLIC OF, 866 United Nations Plaza, Suite 4011, NY 10017	(212) 753-3163
DOMINICAN REPUBLIC, 1715 22nd St. NW., 20008	332-6280
ECUADOR, 2535 15th St. NW., 20009	234-7200
EGYPT, ARAB REPUBLIC OF, 2310 Decatur Pl. NW., 20008	232-5400
EL SALVADOR, 2308 California St. NW., 20008	265-3480
EQUATORIAL GUINEA, 801 Second Ave., Suite 1403, NY 10017	(212) 599-1523
ESTONIA, Legation of, 9 Rockefeller Plaza, NY 10020	(212) 247-1450
ETHIOPIA, 2134 Kalorama Rd. NW., 20008	234-2281
FIJI, 2233 Wisconsin Ave. NW., Suite 240, 20007	337-8320
FINLAND, 3216 New Mexico Ave. NW., 20016	363-2430
FRANCE, 4101 Reservoir Rd. NW.	944-6000
GABON, 2034 20th St. NW., 20009	797-1000
GAMBIA, THE, 1030-15th St. NW., Suite 720, 20005	842-1356
GERMAN DEMOCRATIC REPUBLIC, 1717 Massachusetts Avenue NW., 20036	232-3134
GERMANY, FEDERAL REPUBLIC OF, 4645 Reservoir Rd. NW., 20007	298-4000
GHANA, 2460 16th St. NW., 20009	462-0761
GREECE, 2221 Massachusetts Avenue NW., 20008	667-3168
GRENADA, 1701 New Hampshire Avenue, NW., 20009	265-2561
GUATEMALA, 2220 R St. NW., 20008	745-4952
GUINEA, REPUBLIC OF, 2112 Leroy Pl. NW., 20008	483-9420
GUINEA-BISSAU, REPUBLIC OF, 211 E. 43rd St., Suite 604, NY 10017	(212) 661-3977
GUYANA, 2490 Tracy Place NW., 20008	265-6900
HAITI, 2311 Massachusetts Ave. NW., 20008	332-4090
HOLY SEE, 3339 Massachusetts Ave. NW., 20008	333-7121
HONDURAS, 4301 Connecticut Avenue NW., Suite 100, 20008	966-7700
HUNGARIAN PEOPLE'S REPUBLIC, 3910 Shoemaker St. NW., 20008	362-6730
ICELAND, 2022 Connecticut Avenue NW., 20008	265-6653
INDIA, 2107 Massachusetts Avenue NW., 20008	939-7000
INDONESIA, REPUBLIC OF, 2020 Massachusetts Avenue NW., 20036	775-5200
IRAQ, 1801 P St. NW., 20036	483-7500
IRELAND, 2234 Massachusetts Avenue NW., 20008	462-3939
ISRAEL, 3514 International Dr. NW., 20008	364-5500
ITALY, 1601 Fuller St. NW., 20009	328-5500
JAMAICA, 1850 K St. NW., Suite 355, 20006	452-0660
JAPAN, 2520 Massachusetts Avenue NW., 20008	939-6700
JORDAN HASHEMITE KINGDOM OF, 3504 International Dr. NW., 20008	966-2664
KENYA, 2249 R St. NW., 20008	387-6101

KOREA, REPUBLIC OF, 2320 Massachusetts Avenue NW., 20008   939-5600
KUWAIT, STATE OF, 2940 Tilden St. NW., 20008   966-0702
LAO PEOPLES'S DEMOCRATIC REPUBLIC, 2222 S St. NW., 20008   332-6416
LATVIA, Legation of, 4325 17th St. NW., 20011   726-8213
LEBANON, 2560 28th St. NW., 20008   939-6300
LESOTHO, KINGDOM OF, 1430 K St. NW, 6th Fl. 20005   628-4833
LIBERIA, REPUBLIC OF, 5201 16th St. NW., 20011   723-0437
LITHUANIA, Legation of, 2622 16th St. NW., 20009   234-5860
LUXEMBOURG, 2200 Massachusetts Avenue NW., 20008   265-4171
MADAGASCAR, DEMOCRATIC REPUBLIC OF,
  2374 Massachusetts Avenue NW., 20008   265-5525
MALAWI, 2480 Massachusetts Ave., NW., 20008   797-1007
MALAYSIA, 2401 Massachusetts Avenue NW., 20008   328-2700
MALI, REPUBLIC OF, 2130 R St. NW., 20008   332-2249
MALTA, 2017 Connecticut Avenue NW., 20008   462-3611
MAURITANIA, ISLAMIC REPUBLIC OF, 2129 Leroy Place NW., 20008   232-5700
MAURITIUS, 4301 Connecticut Avenue NW., Suite 134, 20008   244-1491
MEXICO, 2829 16th St. NW., 20009   234-6000
MOROCCO, 1601 21st St. NW., 20009   462-7979
MOZAMBIQUE, PEOPLE'S REPUBLIC OF, 1990 M St. NW., Suite 570, 20037   293-7146
NEPAL, 2131 Leroy Pl. NW., 20008   667-4550
NETHERLANDS, THE, 4200 Linnean Ave. NW., 20008   244-5300
NEW ZEALAND, 37 Observatory Circle NW., 20008   328-4800
NICARAGUA, 1627 New Hampshire Ave. NW., 20009   387-4371
NIGER, REPUBLIC OF, 2204 R St. NW., 20008   483-4224
NIGERIA, 2201 M St. NW., 20037   822-1500
NORWAY, 2720 34th St. NW., 20008   333-6000
OMAN, SULTANATE OF, 2342 Massachusetts Ave., NW., 20008   387-1980
PAKISTAN, 2315 Massachusetts Avenue, NW., 20008   939-6200
PANAMA, 2862 McGill Terrace NW., 20008   483-1407
PAPUA NEW GUINEA, 1330 Connecticut Ave. NW., 20036   659-0856
PARAGUAY, 2400 Massachusetts Ave. NW., 20008   483-6960
PERU, 1700 Massachusetts Avenue NW., 20036   833-9860
PHILIPPINES, 1617 Massachusetts Avenue NW., 20036   483-1414
POLISH PEOPLE'S REPUBLIC, 2640 16th St. NW., 20009   234-3800
PORTUGAL, 2125 Kalorama Rd. NW., 2008   328-8610
QATAR, STATE OF, 600 New Hampshire Avenue NW., Suite 1180, 20037   338-0111
ROMANIA, SOCIALIST REPUBLIC OF, 1607 23rd St. NW., 20008   232-4747
RWANDA, REPUBLIC OF, 1714 New Hampshire Avenue NW., 20009   232-2882
SAINT CHRISTOPHER AND NEVIS, 2501 M St. NW., Suite 540, 20037   833-3550
SAINT LUCIA, 2100 M St. NW., Suite 309, 20037   463-7378
SAUDIA ARABIA, 601 New Hampshire Ave. NW., 20037   342-3800
SENEGAL, REPUBLIC OF, 2112 Wyoming Avenue NW., 20008   234-0540
SEYCHELLES, REPUBLIC OF, 820 Second Ave., Suite 203, NY 10017   (212) 687-9766
SIERRA LEONE, 1701 19th St. NW., 20009   939-9261
SINGAPORE, REPUBLIC OF, 1824 R St. NW., 20009   667-7555
SOMALI DEMOCRATIC REPUBLIC,
  600 New Hampshire Avenue NW., Suite 710, 20037   342-1575

SOUTH AFRICA, 3051 Massachusetts Avenue NW., 20008   232-4400
SPAIN, 2700 15th St. NW., 20009   265-0190
SRI LANKA, DEMOCRATIC SOCIALIST REP. OF, 2148 Wyoming Ave. NW., 20008   483-4025
SUDAN, REPUBLIC OF THE, 2210 Massachusetts Ave. NW., 20008   338-8565
SURINAME, REPUBLIC OF, 2600 Virginia Ave. NW., Suite 711, 20037   338-6980
SWAIZILAND, KINGDOM OF, 4301 Connecticut Ave. NW., 20008   362-6683
SWEDEN, 600 New Hampshire Ave. NW., Suite 1200, 20037   944-5600
SWITZERLAND, 2900 Cathedral Ave. NW., 20008   745-7900
SYRIAN ARAB REPUBLIC, 2215 Wyoming Ave. NW., 20008   232-6313
TANZANIA, UNITED REPUBLIC OF, 2139 R St. NW, 20008   939-6125
THAILAND, 2300 Kalorama Rd. NW., 20008   483-7200
TOGO, REPUBLIC OF, 2208 Massachusetts Avenue NW., 20008   234-4212
TRINIDAD AND TOBAGO, 1708 Massachusetts Ave. NW., 20036   467-6490
TUNISIA, 1515 Massachusetts Ave. NW., 20005   862-1850
TURKEY, REPUBLIC OF, 1606 23rd St. NW., 20008   387-3200
UGANDA, REPUBLIC OF, 5909 16th St. NW., 20011   726-7100
UNION OF SOVIET SOCIALISTS REPUBLICS, 1125 16th St. NW., 20036   628-7551
UNITED ARAB EMIRATES, 600 New Hampshire Ave. NW., Suite 740, 20037   338-6500
UNITED KINGDOM OF GR. BRITAIN & N. IRELAND,
   3100 Massachusetts Ave. NW., 20008   462-1340
URUGUAY, 1918 F St. NW., 20006   331-1313
VENEZUELA, 2445 Massachusetts Ave. NW., 20008   797-3800
WESTERN SAMOA, INDEPENDENT STATE OF, 820 Second Ave., NY 10017   (212) 599-6196
YEMEN ARAB REPUBLIC, 600 New Hampshire Ave. NW., Suite 840, 20037   965-4760
YUGOSLAVIA, SOCIALIST FEDERAL REPUBLIC OF,
   2410 California St. NW., 20008   462-6566
ZAIRE, REPUBLIC OF, 1800 New Hampshire Ave. NW., 20009   234-7690
ZAMBIA, REPUBLIC OF, 2419 Massachusetts Ave. NW., 20008   265-9717
ZIMBABWE, 2852 McGill Terrace NW., 20008   332-7100
COMMISSION OF THE EUROPEAN COMMUNITIES,
   2100 M St. NW., Suite 707, 20037   862-9500

Part 5
Resources

BOOKS ON INVENTIONS

Alexander, R.C. *I Thought of It First: The Joys and Frustrations of Inventing*. Camarillo, CA: Geothermal World.

Bender, Matthew. Edited by *European Patents Handbook*. London, England: Chartered Institute of Patent Agents, 1978. Updates 1985 and 1986.

Einhorn, Harold. *Patent Licensing Transactions*, 2 vol. New York: Matthew Bender, 1968. Updates 1985 and 1986.

Flanagan, John R. *How to Prepare Patent Applications: A Self-Study Course Book Using Actual Inventions*. Boulder, CO: Patent Education Publications, 1983.

Freidel, Robert and Paul Isreal. *Edison's Electric Light: Biography of an Invention*. New Brunswick, NJ: Rutgers University Press, 1985.

Fuller, Melvin L. *Inventor's Guidebook*. Hollywood, FL: Mindsight Publishing.

Gausewitz, Richard L. *Patent Pending: Today's Inventors & Their Inventions*. Greenwich, CT: Devin Adair, 1983.

Greer, Thomas J. *Writing & Understanding U.S. Patent Claims*. Charlottesville, VA: Michie Co., 1979.

Gunn, A.V. *How to Design Better Products for Less Money*. Simi Valley, CA: Halls of Ivy Press, 1976.

Husch, Tony and Linda Foust. *That's a Great Idea: How to Get, Evaluate, Protect, Develop & Sell New Product Ideas*. Berkeley, CA: Ten Speed Press, 1987.

Kivenson, Gilbert. *The Art and Science of Inventing*. New York: Van Nostrand Reinhold, 1982.

MacCracken, Calvin D. *A Handbook for Inventors*. New York: Charles Scribner's Sons, 1983.

Moore, Lois K. and Daniel L. Plung. *Marketing Technical Ideas and Products Successfully*. Washington, D.C.: IEEE Press, 1985.

Norris, Kenneth. *The Inventor's Guide to Low-Cost Patenting*. New York: Macmillan, 1985.

Paige, Richard E. *Little Inventions That Made Big Money*. Camarillo, CA: Geothermal World.

——————. *Simplicity, The Key to Successful Inventions*. Hollywood, FL: Mindsight Publishing.

Pressman, David. *Patent It Yourself*. Berkeley, CA: Nolo Press, 1985.

Reefman, William E. *How To Sell Your Own Invention*. Simi Valley, CA: Halls of Ivy Press, 1977.

Shennan, Anthony. *Nikola Testa, Savant Genius of the Twentieth Century*. Camarillo, CA: Geothermal World.

Steele, J. Rodman. *Is This My Reward? An Employee's Struggle for Fairness in Corporate Exploitation of His Inventions*. West Palm Beach, FL: Pencraft Press, 1986.

BOOKS ON TRADEMARKS

Kuwayama, Yasaburo. *Trade Marks & Symbols,* 2 vol. New York: Van Nostrand Reinhold. 1973.

Murphy, John and Michael Rowe. *How to Design Trademarks and Logos.* Cincinnati, OH: North Light Books, 1988.

New Trade Names. Detroit, MI: Gale Research Company, 1988.

BOOKS ON COPYRIGHTS

Boorstyn, Neil. *Copyright Law.* Rochester, NY: The Lawyers Co-Op, 1981.

Elias, Stephen. *Intellectual Property Dictionary.* Berkeley, CA: Nolo Press, 1985.

Johnston, Donald F. *Copyright Handbook.* New York: R.R. Bowker, 1982.

Miller, Jerome K. *The Copyright Directory.* Friday Harbor, WA: Copyright Information Services, 1985.

Salone, M.J. *How to Copyright Software.* Berkeley, CA: Nolo Press, 1987.

BOOKS BY THE AUTHOR

Barber, Hoyt L. *How to Form a Private Tax-Free Nevada Corporation.* New York: Liberty House, 1990.

_____. *How to Incorporate Your Business In Any State.* New York: Liberty House, 1989.

_____ *How To Make Money In Patent Licensing.* 1989. Patent Licensing Opportunities, Box 18482, Fountain Hills, AZ 85269.

ASSISTANCE FOR INVENTORS

CANADIAN INDUSTRIAL INNOVATION CENTRE
156 Columbia St. West
Waterloo, Ontario, Canada N2L 3L3
(519) 885-5870

BATTELLA DEVELOPMENT CORP.
505 King Ave.
Columbus, OH 43201
(614) 424-6424

AFFILIATED INVENTORS
501 Iowa Ave.
Colorado Springs, CO 80909
(303) 635-1234

KESSLER SALES CORPORATION
Fremont, OH 43420

DR. DVORKOVITZ & ASSOCIATES
P.O. Box 1748
Ormond Beach, FL 32075-1748
904) 677-7033

WISCONSIN INNOVATION SERVICE CENTER
University of Wisconsin
402 McCutchan Hall
Whitewater, WI 53190
(414) 472-1365

SOCIETY OF AMERICAN INVENTORS
505 E. Jackson St.
Suite 204
Tampa, FL 33602
(818) 221-2348

INVENTORS WORKSHOP INTERNATIONAL
  EDUCATION FOUNDATION
3573 Old Conejo Rd.
Suite 120
Newbury Park, CA 91320
(805) 499-1626

INVENTORS CLUB OF AMERICA
Box 450261
Atlanta, GA 30345
(404) 938-5089

THE AMERICAN SOCIETY OF INVENTORS INC.
P.O. Box 58426
Philadelphia, PA 19102
(215) 546-6601

BAYLOR UNIVERSITY
Center for Entrepreneurship
Hankamer School of Business
Waco, TX 76798
(817) 755-2265

GENEXUS
200 N. Main
Suite 200
Salt Lake City, UT 84103
(801) 328-1501

MINDSIGHT
Box 6664
Woodland Hills, CA 91365
(805) 499-8917

For more information concerning regional inventor's
organizations, contact:

NATIONAL CONGRESS OF INVENTOR ORGANIZATIONS
215 Rheem Rd.
Moraga, CA 94556
(415) 376-7541

INVENTION SHOWS

ANNUAL INVENTOR AND ENTREPRENEUR
  CONGRESS
Thomas Lincoln, Conference Chair
P.O. Box 4365
Denver, CO 80204

ANNUAL INVENTORS EXPO
Office of Public Affairs
Patent and Trademark Office
Washington, D.C. 20231

APPALACHIAN INVENTORS FAIR
P.O. Box 388
Oak Ridge, TN 37830

CLEVELAND ENGINEER SOCIETY
3100 Chester St.
Cleveland, OH 44114

INTERNATIONAL INVENTORS EXPO
P.O. Box 20145
Cathedral Finance Station
New York, NY 10025
(212) 666-1874

INVENTION CONVENTION
6860 Canby, Suite 110
Reseda, CA 91335
(818) 344-3375

IWI INVENTORS EXPOSITION
121 N. Fir St.
Ventura, CA 91003

MID-AMERICA NEW IDEAS FAIR
P.O. Box 100
Hill City, KS 67642

MINNESOTA INVENTORS CONGRESS
P.O. Box 71
Redwood Falls, MN 56283

NATIONAL INVENTORS SHOW
New York Hilton Hotel
Avenue of the Americas/53rd St.
New York, NY 10019

NATIONAL INVENTION WORKSHOP
U.S. Dept. of Commerce
National Bureau of Standards
Gaithersburg, MD 20899

NORTH DAKOTA INVENTORS CONGRESS
Jamestown Chamber of Commerce
Box 1530
Jamestown, ND 58402

WORLD FAIR FOR TECHNOLOGY EXCHANGE
Dr. Dvorkovitz & Associates
P.O. Box 1748
Ormond Beach, FL 32074

MAGAZINES FOR INVENTORS

Inventor USA Magazine (bi-monthly)
1 year—$20
505 E. Jackson St., Suite 204
Tampa, FL 33602
(818) 221-2343

Invent! Magazine
Published bi-monthly by Mindsight Publishing
3201 Corte Malpaso, #304
Camarillo, CA 93010
(805) 388-3097

INTERNATIONAL TRADE NEWSLETTERS

American Exporter Marketer
Newsletter Management Corporation
10076 Boca Entrada Blvd.
Boca Raton, FL 33433

Doing Business in Europe
Commerce Clearing House, Inc.
4025 W. Peterson Ave.
Chicago, IL 60646

International Electronic Trade Opportunities
Elmatex International
3640 Sepulveda Blvd.
Los Angeles, CA 90034

International Intertrade Index
Box 636 Federal Square
Newark, NJ 07101

International New Product News
U.S. International Marketing Co., Inc.
17057 Bellflower Blvd.
Bellflower, CA 90706

World Convention Dates
Hendrickson Publishing Co., Inc.
79 Washington St.
Hempstead, NY 11550

New From Europe Newsletter
New From Japan Newsletter
New From U.S. Newsletter
Prestwick International, Inc.
P.O. Box 205
Burnt Hills, NY 12027

BUSINESS NEWSLETTERS

Business Ideas
Dan Newman Co.
57 Lakeview Ave.
Clifton, NJ 07011

Leads USA
5 Auburn St.
Framingham, MA 01701

Business Opportunities Digest
301 Plymouth Dr. NE
Dalton, GA 30720

Money Makers Newsletter
Box 752
Orange Park, FL 32067-0752

Creative Ideas Newsletter
Castle Publishing Co.
1422 Kilcrease Circle
Paradise, CA 95969

New Product Development Newsletter
Point Publishing Co.
P.O. Box 1309
Point Pleasant, NJ 08742

Drop Shipping News
Consolidated Marketing Services, Inc.
P.O. Box 3328
New York, NY 10017

Tradeshow Week
Tradeshow Week International
12233 W. Olympia Blvd., #236
Los Angeles, CA 90064

Hoyt Barber Reports
P.O. Box 18482
Fountain Hills, AZ 85269
(Incorporates ''Patent Licensing Opportunities'')

Your Product and the Law
Business Research Publications, Inc.
817 Broadway
New York, NY 10003

DIRECTORIES

The Directory of Directories
A Directory of Research Centers
Encyclopedia of Associations
Directory of British Associations
Directory of European Associations
Gale Research Company
2200 Book Tower
Detroit, MI 48226

MacRae's Blue Book
MacRae's Blue Book Company
100 Shore Drive
Hinsdale, IL 60521

National Telephone Directories
(800) 551-4400

STANDARD RATE AND DATA SERVICE
5201 Old Orchard Rd.
Skokie, IL 60076

Bacon's Publicity Checker
Bacon's Publishing Company, Inc.
332 S. Michigan Ave.
Chicago, IL 60604

Literary Market Place
R.R. Bowker Company
245 W. 17th St.
New York, NY 10011

The Klein Guide to American Directories
B. Klein Publications
P.O. Box 8503
Coral Springs, FL 33065

INVENTION BOOKS
ILMA Printing & Publishing:
P.O. Box 251
Tarzana, CA 91356
(818) 344-3375

Thomas Register of American Manufacturers
Thomas Publishing Company
One Penn Plaza
New York, NY 10001

Kelly's Manufacturers and Merchants Directory
Kelly's Directories, Ltd.
Neville House, Eden St.
Kingston Upon Thomas
KT1 1BY Surrey, England

Sources of state information and state
    industrial directories:
State Chamber of Commerce Dept.
Chamber of Commerce of the U.S.
1615 H Street, NW
Washington, D.C. 20006

Artist's Market
Fiction Writer's Market
Photographer's Market
Writer's Market
Writer's Digest Books
9933 Alliance Rd.
Cincinnati, OH 45242

Oxbridge Directory of Newsletters
Oxbridge Communications, Inc.
150 Fifth Ave.
New York, NY 10011

Trade directories of the world:
CRONER PUBLICATIONS
211-03 Jamaica Ave.
Queens Village, NY 11429

SELECT INFORMATION EXCHANGE
(A newsletter subscription service;
annual catalog—$2)
2095 Broadway
New York, NY 10023
(212) 874-6408

LITERARY ASSOCIATIONS

THE ACADEMY OF AMERICAN POETS
177 E. 87th St.
New York, NY 10128
(212) 427-5665

AMERICAN MEDICAL WRITERS ASSOCIATION
572 River Rd., Suite 410
Bethesda, MD 20816
(301) 986-9119

AMERICAN WOMEN IN RADIO & TV
1101 Connecticut Ave.
Washington, DC 20036
(202) 296-0008

THE AUTHOR'S LEAGUE FUNDS
234 W. 44th St.
New York, NY 10036
(212) 391-3966
Extend interest-free loans to
professional authors who need
financial assistance.)

THE AUTHOR'S LEAGUE OF AMERICA, INC.
234 W. 44th St.
New York, NY 10036
(212) 391-9198

CHRISTIAN WRITERS GUILD
260 Fern Lane
Hume, CA 93628
(209) 335-2333

COUNCIL OF WRITERS ORGANIZATIONS
1501 Broadway, Suite 1907
New York, NY 10036
(212) 997-0947

EDITORIAL FREELANCERS ASSOCIATION
20 E. 20th St., Room 305
New York, NY 10011
(212) 677-3357

THE INTERNATIONAL SOCIETY OF DRAMATISTS
Box 1310
Miami, FL 33153
(305) 756-8313

THE INTERNATIONAL WOMEN'S WRITING GUILD
Gracie Station
Box 810
New York, NY 10028
(212) 737-7536

MYSTERY WRITERS OF AMERICA, INC.
150 Fifth Ave.
New York, NY 10011
(212) 255-7005

THE NATIONAL WRITERS CLUB, INC.
1450 S. Havana, Suite 620
Aurora, CO 80012
(303) 751-7844

OUTDOOR WRITERS ASSOCIATION OF AMERICA
2017 Cato Ave., Suite 101
State College, PA 16801
(814) 234-1011

PEN AMERICA CENTER (INTERNATIONAL)
568 Broadway
New York, NY 10012
(212) 334-1660

THE POETRY SOCIETY OF AMERICA
15 Gramercy Park
New York, NY 10003
(212) 254-9628

WOMEN IN COMMUNICATION, INC.
Box 9561
Austin, TX 78766
(512) 346-9875

ROMANCE WRITERS OF AMERICA
5206 FM 1960 West, Suite 207
Houston, TX 77069
(713) 440-6885

WRITERS GUILD OF AMERICA, WEST, INC.
8955 Beverly Blvd.
Los Angeles, CA 90048
(213) 550-1000

SOCIETY OF CHILDREN'S BOOK WRITERS
Box 296, Mar Vista Station
Los Angeles, CA 90066
(818) 347-2849

INTELLECTUAL PROPERTY NEWSLETTERS

United States Patent Quarterly
BNA's Patent, Trademark and Copyright Journal
The Bureau of National Affairs, Inc.
1231-25th St. NW
Washington, DC 20037

Trademark Trends
Board Publishing Co., Inc.
Box 1561
Harrisburg, PA 17105

World Patent Law: Patent Statutes, Regulations & Treaties
Mathew Bender, Inc.
235 E. 45th St.
New York, NY 10017

Copyright Management
Institute for Invention & Innovation, Inc.
85 Irving St., P.O. Box 436
Arlington, MA 02174

I.N. Invention News
Oracle Publishing Co.
OMSR 2648
Oracle, AZ 85263

International Invention Register
(Listings of patents for sale or license):
Catalyst
420 Ammunition Rd., P.O. Box 547
Fallbrook, CA 92028

Invention Management
Institute for Invention & Innovation, Inc.
85 Irving St., P.O. Box 436
Arlington, MA 02174

INTERNATIONAL NEW PRODUCT NEWSLETTER
6 Saint James Ave.
Boston, MA 02116

Patent Licensing Gazette
Techni Research Assn., Inc.
Professional Center Building
41 Easton Rd.
Willow Grove, PA 19090

GOVERNMENT PUBLICATIONS

U.S. Government Book Catalog. Excellent source of informative books. Free.

Annual Indexes. Two volumes. Patentees and titles of inventions. Price varies from year to year, depending upon size of publication.

A Basic Guide to Exporting. A step-by-step guide to establishing profitable international trade. Tells how to get assistance in reaching this goal. 133 pgs. #003-009-00349-1. $6.50.

European Trade Fairs: A Guide for Exporters. How to choose a market in Europe, how to identify the right fairs, and how to make fairs as productive as possible. 75 pgs. #003-009-00341-5. $5.00.

Foreign Consulate Offices in the United States. Contains a complete and official listing of the foreign consulate offices in the U.S., together with their jurisdictions and recognized consulate officers. #004-000-10965-5. $6.50.

General Information Concerning Patents. Contains a brief introduction to patent matters, including the working of the Patent and Trademark Office, what applicants must do, and definitions of patents, copyrights, and trademarks. 46 pgs. #003-004-00596-3. $3.50.

General Information Concerning Trademarks. $2.00.

How to Build an Export Business. A step-by-step guide for small businesses. 168 pgs. #003-000-00532-1. $6.00.

Manual of Classification. A loose-leaf volume listing the numbers and descriptive titles of the more than 390 classes and 115,000 subclasses used in subject classification. Substitute and additional pages, which are included in the subscription service, are issued from time to time. Subscription is $77.00.

Manual of Patent Examining Procedure. A loose-leaf manual which serves primarily as a detailed reference work on the patent-examining practice and procedure for the Patent Examining Corps. Subscription service includes basic manual, quarterly revisions, and change notices. Subscription is $70.00.

Monthly Catalog of United States Government Publications. Lists the U.S. Government publications issued each month. Subscriptions are entered for the calendar year only. Back issues from January are furnished. A one-year subscription is $215.00 to domestic addresses.

Official Gazette of the United States Patent and Trademark Office: Patents. Contains the patents, Patent Office notices, and designs issued each week. Weekly. One-year subscriptions are $523.00 (priority) or $347.00 (non-priority) to domestic addresses. Single copy is $21.00.

Official Gazette of United States Patent and Trademark Office: Trademarks. Contains trademarks, trademark notices, marks published for opposition, trademark registrations issued, and index of registrations. Weekly.

Overseas Business Reports. Monthly publication. Subscription $26.00 yearly.

Patent Attorneys and Agents Registered to Practice Before the U.S. Patent and Trademark Office. #003-004-00573-4. $21.00.

Selling to the Military. Tells how business owners can locate sales opportunities within the Department of Defense and explains the military procurement process. Copies of the Bidders Mailing List Application and Department of Defense Contract Proposal Pricing form are included. 141 pgs. #008-000-00392-1. $6.00

Selling to the U.S. Government. Tells how to secure government business and details ways the Small Business Administration can help. 20 pgs. #045-000-00160-1. $2.50.

Small Business and Government Research and Development. Helps small-business owners determine if they qualify for government R&D contracts and tells how to market these services to the government. 41 pgs. #045-000-00130-0. $4.25.

Small Business Guide to Federal R&D Funding Opportunities. Outlines the steps in the Federal R&D funding process and identifies government sources of fundings and technical information. 136 pgs. #038-000-00522-7. $6.00.

Story of the Patent and Trademark Office. #003-004-00579-3. $4.75.

Trademark Manual of Examining Procedures. $24.00.

All government publications mentioned above can be ordered from:

> SUPERINTENDENT OF DOCUMENTS
> U.S. Government Printing Office
> Washington, D.C. 20402

The PCT Applicant's Guide. Free brochure. Write:

> PCT DEPT
> Patent and Trademark Office
> Washington, DC 20231

The PCT Applicant's Guide. Book. Write:

> WORLD INTELLECTUAL PROPERTY ORGANIZATION
> 34 Chemin des Colombettes
> 1211 Geneva 20, Switzerland

In the U.S., write:

RAPID PATENT SERVICE
1921 Jefferson Davis Hwy.
Suite 1821D
Arlington, VA 22202
(703) 920-5050

A Guide for Applicants—How to Get A European Patent. Write:

EUROPEAN PATENT OFFICE (EPO)
Motorama-Haus
Rosenheimer Strasse 30
Munich, Germany

COPYRIGHT PUBLICATIONS

Copyright Fees—Circular 4
Blank Forms and Other Works Not Protected by Copyright—Circular 32
The Certification Space of the Application Form—Circular 1e
Cartoons and Comic Strips—Circular 44
Computing and Measuring Devices—Circular 33
Copyright Notice—Circular 3
Copyright Protection Not Available for Names, Titles or Short Phrases—Circular 34
Copyright Registration for Multimedia Works—Circular 55
Copyright Registration for Computer Programs—Circular 61
Copyright Registration for Motion Pictures Including Video Recordings—Circular 45
Copyright Registration for Automated Databases—Circular 65
Copyright Registration for Musical Compositions—Circular 50
Copyright Registration for Musical Compositions and Sound Recordings—Circular 56a
Copyright Registration for Serials on form SE—Circular 62
Copyright Registration for Secure Tests—Circular 64
Copyright for Sound Recordings—Circular 56
Extension of Copyright Terms—Circular 15t
Federal Statutory Protection for Mask Works—Circular 100
How to Open and Maintain a Deposit Account in the Copyright Office—Circular 5
Ideas, Methods or Systems—Circular 31
Registration for Video Games and Other Machine Readable Audiovisual Works—Circular 49
Renewal of Copyright—Circular 15
Reproduction of Copyrighted Works for Blind and Physically Handicapped Individuals—Circular 63
Special Postage Rates for Deposit Copies Mailed to the Copyright Office—Circular 30

Deposit Requirements for Registration of Claims to Copyright Visual Arts Materials—
Circular 40a
*Supplementary Copyright Registration—*Circular 8
*Trademarks—*Circular 13
*Works-Made-for-Hire Under the 1976 Copyright Act—*Circular 9
*"Best Edition" of Published Copyrighted Works for the Collections of the Library of Congress—*Circular 7b
*Mandatory Deposit of Copies or Phonorecords for the Library of Congress—*Circular 7d
*Copyright Law of the United States of America—*Circular 92
*Copyright Basics—*Circular 1
*Duration of Copyright—*15a
*Compulsory License for Making and Distributing Phonorecords—*Circular 73
Correcting Errors in Jukebox Certificates and Securing Appropriate Refunds—
    Circular 72
*The Licensing Division of the Copyright Office—*Circular 75
Performances of Music on Coin-Operated Phonorecord Players (Jukeboxes)—
    Circular 70
*Repeal of Notice of Use Requirement—*Circular 51
*International Copyright Conventions—*Circular 38c
*International Copyright Relations of the United States—*Circular 38a
*Selected Biographies of Copyright—*Circular 2b
*The Copyright Catalog Card and the Online Files of the Copyright Office—*Circular 23
The Effects of Not Replying Within 120 Days to Copyright Office Correspondence—
    Circular 7c
*How to Investigate the Status of a Work—*Circular 22

To order Copyright Office publications, call the Forms and Publications Hotline or write:

COPYRIGHT OFFICE
Publications Section, LM-455
Library of Congress
Washington, D.C. 20559
Hotline: (202) 287-9100

GOVERNMENT BOOKSTORES

ALABAMA
Roebuck Shopping City
9220-B Parkway East
Birmingham, AL 35206
(205) 254-1056
9:00 A.M.-5:00 P.M.

CALIFORNIA
ARCO Plaza, C-Level
505 S. Flower St.
Los Angeles, CA 90071
(213) 688-5841
8:30 A.M.-4:30 P.M.

Room 1023, Federal Building
450 Golden Gate Ave.
San Francisco, CA 94102
(415) 556-0643
8:00 A.M.-4:00 P.M.

COLORADO
Room 117, Federal Building
1961 Stout St.
Denver, CO 80294
8:00 A.M.-4:00 P.M.

World Savings Building
720 North Main St.
Pueblo, CO 81003
(303) 544-3142
9:00 A.M.-5:00 P.M.

DISTRICT OF COLUMBIA
U.S. Government Printing Office
710 North Capitol St.
Washington, DC 20402
(202) 275-2091
8:00 A.M.-4:00P.M.

Commerce Department
Rom 1604, 1st Floor
14th & E Streets, NW
Washington, DC 20230
(202) 377-3527
8:00 A.M.-4:00 P.M.

Dept. of Health & Human Services
Room 1528, North Building
330 Independence Avenue, SW
Washington, DC 20201
(202) 472-7478
8:00 A.M.-4:00 P.M.

Pentagon
Room 2E172
Main Concourse, South End
Washington, DC 30210
(703) 557-1821
8:00 A.M.-4:00 P.M.

FLORIDA
Room 158, Federal Building
400 W. Bay St.
P.O. Box 35089
Jacksonville, FL 32292
(904) 791-3801
8:00 A.M.-4:00 P.M.

GEORGIA
Room 100, Federal Building
275 Peachtree St., NE
Atlanta, GA 30303
(404) 221-6947
8:00 A.M.-4:00 P.M.

ILLINOIS
Room 1365, Federal Building
219 S. Dearborn St.
Chicago, IL 60604
(312) 353-5133
8:00 A.M.-4:00 P.M.

MASSACHUSETTS
Room G25, Federal Building
Sudbury St.
Boston, MA 02203
(617) 223-6071
8:00 A.M.-4:00 P.M.

MICHIGAN
Suite 160, Federal Building
477 Michigan Ave.
Detroit, MI 48226
(313) 226-7816
8:00 A.M.-4:00 P.M.

MISSOURI
Room 144, Federal Building
601 East 12th St.
Kansas City, MO 64106
(816) 374-2160
8:00 A.M.-4:00 P.M.

NEW YORK
Room 110
26 Federal Plaza
New York, NY 10278
(212) 264-3825
8:00 A.M.-4:00 P.M.

OHIO
1st Floor, Federal Building
1240 E. 9th St.
Cleveland, OH 44199
(216) 522-4922
9:00 A.M.-5:00 P.M.

Room 207, Federal Building
200 N. High St.
Columbus, OH 43215
(614) 469-6956
9:00 A.M.-5:00 P.M.

PENNSYLVANIA
Room 1214, Federal Building
600 Arch St.
Philadelphia, PA 19106
(215) 597-0677
8:00 A.M.-4:00 P.M.

Room 118, Federal Building
1000 Liberty Ave.
Pittsburgh, PA 15222
(412) 644-2721
9:00 A.M.-5:00 P.M.

TEXAS
Room 1C50, Federal Building
1100 Commerce St.
Dallas, TX 75242
(214) 767-0076
7:45 A.M.-4:15 P.M.

45 College Center
9319 Gulf Freeway
Houston, TX 77017
(713) 229-3515
10:00 A.M.-6:00 P.M.

WASHINGTON
Room 194, Federal Building
915 Second Ave.
Seattle, WA 98174
(206) 442-4270
8:00 A.M.-4:00 P.M.

WISCONSIN
Room 190, Federal Building
517 E. Wisconsin Ave.
Milwaukee, WI 53202
(414) 291-1304
8:00 A.M.-4:00 P.M.

RETAIL SALES OUTLET
8660 Cherry Lane
Laurel, MD 20707
(301) 953-7974
8:00 A.M.-4:00 P.M.

Index